University Press of Florida

Gainesville/Tallahassee/Tampa/Boca Raton

Pensacola/Orlando/Miami/Jacksonville

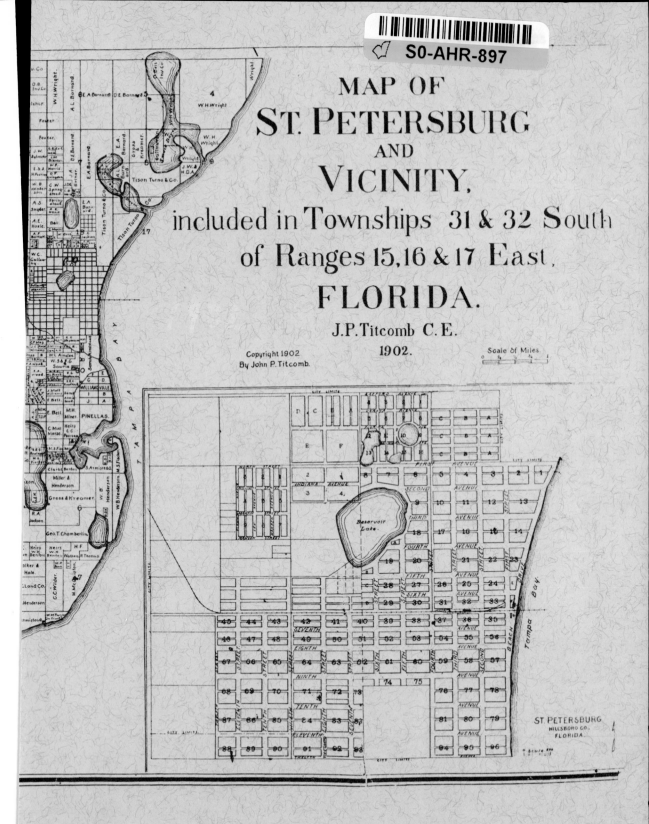

MAP OF
ST. PETERSBURG
AND
VICINITY,

included in Townships 31 & 32 South

of Ranges 15, 16 & 17 East,

FLORIDA.

J.P. Titcomb C.E.

Copyright 1902
By John P. Titcomb.

1902.

Scale of Miles.

ST. PETERSBURG
HILLSBORO CO.
FLORIDA.

St. Petersburg and the
Florida Dream, 1888–1950

ST PETERSBURG

and the Florida Dream, 1888–1950

Raymond Arsenault

Copyright 1996 by the Board of Regents of the State of Florida
Original cloth edition published 1988 by The Donning Company/Publishers
Printed in the United States of America on acid-free paper
All rights reserved

01 00 99 98 97 96 C 6 5 4 3 2 1

Library of Congress Cataloging-in-Publication Data

Arsenault, Raymond.
  St. Petersburg and the Florida dream, 1888–1950 / by Raymond Arsenault.
    p. cm.
  Originally published: Norfolk: Donning Co., 1988.
  Includes bibliographical references and index.
  ISBN 0-8130-1442-5 (alk. paper)
  1. Saint Petersburg (Fla.)—History—Pictorial works. 2. Saint Petersburg
(Fla.)—History. I. Title.
[F319.S24A77 1996]
975.9'63—dc20 96-3863

The University Press of Florida is the scholarly publishing agency for the
State University System of Florida, comprised of Florida A & M University,
Florida Atlantic University, Florida International University, Florida State
University, University of Central Florida, University of Florida, University of
North Florida, University of South Florida, and University of West Florida.

University Press of Florida
15 Northwest 15th Street
Gainesville, FL 32611

Contents

For
Oscar W. Arsenault
and
Robert M. Garrels

Preface and Acknowledgments

This book explores the history of St. Petersburg and the lower Pinellas Peninsula from the recesses of prehistory to the middle of the twentieth century. It does not deal with the recent history of St. Petersburg, which deserves to be treated in detail in a separate volume. In the decades since 1950, several powerful historical forces—the emergence of the Sunbelt, the mass in-migration of senior citizens, the drama of desegregation, and a spiralling pattern of growth and development—have altered the city's character, separating it from the culture and experience of "old" St. Petersburg. At midcentury, the age of expressways, heat pumps, fast-food restaurants, and suburban shopping malls was yet to come. Instead, local life revolved around a number of unique institutions and traditions that reflected the city's long association with the Florida Dream—the centuries-old promise of perpetual warmth, health, comfort, and leisure. Old St. Petersburg never achieved this mythic ideal, but the continuing effort to create a subtropical dreamland gave the city a distinctive and colorful history.

Recapturing the history of a city is almost inevitably a communal enterprise, a process of collective rediscovery that draws upon the talents and resources of numerous individuals and local institutions. *St. Petersburg and the Florida Dream, 1888-1950* is a good case in point. This book would not have become a reality without the joint sponsorship and generous support of the Orange Belt Express, Inc. Centennial Committee and the St. Petersburg Historical Society. I am especially grateful to C. W. McKee, Jr., president of the Orange Belt Express's Board of Trustees; Mary Wyatt Allen, president of the Orange Belt Centennial Activities Council and the St. Petersburg Historical Society; and Professor David Carr, the history coordinator for the Orange Belt Express. I would also like to express my apprecia-

tion to Andrew Barnes, the editor of the *St. Petersburg Times*, for his support and encouragement. This study was partially funded by a grant from the *St. Petersburg Times*, and my research was aided by unlimited access to the *Times'* news and photographic files.

I would like to thank the University of South Florida for granting me a sabbatical leave during the academic year 1984-85. I am especially indebted to Dean Lowell Davis, Associate Dean William Garrett, and History Department Chairman James Swanson for helping to arrange my leave of absence. Several of my friends and colleagues in the history department also deserve thanks. John Belohlavek, David Carr, Gary Mormino, James Swanson, and Nick Wynne were always willing to listen to my ideas and to help in any way that they could. Gary Mormino deserves special thanks, not only for sharing his vast knowledge of Florida history and editing several chapters, but also for temporarily overcoming his fierce loyalty to the Tampa side of the bay. I would also like to acknowledge the intellectual and moral support that I received from a number of my nonhistory colleagues at the University of South Florida at St. Petersburg—Winston Bridges, Regis Factor, Cliff Holmes, Danny Jorgensen, Darryl Paulson, Harry Schaleman, Sudsy Tschiderer, and Steve Turner—all of whom are undoubtedly tired of hearing about the history of St. Petersburg.

During the past year and a half, I have leaned heavily on the small but talented staff of the St. Petersburg Historical Society. Curator Ellen Babb, Registrar Julia Robinson, Assistant Curator Lisa Budreau, Haas Museum Manager Catherine Hull, and clerical assistant Lila Gordon have been unfailingly helpful and gracious in their efforts to point me in the right direction whenever I descended upon the Society's archives for information or photographs. Ellen Babb, in particular, devoted countless hours to this project.

I would also like to express my appreciation to the members of the St. Petersburg Historical Society's Board of Directors, both past and present, for their numerous contributions to this book. Tom Fisher was the first person to urge me to write a history of St. Petersburg, and he has been a great source of encouragement and advice throughout this project. He took time out from a busy schedule to read and comment on several chapters, and his attention to detail prevented me from committing several factual errors. I also owe special debts of gratitude to: David Shedden, for acting as my unofficial research associate and for allowing me to benefit from his intelligence and common sense on numerous occasions; Earnest Foster, for spearheading the marketing campaign for the book; Jake Vonk, for helping with the financial record keeping and for unselfishly sharing the results of his pioneering study of St. Petersburg's Jewish community; Samuel Davis, for writing several insightful essays on the history of St. Petersburg's black community; Fritz Wilder, for providing me with information on the history of St. Petersburg's trailer parks; Sophia Daily and Peter Sherman, for sharing their extensive knowledge of Snell Isle; Mo and Jeanette Wenzel, for their tireless and invaluable cataloging of the Society's photographic collection; Lyn Homan, for her many months of work identifying and reproducing the Society's photographs; and John Warren, for his leadership in reestablishing the Society's commitment to local history.

I am also deeply indebted to the many individuals who were involved, in one way or another, in the complex process of locating, selecting, identifying, and reproducing the historic photographs that appear in this volume. In addition to those noted above, several individuals deserve special mention in this regard: David Shedden, the audio-visual archivist of the Poynter Institute for Media Studies, who rearranged his busy scheduled so that he could guide me through the voluminous photographic files of the *St. Petersburg Times*; Cary Kenney, Pete Basofin, and Barbara Hijek of the *St. Petersburg Times* library, who facilitated my use of their library's photographic holdings; Oscar W. Arsenault, who spent an entire weekend reproducing prints from the Earl Jacobs Collection and who served as an invaluable photographic consultant throughout the preparation of this book; Director Samuel Fustukjian and Audio-Visual Librarian Jerry Notaro of the Nelson Poynter Library, who graciously allowed me to use the Earl Jacobs Collection; Bob Harris and Ken Ford of the Heritage Park and Historical Museum, who gave me access to the Museum's rich collection of photographs and maps; Jay Dobkin and Paul Camp of the University of South Florida Library's Special Collections, who were able to locate several important maps and photographs; and Joan Morris, the photographic curator at the Florida State Archives in Tallahassee. I would also like to thank Diane Anderson, Bill and John Wallace, Brian Evensen, Joseph Albury, Jr., Shirlye Whiting, Arline McCray, Freddie Dyles, Robin Mitchell, Helen Edwards, Niko Pavan, Don and Lisa Munafo, Pat Costrini, the photography lab of the University of South Florida, Tom Rawlins and the staff of the *St. Petersburg Times* photography lab, and Robert Danielson of the City of St. Petersburg's Department of Marketing and Public Information.

Much of the research for this study was conducted in local libraries, most notably the St. Petersburg Public Library (Main Branch), the University of South Florida Library in Tampa, the Nelson Poynter Library at the University of South Florida's St. Petersburg campus, and the *St. Petersburg Times* library. I would like to thank the staffs of these institutions for their cooperation and assistance. I am also indebted to Debbie Factor, Lynn Fox, and the other members of the St. Petersburg League of Women Voters Historical Committee for allowing me to use their files. John Robinson of the City of St. Petersburg's Department of Central Records and Lynn Rosetti of the city's Planning Department also deserve thanks for their help.

A number of the city's longtime residents provided me with invaluable information on various aspects of local history. Their candor and their willingness to share memories of personal experiences, both pleasant and unpleasant, enabled me to recapture some of the hidden or forgotten recesses of the city's past. I am deeply indebted to Joseph Albury, Jr., Harold Anderson, Gardner Beckett, Jr., Joseph Berkowitz, L. D. Brown, Sr., Mamie Brown, Frederick Burney, Leonard Cooperman, Alvin Downing, Freddie Dyles, C. Gray Egerton, Helen Edwards, E. Thomas Fisher, Sr., Ruth Fisher, A. B. "Babe" Fogarty, Jerome "J. D." Girard, Lula Grant, Robert Harper, Margaret Harris, Margaret Hart, Bunny Katz, Cecil B. Keene, Paul Krayer, Leonard Lubin, Arline McCray, Dorothy Morrison, Matty Morrison, Catherine Moses, Peggy Peterman, E. A. Ponder, Katie Postell, Annie Reddick, John Rembert, Laura Rosse, Goldie Schuster, Harry Scott, Jay Starkey, Virginia Stewart, David Susskind, Dorotha Tanner, William Bell Tippetts, Jr., Herschel Vrooman, Dr. Lyman Warren, Shirlye Whiting, and Phil Williams.

During the past eight years, many of my students at the University of South Florida have undertaken research projects on the history of St. Petersburg. I have appreciated their enthusiasm and commitment, and in several cases I have learned a great deal from their research in previously unexplored areas of local history. I am grateful to all of them, but I especially want to thank Ellen Babb, Jack Davis, Samuel Davis, Curtis Kuppler, Robin Nitz, Milly St. Julien, David Shedden, James Tidd, Jake Vonk, William Watts, and Jon Wilson.

Marion Ballard, Marianne Rucker, Marty Wallace, and Sally Wallace, the irrepressible bibliophiles of Bayboro Books, were among the first to encourage me to write a history of the city. I owe them a debt of gratitude and hope that they are pleased with the final product. Others who have earned my sincere thanks for their help and encouragement include Steve Baal, Bob Bradshaw, Russell Buchan, Bethia Caffery, Tim Clemmons, Winnie Foster, Bill Fox, Cynthia Garrels, Rita Gould, James Horton, Lee Malone, Mary Mellstrom, Jon Nelson, Albert Parry, Jr., William Parsons, David Scussel, Mike Slicker, Laura Stewart, Robert Thrush, Diane Tonelli, Jeanne Trudeau, Jay Warthen, Margo Yazell, Ray Yazell, and the valiant historic preservationists of Save Our St. Petersburg.

I would also like to thank the editors and designers of the Donning Company for their flexibility and patience. I am especially grateful to Beverley Hainer, Richard A. Horwege, and Nancy O. Phillips.

Finally, I want to acknowledge the support of my family. I owe a special debt to my father, Oscar W. Arsenault, a professional photographer who nurtured my appreciation for the power and beauty of the photographic art. As always, my wife Kathy and my daughters Amelia and Anne—all of whom love St. Petersburg beyond reason—were there when I needed them most. Somehow they managed to adapt to the demands of the past year without sacrificing their high spirits and good humor.

This book is dedicated to Oscar W. Arsenault and Robert M. Garrels, two men of uplifting wisdom and uncommon grace.

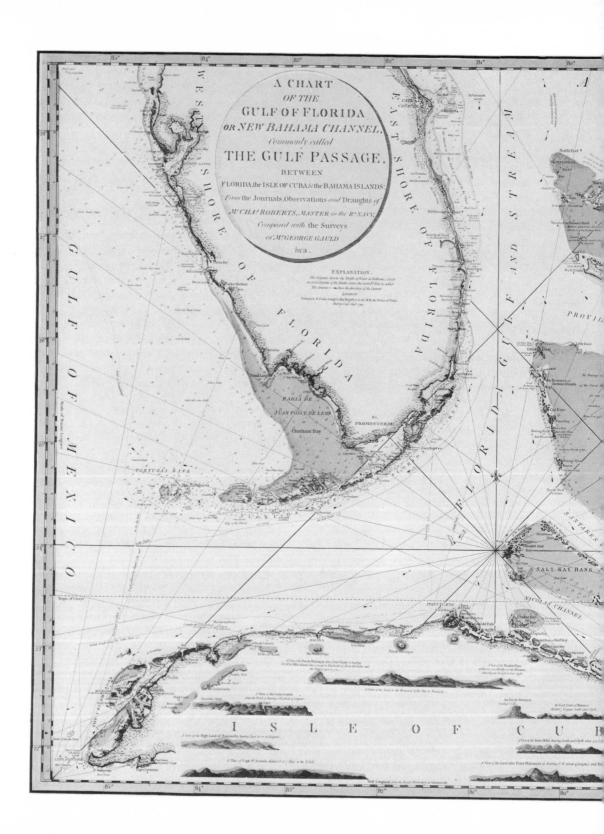

Chapter One

Natives and Strangers

1500-1848

Chartmaker Charles Roberts of the British Royal Navy drafted this map of southern Florida and "The Gulf Passage" in 1794. Roberts's map was based, in part, on the surveys of George Gauld, a noted cartographer who spent three months in the Tampa Bay region in 1765. Reproduced from an engraving in the collection of Historic Urban Plans, Ithaca, New York

The city of St. Petersburg has achieved a century of urban growth and development—a milestone worth celebrating in an age of impermanence and enforced obsolescence. And yet, in the grand scheme of things, the development of a city is less impressive than the long life of the land and water on which it sits. The human saga of the teardrop of land that evolved into St. Petersburg began a full 20 million years after Florida's emergence from the waters of the Atlantic, and more than 180 million years after the onset of continental drift. Here, as elsewhere, the relative brevity of human history reinforces one's faith in the primacy of earth and sky and water. The history of St. Petersburg is ultimately the history of a place; and however complex or interesting the chronicle of its human accomplishments and follies may be, that chronicle is but a part of a larger story bounded only by time and space.

Florida's first human inhabitants may have arrived on the peninsula as early as 35,000 years ago, a few centuries after the nomadic hunters of eastern Siberia discovered the intercontinental land bridge between Asia and Alaska. Or they may have come as late as 11,500 years ago, when a second wave of Asian migrants wandered southward into the Americas. But, whatever the exact date of their arrival, these early settlers found themselves in a cold, semiarid land that no modern Floridian would recognize. The climatic extremism of the late Pleistocene Ice Age dominated the earth for approximately 60,000 years, from 70,000 B.C. to 8000 B.C., and the Florida Suncoast was no exception.

During the coldest period of the Ice Age, from 30,000 to 20,000 B.C., overland migration from Asia became all but impossible, as thick sheets of ice covered North America as far south as Long Island. However, this period of frigid isolation was followed by a slow but steady warming, and gradually the glaciers receded northward. By 10,000 B.C., the warming trend had produced an ice-free corridor in western Canada—a narrow highway that once again allowed Asian animals and hunters to pass southward into the Americas. In less than a millennium, this new wave of intercontinen-

tal migrants fanned out across all of North and South America, from Alaska to Tierra del Fuego.

These Paleo-Indian nomads probably reached the rich hunting grounds of Florida sometime around 9500 B.C., and for a thousand years or more, they lived off the herds of mastodons, giant bison, ground sloths, woolly mammoths, musk oxen, sabre-toothed tigers, tapirs, and other large mammals that roamed the peninsula. Living in small, kin-based groups, the Paleo-Indians survived by knowing the location of fresh-water springs, which were relatively scarce in late Pleistocene Florida, and by adapting to the migratory habits of their food supply. Using flint-tipped spears with deadly accuracy, they more than held their own against the peninsula's larger but more vulnerable mammals.

Over time the great Florida herds were severely depleted by overhunting, but the hunters' lack of restraint only accelerated a biological decline that had already been set in motion by climatic change. When the Paleo-Indians arrived in late Pleistocene Florida, they entered a world that was already in the process of massive change. The last great Ice Age was coming to an end, and the days of the mastodon and the ground sloth were numbered. When the Ice Age finally came to a close around 8000 B.C., the environment that had nurtured both the hunter and the hunted disappeared, propelling the natural and human history of Florida into a new epoch. The rise in global temperatures, which had begun around 20,000 B.C., accelerated after 8000 B.C., eventually melting all of the world's great glaciers, with the exception of the polar ice caps. The result was a sharply elevated sea level that altered the shoreline of every land mass on the planet. Not only did the land bridge between Asia and Alaska disappear—an epochal development that shut off the flow of intercontinental migration for ten thousand years—but also the width of the Florida peninsula was reduced by more than two hundred miles, forcing the abandonment of hundreds of traditional Paleo-Indian sites. The narrowing of Florida resulted in countless new configurations of land and water, including Tampa Bay and the spit of

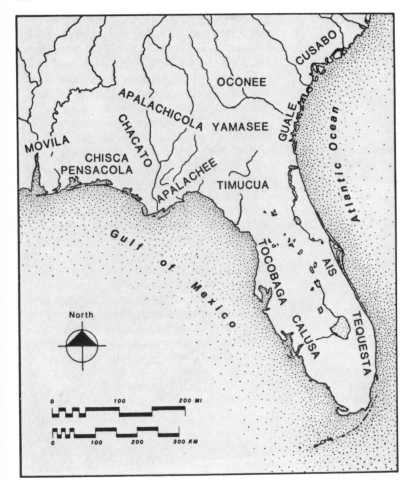

Indian cultures of Florida and the lower Southeast in the sixteenth century. Reprinted from John H. Hann, Apalachee: The Land between the Rivers *(1988), p. 6. Courtesy of John H. Hann and the University Presses of Florida*

limestone, sand, and coquina marl later known as the Pinellas Peninsula.

In the Pinellas region, as in most areas of lower North America, the post-Ice Age (Holocene) environment bore little resemblance to that of the late Pleistocene era. As the climate became warmer and more humid, subtropical forests of pine and palmetto and mangrove supplanted the oak and hardwood forests that had covered Florida for thousands of years. In less than a millennium, virtually all of the large Pleistocene quadrupeds—including the sabre-toothed tiger, the mastodon, the ground sloth, and even the horse—vanished from the Florida landscape. Fortunately for the Paleo-Indians, the loss of the large quadrupeds was partially balanced by a proliferation of fresh-water ponds, salt marshes, and estuaries,

all of which spawned new species of plant, animal, and marine life. The Holocene environment would take several thousand years to evolve into its modern form. But by the second millennium B.C., most of the flora and fauna that would characterize Florida during the late pre-Columbian era had taken hold.

With this new environment came new cultural opportunities and new cultural forms. Sometime around 6500 B.C., Florida's Indians moved into what archaeologists generally refer to as the Archaic stage of development. During the Archaic era, which lasted approximately five thousand years in Florida, the region's inhabitants developed an increasingly sophisticated hunting and gathering society. The range of nomadic migration became narrower and patterns of migration became somewhat regularized; tools and projectile points became more efficient; food resources became much more varied; and burial practices became more elaborate, with some groups burying their dead in ponds or marshy wetlands. Perhaps most important, with respect to the development of Pinellas's Indian culture, the coastal orientation of Florida's Indians became much more pronounced, especially during the late Archaic era (3000-1200 B.C.). As oysters and other shellfish became an increasingly important food source—and archaeological evidence suggests that this trend began as early as 2500 B.C.—the Indians of central Florida gravitated to the estuarial areas of the Tampa Bay region. Many of these coastal Indians gradually adopted a semisedentary lifestyle, and a few groups even began to produce a primitive form of pottery tempered with plant fibers.

The utilization of semipermanent habitation sites and the manufacture of pottery, however crude, were sure signs that the Indians of west central Florida were entering the Formative (post-hunting and gathering) stage of development. Historians and archaeologists generally divide west central Florida's Formative stage into five periods of cultural evolution: the Florida Transitional (1200-500 B.C.), Manasota (500 B.C.-A.D. 200), Manasota/Weeden Island-related (A.D. 200-1000), Safety Harbor (A.D. 1000-1700), and Seminole (A.D. 1700-1860).

During the first of these periods, the Florida Transitional, small bands of natives began to exhibit some of the traits associated with the Neolithic Revolution, the process of community and cultural development that first appeared in Sumeria during the sixth millennium B.C. The creation of villages, the emergence of identifiable local cultures and dialects, the division of labor, the acceptance of social stratification, and the development of intertribal trade were all part of this transition to organized community life. At the same time, sand-tempered pottery replaced the fiber-tempered ceramics of the Archaic era, and dependence on shellfish and other estuarine resources became the central fact of local economic life. Although hunting and gathering activities remained important, the Indians of Tampa Bay had reached the point where most of their material culture was derived from the world of the bayou and the barrier island.

The cultural developments of the Florida Transitional era were extended, refined, and particularized during the Manasota period. The domain of the Manasota culture stretched from Charlotte Harbor to Anclote Bay, and included all of the Pinellas Peninsula. Although there is no evidence that the Manasota peoples constituted a well-defined or even a loosely aggregated tribe, interaction between the region's coastal bands produced a striking cultural convergence. A preference for tools made of shell or bone, the use of ornamental beads made of oliva shell or shark vertebra, the production of undecorated sand-tempered ceramics, the placement of villages on or near the shoreline, and the practice of burying the dead in a flexed position in shell middens were common characteristics throughout the region. For approximately seven hundred years, these cultural traits evolved in relative isolation. Although there was undoubtedly intermittent contact with the Indians of southern Florida—contact which may have given the Manasota some familiarity with the cultivation of domesticated plants—the hegemony of Manasota traditions apparently faced few challenges until the third century A.D., when all of central Florida came under the influence of the Weeden Island cultural complex.

The initial archaeological identification of this expansive and sophisticated Indian culture occurred at St. Petersburg's Weedon Island site in 1924. However, later archaeological investigations revealed that Weeden Island culture (the Smithsonian researcher who named the culture misspelled the name of the island, changing "Weedon" to "Weeden") was actually centered in northern Florida, southern Georgia, and Alabama. Distinguished by its wide-ranging trade networks, complex social and religious structures, elegant ceramics, and elaborate burial rites, Weeden Island culture gradually absorbed hundreds of less sophisticated regional cultures. In the Tampa Bay region, this process of cultural absorption took several centuries to complete.

Eventually it reshaped all aspects of Manasota life, from ceramic styles to religious practices. The triumph of Weeden Island culture was particularly evident in burial customs. By the eighth or ninth century A.D., traditional Manasota burial practices had been replaced by a highly stylized form of mound burial. In the Weeden Island-related style of interment, the body was defleshed and dismembered, and the bones of the deceased were placed in a bundle which was later buried in a mound of sand. Sometimes ornate ceremonial pots were interred with the bundles, but, with or without ceramic accessories, elongated sand mounds became the telltale sign of Weeden Island influence.

The burial mounds and ceramic creations of the Weeden Island phase were impressive accomplishments which represented important advances in cultural evolution. Nevertheless, sometime during the tenth century the Weeden Island culture gave way to an even more sophisticated mound-building culture, that of the Mississippians. The Mississippian culture took shape in the central Mississippi Valley during the seventh century, and over the next eight hundred years it spread throughout most of the American Southeast. Inspired by the earlier Adena-Hopewell culture of the Midwest and the Northeast, and heavily influenced by indirect contact with the Mayan and Aztec peoples of Mexico and Guatemala, the Mississippian culture was characterized by well-structured chiefdoms, territoriality and militarism, complex patterns of social stratification, an elaborate religious life that required the construction of large truncated pyramidal mounds, intensive agriculture, and, in some areas, death cults involving torture and human sacrifices.

By the beginning of the eleventh century, the Indians of west central Florida had adopted most, although not all, of the dominant Mississippian traditions. Archaeologists generally refer to this local variation of Mississippian culture as the Safety Harbor culture, but most historians prefer to use the tribal name *Tocobaga*. Following the custom of the Indians themselves, historians also refer to the tribe's principal chief, and to the large village where he resided, as *Tocobaga*. Located on the western shore of Old Tampa Bay, on the present-day site of Safety Harbor, the village of Tocobaga served as the political and religious center of the Tampa Bay region throughout the late pre-Columbian era.

By the end of the fifteenth century, the Tocobaga's coastal domain extended from Charlotte Harbor to Crystal Bay, an area that encompassed dozens of large towns and scores of smaller villages. For the most part, the leaders at Tocobaga practiced a loose form of federal control, and each large town had its own temple mound, ceremonial plaza, and sub-chief. The subchiefs exhibited varying degrees of loyalty to the principal chief at Tocobaga, and intratribal warfare was not uncommon. Indeed, like the Timucua and Apalachee cultures of northern Florida, the Tocobaga regime was not so much a tribe as it was a confederation of culturally and linguistically linked clans. At times, the Tocobaga may have been involuntarily incorporated into the much larger Timucuan confederation. But, in general, the Tocobaga seem to have acted as an independent political and military buffer between the Timucua to the north and the Calusa to the south.

Culturally and geographically, the Tocobaga occupied the middle ground between the semiagricultural society of the Timucua and the nonagricultural maritime society of the Calusa. However, the role of agriculture in Tocobaga society has been a subject of sharp debate among Florida archaeologists and historians. While some scholars maintain that the Tocobaga must have spent at least part of their time cultivating maize and other crops, others argue that there is no solid archaeological evidence to support this claim. Although the archaeological record on this point is indeed murky, fragmentary historical evidence from the early post-European contact period seems to support the view that the Tocobaga supplemented their primary diet of fish and game with maize, pumpkins, and squash. Chronicles compiled during the Narváez and de Soto expeditions of the early sixteenth century indicate that, at least in the northern half of the Tocobaga realm, in the region above Tampa

The paintings of Jacques Le Moyne, a Frenchman who visited Fort Caroline and its environs in 1564, provide us with an invaluable visual depiction of sixteenth-century Timucua society. Le Moyne's forty-two paintings were transferred to engravings and published by Flemish artist Theodore de Bry in 1591. The de Bry engraving above depicts an alligator hunt. Aside from its heavy reliance on corn cultivation, the Timucua culture of northeastern Florida was similar to the Tocobaga culture that dominated the Tampa Bay region. Courtesy St. Petersburg Historical Society

In this Le Moyne/de Bry engraving, Timucua men and women are using a dugout canoe to transport produce to a tribal granary. Courtesy St. Petersburg Historical Society

Bay, maize cultivation was a common activity. Unfortunately, we do not know the extent to which these interior fields were used by the Tocobaga living in coastal villages. Nor do we have any evidence that the Tocobaga adopted the general Mississippian custom of holding a spring "green corn" celebration. In all likelihood, the Tocobaga were a maritime people who dabbled in agriculture—a people who remained more familiar with oyster beds than corn fields. But definitive answers to these questions await further research.

Whatever the balance between horticulture, hunting, and estuarial activities, the Tocobaga were able to raise themselves well above the level of mere subsistence. There is every indication that, prior to the arrival of the Europeans, the Tocobaga were more than holding their own demographically; indeed, archaeological evidence suggests that the Tocobaga population may have been as high as twenty or even thirty thousand during the late pre-Columbian era. The Tocobaga lived in simple, palm-thatched huts and were more inclined to tattoo their bodies with vegetable dyes than to wear clothes. But this superficial primitivism should not obscure the fact that Tocobaga culture represented a successful and sophisticated adaptation to the surrounding environment. The ability to maintain complex social structures and long-distance trade networks, the capacity to produce ornate ceramics and beautifully crafted jewelry, and the decision to devote considerable time and energy to the construction of temple and burial mounds all testify to the richness and vitality of Tocobaga life. On the Pinellas Peninsula alone, there were scores of mounds during the late pre-Columbian era. Although some were nothing more than kitchen middens, others were massive earthworks adorned with wooden temples and charnel houses. The largest of the temple mounds were fifty feet high and more than a hundred feet long, a magnitude that impressed the haughtiest of Spanish conquistadors.

The historical record provides us with few specific clues about what went on in the temples and charnel houses of the Tocobaga. We can be reasonably confident that Tocobaga religion derived much of its structure and meaning from the rhythms of the natural world. Unlike modern Christianity and Judaism, where the historical dimension is paramount, most forms of Mississippian religion sought to explain and enhance a recurring pattern of birth, life, death, and renewal. The Tocobaga Mississippians lived in a world of cyclical equilibrium and subtle adaptation, a world where there was little need for a linear sense of time or development. Although some years were more memorable than others, the basic rhythm of life was dictated by seasonal variation. Tropical storms and winter freezes came and went, but the governing principle of Tocobaga life remained the same; as always, the cultural and physical survival of the tribe depended on an unbroken symbiosis with the surrounding environment. Despite the inevitable temptations of territoriality and cultural pride, the Tocobaga could ill afford a growth mentality, or any other philosophy that pitted human striving against natural limits. The maintenance of ecological balance took precedence over individual or collective ambition, and the Tocobaga saw to it that this calculus was ruthlessly enforced by religious ritual and communal pressure.

For at least a dozen millennia, a succession of native peoples extracted what they needed from the land and sea of the lower Gulf coast without destroying the environment that sustained them. They probably would have gone on in this way indefinitely had it not been for the advent of the European age of exploration and discovery. In the late fifteenth and early sixteenth centuries, the cyclical equilibrium of the Tocobaga and other New World societies was swiftly and irrevocably shattered by the coming of the Europeans. Beginning with the voyages of Columbus, the process now known as the Columbian Exchange gradually melded the biological and cultural systems of the Old and New Worlds.[1] The discovery and exploration of the Americas redefined the boundaries of European intellectual thought, and for better or worse, colonization brought Christianity and European technology to hundreds of previously isolated cultures.

Perhaps even more importantly in the

Real estate developer and local historian Walter P. Fuller erected this sign in the Jungle area of northwestern St. Petersburg during the 1920s to mark the location of Spanish explorer Panfilo de Narváez's arrival in central Florida in 1528. Despite Fuller's claim, the exact location of the Narváez landing is still a subject of debate among archaeologists and historians. Courtesy St. Petersburg Times

long run, the Columbian Exchange included a massive two-way transfer of plants and animals. During the sixteenth century, the Old World had its first encounter with such novelties as chocolate, tomatoes, potatoes, peanuts, maize, bison, hummingbirds, and rattlesnakes. In return, horses, cattle, sheep, pigs, oranges, melons, bananas, coconut palms, daisies, dandelions and hundreds of other "oddities" from Europe, Asia, and Africa were introduced to the American landscape. Many of these Old World species were useful additions to the American scene, but unfortunately for the aborigines of the New World, a number of deadly Old World diseases also migrated across the Atlantic. The result was a demographic disaster of monumental proportions, a nightmarish spiral of depopulation and cultural disintegration that facilitated the Europeanization of two continents.

The Columbian Exchange began relatively early on the lower Gulf coast of Florida, although the date of initial contact between the Tocobaga and the Europeans was probably later than some historians have claimed. During the early sixteenth century, a number of Spanish explorers landed on Florida's lower Gulf coast: Juan Ponce de Léon (1513 and 1521), Diego Miruelo (1516), Francisco Hernandez de Cordoba (1517), Francisco de Garay (1519), and Panfilo de Narváez (1528). But, with the exception of Narváez, there is no hard evidence that any of these explorers encountered the Tocobaga. Although Walter Fuller and other local historians have insisted that the fabled Ponce de Léon visited the Pinellas Peninsula twice, the probability that these visits actually occurred is extremely low. In 1513, after exploring most of Florida's Atlantic coast and the Florida Keys, Ponce de Léon did indeed head north along the lower Gulf coast. But few, if any, serious historians believe that he went much beyond the mouth of the Caloosahatchie River. Eight years later the peripatetic governor of Puerto Rico returned to the lower Gulf coast, with the intention of establishing Florida's first Spanish colony. But a phalanx of native warriors drove the Spanish intruders away, fatally wounding Ponce de Léon in the process. Although the exact location of this fatal skirmish is unknown, most scholars feel that it was somewhere in Calusa territory well to the south of Tampa Bay.

Of course, wherever it occurred, the Tocobaga probably knew about the Ponce de Léon episode. And, even if they knew nothing of this particular incident, the Tocobaga were undoubtedly aware of the Europeans' presence in the Caribbean basin by the time of Ponce de Léon's second voyage. Spanish slavers and freebooters had been prowling the Florida coast since the beginning of the sixteenth century, and it seems highly unlikely that a coastal tribe like the Tocobaga could have avoided these early intruders altogether. Indeed, the overnight departure of the first villagers Narváez encountered in 1528 suggests that prior contact with Europeans had already made the Tocobaga wary of pale-skinned visitors in square-rigged ships.

When Narváez splashed ashore in the spring of 1528, the long history of the Tocobaga entered a final and ultimately tragic phase. Any visitor carrying European pathogens and European ideas of sanctified conquest would have disrupted the biological and cultural balance of Tocobaga society. But Narváez, a man described by Samuel Eliot Morison as "both cruel and stupid," was a particularly unsavory intruder. According to Morison, Narváez was "the most incompetent of all who sailed for Spain in this era."[2] Unfortunately, his incompetence as a leader did not prevent him from rising to prominence in an imperial army that generally valued ruthlessness more than intelligence or compassion. Born in Valladolid in 1480, Narváez served under Juan de Esquivel in Jamaica, where he earned a reputation as a consummate Indian killer. Later, during the conquest of Cuba, he extended his reputation by directing several mass slaughters that helped to break native resistance. In 1520, he was sent to Mexico to arrest Hernando Cortez, whose expansive activities, according to the governor of Cuba, had gotten out of hand. In this case, Narváez's martial skills failed him, and Cortez got the better of the exchange. Wounded in battle (he lost an eye) and later imprisoned, he eventually had no choice but to side with Cortez in the disagreement over the imperial chain of command.

Despite his humiliation at the hands of Cortez, Narváez remained a favorite of Emperor Charles V, who appointed him *adelantado* of Florida in 1527. With this title came the right to conquer and colonize the entire Gulf coast area stretching from the Florida Keys to Rio de las Palmas (later known as Soto la Marina) in northeastern Mexico. Determined to succeed where Ponce de Léon and others had failed, Narváez gathered together a massive invasion force of soldiers, colonists, and missionaries. In February 1528, Narváez's armada of five ships, loaded down with four hundred men and women, eighty horses, and tons of supplies, left Trinidad bound for Rio de las Palmas. However, a series of severe storms forced the fleet to turn to the northeast and sail along Florida's lower Gulf coast.

In mid-April, Narváez's ships dropped anchor in a small bay somewhere along the coast. Although there is still some uncertainty about the bay's location, most available evidence points to a landing somewhere in or near Boca Ciega Bay. (Other historians have placed the Narváez landing on the Manatee River, near Bradenton, and some have even argued that it was as far south as the Caloosahatchie River.) Wherever the spot was located, a small cluster of *bohios* (palmetto-thatched huts) could be seen on the shore, and Narvaez dispatched a scouting party to investigate the scene. The scouts made contact with a small group of seemingly friendly natives, but when Narváez himself went ashore the next day, he found that the village was deserted. A thorough search of the village uncovered only one object of value—a small rattle made of gold—but this was enough to pique Narváez's interest. After claiming the village and all surrounding lands for Spain, the conquistador spent ten days exploring the area. The Spaniards hacked their way across a wide peninsula, eventually coming upon a large bay which Narváez christened *La Bahia de la Cruz* (the Bay of the Cross). At this point, Narváez was growing impatient, having found no one to plunder. But, to his relief, he soon encountered a small band of natives who directed him to the nearby village of Ucita.

At Ucita, Narváez was introduced to Chief Hirrihigua, an imposing but not unfriendly man who took his visitors on a tour of the village. All went well until the party inspected the tribal burial ground which, to the Spaniards' astonishment, was littered with Castillian cases. The cases apparently had been retrieved from a shipwreck, and the resourceful natives of Ucita had turned them into makeshift coffins. To Narváez's horror, the cases were filled with corpses wrapped in painted deer skins. Offended by this alleged sacrilege, he ordered his soldiers to burn the cases. In the melee that followed, Chief Hirrihigua was wounded in the face, and his mother, who had rushed forward in an effort to protect her son, was hacked to death and fed to Narváez's greyhounds. This particular atrocity would have deadly repercussions a decade later when Hernando de Soto visited the village, but at the time the outnumbered warriors of Ucita could only look on in disbelief. As Hirrihigua lay bleeding on the ground, Spanish soldiers ransacked the village looking for gold and silver. When they emerged from the bohios with a few golden trinkets, Narváez demanded to know where he could find more. Anxious to get rid of their brutish guests, several quick-thinking warriors pointed north and shouted, "Apalachen!"

At this time, the Spanish knew nothing about the Apalachee Indians who inhabited the Florida panhandle, but the feigned enthusiasm of the Ucita warriors was more than enough to stir the fertile imagination of Narváez. Intoxicated with visions of an Aztec-like empire to the north, he decided to undertake an overland march in search of Apalachen riches. Nuñez Cabeza de Vaca, Narváez's top aide and the treasurer of the expedition, counseled against an extended march that would separate the expedition's soldiers from their supply ships. But the impetuous Narváez refused to listen. Led by a handful of Indian guides, Narváez, Cabeza de Vaca, and more than three hundred Spanish soldiers headed north on May 1. For weeks they wandered through the overgrown interior of central Florida, battling the heat and the mosquitoes and the swamps, but always pressing on. Along the way, they encountered several large Indian villages and numerous cornfields, but not an ounce of gold. By late summer, the exhausted Spaniards had reached the heart of the Apalachee Indian country, near present-day Tallahassee, but even here they found nothing but death and disappointment.

In the meantime, the supply ships followed the coastline north, hoping to meet their conquistador's land force. But the projected rendezvous never took place. Unable to re-establish contact with Narváez's wandering band, the flotilla's commander had no choice but to return to Cuba, leaving the *Adelantado* to his own devices. Narváez eventually made his way back to the coast, emerging somewhere near St. Mark's Bay (which the Spanish called *La Bahia de Caballos*), but by that time the supply ships were long gone. Undaunted, the conquistador supervised the construction of five small boats designed to carry the expedition's 245 survivors to safety in Mexico. With only one carpenter and no experienced boatbuilders, Narváez's force produced an unseaworthy fleet that had little chance of successfully crossing several hundred miles of open water.

By hugging the coastline as much as possible, all five boats managed to sail as far west as Louisiana, but eventually all but one of the boats were lost. In November 1528, Cabeza de Vaca and eighty other survivors landed on the Texas coast, but after eight years of starvation, disease, and skirmishes with hostile natives, the only survivors were Cabeza de Vaca and three companions. In July 1536, after walking through much of central Texas and the Gulf coast backcountry, the four men staggered into a Spanish settlement in northern Mexico. Cabeza de Vaca's chronicle of his adventures, published in 1542, became one of sixteenth-century Europe's most popular literary creations, ensuring the Narváez expedition's place in recorded history. But in the land of the Tocobaga no such chronicle was necessary to sustain the bitter legacy of the red-bearded stranger. The Spaniards had marked the land with their cruelty, and the humiliations suffered at Ucita and elsewhere would not be forgotten.

As remarkable as it was, the Narváez expedition spawned an equally remarkable sequel—the saga of Juan Ortiz, a young sailor who participated in the 1528 expedition but who returned to Cuba before Narváez marched north. Having some knowledge of Narváez's travels in central Florida, Ortiz was asked to join a search party commissioned by Narváez's wife. After helping to locate the village of Ucita, Ortiz and a friend went ashore to inquire about Narváez's fate. But Hirrihigua and his followers had not forgotten the brutality of the Narváez invasion, and as soon as the pair stepped onto the beach the friend was killed and Ortiz was taken captive. Brought before Hirrihigua, Ortiz soon found himself being roasted alive over an open fire. As the flames rose, he filled the air with piercing screams, prompting Hirrihigua's daughter Ulela to intercede on his behalf. Thus, despite Hirrihigua's desire to wreak vengeance against all Spanish invaders, the terrified sailor was allowed to survive. With Ulela as his patroness, a grateful Ortiz subsequently became a member of the Ucita tribe. It is said that Captain John Smith later read Ortiz's story and was inspired to claim a similar history of succor by another Indian maiden, Pocahontas.

Ortiz never gained the complete trust of Hirrihigua. After an unsuccessful skirmish with an enemy tribe, Hirrihigua accused him of treachery, and once again Ulela had to intervene to save his life. This time she helped him to relocate in the village of Mocoso, where the cacique—a longtime rival of Hirrihigua's—promised to protect him. Ortiz lived at Mocoso for nearly a decade and probably would have remained there until his death had it not been for the unexpected appearance of Hernando de Soto.

A native of Barracota and a veteran of Francisco Pizarro's Peruvian campaign, de Soto was at the court of Charles V in Seville when Cabeza de Vaca returned from Mexico in 1537. De Soto was already in the midst of organizing an expedition to Florida, and Cabeza de Vaca's tales of the Narváez expedition confirmed his suspicion that Florida could be turned into a grand vice-royalty similar to Mexico and Peru. This prospect prompted Charles V to appoint de Sotoa governor of Cuba and *Adelantado* of Florida, and in April 1538 de Soto and an armada of seven ships sailed for Florida by way of Havana. After more than a year of preparation in Cuba, the de Soto expedition—comprised of 570 soldiers and 223 horses—landed near the village of Mocoso (probably in the vicinity of the Little Manatee River) on Whitsunday, May 25, 1539. There, to his amazement, de Soto encountered Juan Ortiz, who remembered enough Spanish to blurt out an incredible story of captivity and survival. Ortiz helped de Soto to establish a presidio at Ucita and eventually became the conquistador's most valued interpreter and guide. When de Soto headed north in search of gold and other plunder, Ortiz went with him.

As far as we can tell, de Soto's route north—still a subject of sharp debate among historians—did not pass through the Pinellas Peninsula; and there is no evidence that de Soto or any of his men visited the village of Tocobaga. Nevertheless, there can be little doubt that all of the inhabitants of the Tocobaga realm knew of the conquistador's presence. Fortunately for the Tocobaga, de Soto did not stay in the area for very long, although he did stay long enough to rename the bay *La Bahia de Espíritu Santo*—the "Bay of the Holy Spirit." Most importantly, when de Soto marched north he took most of his soldiers with him, leaving behind only a small garrison at Ucita.

For almost three years, de Soto and his men wandered from village to village, spreading disillusionment and suffering all across the American southeast. De Soto's method of conquest, as described by historian Samuel Eliot Morison, was "to enter an Indian village, seize the cacique and others as hostages, demand and receive provisions for man and beast, and after a tense rest, proceed to the next town with the captive cacique and hostages. These were allowed to go home when the second town capitulated."[3] This slash-and-burn style of diplomacy took its toll on scores of native tribes, but it eventually wore down the Spaniards as well. Warfare and disease thinned the ranks, and in May 1542 de Soto himself succumbed to fever on the banks of the Mississippi River. Luis Moscoso, who succeeded de Soto as *adelantado*, led a surviving remnant of 311 soldiers to the Mexican settlement of Rio Pánuco in September 1543. Ini-

This photograph of a large sand and shell mound was taken in 1903. Photograph by James Hamilton, courtesy Florida State Archives

tially, the survivors were hailed as conquering heroes, but the subsequent accounts of the four-year saga, although fascinating, revealed that the de Soto expedition had found more corn than gold in the southeastern interior. The North American landscape had been explored as never before, but at the expense of brutalizing and alienating an entire region of native peoples.

In the wake of the ill-fated de Soto expedition, several religious leaders urged the Spanish Crown to adopt a more humane, soul-saving approach to New World colonialism. The curse of the Black Legend (the notion that Spaniards—especially Spanish colonials—were unduly cruel) could only be undone, they argued, by a change in emphasis throughout the empire. Such reform seemed particularly appropriate in Florida, where de Soto's brutality had already backfired and where the acquisition of converts was more likely than a bounty of gold or silver. In 1547, two well-known Dominican priests with extended experience in Mexico and Central America, Bishop Bartolomé de las Casas and Fray Luis

Cancer de Barbastro, successfully petitioned for a royal patent that would allow them to establish missions among the Indians of Florida. Two years later, armed with bibles, crucifixes, and hopeful expectations, Fray Luis Cancer and four Dominican brothers left Vera-cruz for the Gulf coast of Florida. After a brief stop in Havana, where they acquired a Christianized Indian interpreter named Magdalena, the friars sailed into Tampa Bay aboard the caravel *Santa Maria de la Encina*. Although the captain had orders to avoid areas where there was any history of hostility between natives and Spaniards, the unsuspecting friars were ferried to the northern recesses of Tampa Bay, in the heart of Tocobaga territory. This mistake would cost them their lives.

As soon as the Dominicans made landfall, Magdalena defected, helping a group of Tocobaga warriors to kidnap a sailor and two of the priests. A shaken but resolute Fray Luis Cancer managed to return to the *Santa Maria*, but the missing priests and the sailor were never seen again. After several days of searching for his lost colleagues, Fray Luis reen-

A 1909 postcard view of a St. Petersburg mound. Courtesy St. Petersburg Historical Society

countered Magdalena who warned him that the natives were in no mood to discuss religious doctrine. He also received an ominous warning from Juan Muñoz, a Spanish soldier who had lived with the Tocobaga since his capture ten years earlier. Muñoz paddled out to the *Santa Maria* to inform Fray Luis that the missing priests had already been tortured to death. This convinced the disappointed friar that he had better look elsewhere for potential converts, but he foolishly made one last trip to the shore in search of drinking water and further confirmation that his colleagues were dead. Once on the beach, he was immediately bludgeoned to death by two native executioners.

The celebrated martyrdom of Fray Luis Cancer delayed Spain's colonization of Florida for more than a decade. Although Spanish galleons continued to fill the sea lanes on all sides of the peninsula, Florida itself was left undisturbed. Indeed, the expectation of fierce Indian resistance might have kept the Spanish away for a much longer period if a group of French Huguenots, led by Jean Ribault, had not established a colony at Fort Caroline, on the St. Johns River, in 1564. The appearance of this Protestant enclave was a provocation which King Phillip II, a devout Roman Catholic, could not ignore. Hoping to save Florida from heretics and savages, the king commissioned Pedro Menéndez de Avilés to secure the claims of Ponce de Léon and de Soto. One of Spain's most talented conquistadors, Menéndez fulfilled his commission with astounding speed and uncompromising ruthlessness. After slaughtering more than four hundred Frenchmen on the beaches of northern Florida, he founded the colonial stronghold of St. Augustine. Through a combination of bribery and intimidation, he pacified the local Timucua Indians, and by 1566 Spanish authority in northeastern Florida was secure.

Pleased with this success, Menéndez soon turned his attention to the unexplored and unconquered central and southern portions of the peninsula. Menendez was determined to bring all of Florida under his control, and in February 1566 he led an expedition to the lower Gulf coast. His first landing was in Calusa territory, near Charlotte Harbor, where he was greeted with an elaborate procession of three hundred warriors. After several rounds of gift giving, the chief of the Calusa tribe, whom the Spanish called Cacique Carlos, urged Menéndez to form a military alliance with his tribe. Together, he argued, the Calusa and the Spanish could destroy the hated Tocobaga, a villainous tribe to the north that was holding his sister captive. A wary Menéndez refused Carlos's offer, but he was intrigued by Carlos's tales of the Tocobaga. His desire to head north into Tocobaga territory was also encouraged by his conversations with Domingo Escalante de Fontaneda, a shipwrecked Spanish sailor who had lived among the Calusa since 1545. Fontaneda would eventually return to Spain with the first book on Florida, but not before he had filled Menéndez's head with stories of native savagery and hidden treasure troves.

In March 1567, the Menéndez flotilla sailed into Tampa Bay, which the Spanish then called *Las Bahias de Espíritu Santo*. At the village of Tocobaga (Safety Harbor), Menéndez met with the Tocobaga cacique, who seemed interested in the Spaniard's proposal to use Spanish soldiers as a peacekeeping buffer between the Calusa and the Tocobaga. This proposal, plus an offer to teach the Tocobaga the principles of Christianity, led to a four-day conference which brought together twenty-nine caciques (including Carlos and Tocobaga), a hundred subchiefs, and more than fifteen hundred warriors. At the end of this remarkable conference, Menéndez was given permission to set up a mission and a small presidio at Tocobaga village. After assigning Capt. Garcia Martinez de Cos to command the presidio and a Jesuit priest, Father Juan Rogel, to lead the mission effort, Menéndez sailed for Havana, confident that he had established an entering wedge among the Tocobaga. However, as soon as Menéndez left the scene, relations between the Tocobaga and their Spanish guests soured. The situation reached a crisis in December 1567, when the Tocobaga cut off the garrison's food supply, forcing Father Rogel to sail to Havana for help. By the time Rogel returned a month later, all but three of Captain de Cos's men had been killed. And, as Rogel soon dis-

covered, the three survivors had been kept alive only for his benefit. As the Jesuit looked on in horror from the deck of a Spanish caravel, the Tocobaga hacked their three prisoners to death on the beach. Once again the sword and the cross had been rudely dispatched from the seemingly bedeviled Bay of the Holy Spirit.

Following the fiasco of 1567, Menéndez returned to Spain to convince Phillip II to bankroll a major colonization effort on the Florida Gulf coast. But the crown, which was having enough trouble holding its position in northern Florida, gave him only lukewarm support. Menéndez pressed on with his plans until his death in 1574, but the *adelantados* who succeeded him displayed little interest in Florida's lower Gulf coast. Thus, well before the end of the century the hegemony of the Tocobaga and the Calusa had been restored. When a Spanish frigate captained by Fernando Valdés surveyed the lower Gulf coast in 1603, no traces of European colonization could be found.

Unfortunately for the Tocobaga, the Spanish withdrawal from Tampa Bay did not presage a return to the splendid isolation of the fifteenth century. Although the Spanish were gone, many of the plants, animals, and diseases that had accompanied them remained. Moreover, the growing Spanish presence in northern Florida, where several Franciscan missions were established in the late sixteenth and early seventeenth centuries, ensured that the flora, fauna, and pathogens of southern Europe would continue to advance across the Florida peninsula. The Europeanization of Florida's landscape created an ecological panoply that would astound and benefit later settlers, but its impact on the natives was catastrophic. Ravaged by smallpox, measles, and other European diseases for which they had no natural immunities, the Tocobaga of the Pinellas Peninsula were reduced to a dispirited remnant by the end of the seventeenth century.

For the once-proud Tocobaga, the final blow came not from disease but from the vicissitudes of imperial rivalry. After the establishment of South Carolina in 1670, the British posed a direct threat to Spanish Florida, which then stretched all the way to the Savannah River. Driven by religious conviction and a hunger for Spanish gold and Indian slaves, the British colonials encouraged their Indian allies, the Creeks and the Yamasee, to plunder the Spanish missions that had been established among the Guale, the Apalachee, and the Timucua. By 1690, the Spanish friars had been forced to abandon the Guale region along the Georgia coast. During Queen Anne's War (1702-1713), a large raiding party led by former South Carolina governor James Moore overran the missions of Apalachee and Timucua. Although the fortress city of St. Augustine withstood the invasion, the Spanish were powerless to protect the outlying mission Indians from annihilation or enslavement. By the end of the war, tens of thousands of Apalachee and Timucua had been sold into slavery, and thousands more had been butchered. The British-sponsored raids eventually probed beyond the mission country, reaching the Tampa Bay area by 1709. In that year, according to a map in the British Colonial Office, the Tocobaga tribe was destroyed. Some Tocobaga were undoubtedly absorbed by the conquering Creeks and Yamasee, and a few survivors reportedly fled southward to merge with what was left of the Calusa and the Tequesta. After two centuries of decline and demoralization, the Tocobaga as a distinct people ceased to exist.

For several decades after the destruction of the Tocobaga, the Pinellas Peninsula was all but deserted. In northern Florida the former domains of the Apalachee and the Timucua were quickly repopulated with thousands of Creek settlers, but very few Creeks migrated as far south as Tampa Bay. Although roving bands undoubtedly visited the area from time to time, there is no evidence that the Creeks established any permanent settlements there prior to 1750. By mid-century the Pinellas Peninsula was overgrown with vegetation, its past civilizations reduced to pottery shards, rotting canoes, and mounds of earth and shell. Standing amidst the scrub oaks and palm thickets, the massive temple and burial mounds of the Tocobaga were ghostly reminders of a lost humanity. Human activity on the

Pinellas, insofar as it continued to exist, was generally confined to the coast, where, from the early eighteenth century on, small groups of Cuban fishermen gathered to dry and salt their fish. Living in palm-thatched huts near the shore, the Cubans maintained a lucrative trade with Havana's fish markets. The Pinellas coast also attracted its share of pirates and privateers, but for the most part the area went unnoticed by the outside world. To the Spanish, who still nominally controlled Florida, and to the French and the British, who hoped to drive the Spanish out, this unheralded spit of land was nothing more than an obscure geographic point somewhere between Pensacola and St. Augustine. Even the mapmakers were a little hazy about its location.

The Pinellas Peninsula became somewhat less obscure in the mid-eighteenth century, even though the area remained semideserted. With the outbreak of the War of Jenkins' Ear in 1743, the colonial rivalry between Spain and Britain intensified, making Florida's Gulf coast a strategically important region. In the ensuing struggle to control the seas, the Tampa Bay area, with its numerous harbors and unattended natural resources, was literally rediscovered by the imperial powers of Europe. In 1745, a British mapping expedition under the command of Capt. David Cutler Braddock surveyed much of Tampa Bay and the Pinellas coast. This enemy incursion into Spanish territory alarmed officials in Madrid and St. Augustine, who eventually countered with several expeditions of their own. In 1756, the noted chartmaker Juan Baptista Franco spent several days in and around Tampa Bay, mapping the coast, exploring the interior, and gathering information on local timber resources for the Spanish navy. Franco made a second voyage in 1757, setting the stage for the most ambitious Spanish expedition of the period, that of Don Francisco Maria Celi.

The pilot of the Royal Spanish Fleet in Havana, Celi set sail for *La Bahia de Tampa* in mid-April 1757. Upon his arrival, he renamed the bay *La Bahia de San Fernando*, honoring King Ferdinand VI. For more than a month Celi and his crew roamed the area, exploring the coastline, taking soundings in the bay, and

Shell Mound Park
St. Petersburg Fla.

AUGUSTA MEMORIAL HOSPITAL

occasionally going ashore to study the land-scape. Through it all, Celi kept a detailed journal that described his wanderings. Along with the elaborately illustrated map which resulted from the expedition, Celi's journal indicates that his men explored the entire region, from several miles up the Hillsborough River, which he named *El Rio de San Julian y Arriaga*, to Egmont Key, which he called *Ysla de San Blas Barreda*. Celi spent several days on the Pinellas Peninsula, examining local plants and animals, and searching for water and timber resources. In the process, he discovered Lake Maggiore, which he named *Aguada de San Francisco*.

Much to his relief, Celi found no Indian settlements on either side of the bay, although he did encounter a few Indians in canoes who boldly paddled up to his three-masted xebec, the *San Francisco de Asis*. The Indians were armed with muskets, which led Celi to believe that they were Creeks who had been in contact with British traders to the north. After accept-ing gifts of tobacco, honey, and corn, and after sampling the Spaniards' rum, the mysterious

natives disappeared. Before Celi himself departed, he made a lasting contribution by naming the point at the entrance of the bay, *Punta de Pinal de Jiminez*. The naming was in honor of Jose Jiminez, the captain of the *San Francisco de Asis*, and in recognition of the pine forest that blanketed the point. In time, of course, the name was shortened and anglicized to Point Pinellas.

The Celi expedition signaled a renewal of Spanish interest in Florida's lower Gulf coast, but any chance of recolonizing the region dis-appeared in 1761, when Spain belatedly sided with France in the French and Indian War, which was ultimately won by the British. With the cessation of hostilities in 1763, Spanish Florida was given to Britain in exchange for Cuba, which had been captured by the British navy during the war. The period of British sovereignty lasted for twenty years, but the British government, consumed with the task of holding on to Massachusetts, Virginia, and other established colonies, displayed little interest in its colonial stepchild. When British officials did concern themselves with Florida,

Shell Mound Park and Augusta Memorial Hospital, near the corner of Sixth Avenue South and Seventh Street, circa 1915. The name of the hospital was changed to Mound Park Hospital in 1923. Prior to the founding of St. Petersburg, there were at least seven mounds in the Booker Creek-Big Bayou area of the peninsula. Shell Mound Park was built to preserve the area's last surviving mound, but it later fell victim to hospital expansion. Courtesy St. Petersburg Historical Society

their attention focused on the lucrative Indian trade of northern Florida or on Atlantic settlements such as Andrew Turnbull's Minorcan colony at New Smyrna. Although the British rarely ventured into southern Florida, one notable exception was the Gauld expedition of 1765. Along with the crew of the HMS *Alarm*, the cartographer George Gauld spent nearly three months in the Tampa Bay area. In addition to charting the bay, Gauld explored the interior of the Pinellas Peninsula, identifying topographical contours, locating sources of fresh water, and anglicizing local place names. More than a century before the incorporation of St. Petersburg, he concluded that the southeastern corner of the peninsula was "a good place for a settlement."[4]

Gauld's findings were welcome news to the earl of Hillsborough, the one British leader who had ambitious plans for Florida. After Lord Hillsborough became colonial secretary in 1768, he commissioned the noted surveyor Bernard Romans to explore the entire Florida coast, from Amelia Island to Perdido Bay. Romans never completed this Herculean assignment, but he did make several reconnaissance visits to the Tampa Bay area, sometimes traveling overland from St. Augustine. Like Francisco Maria Celi, Romans became captivated with the natural beauty of the region and sent back glowing reports of its potential for colonization and profitable staple agriculture. He also claimed, with a measure of hyperbole, that Tampa Bay was "the most proper place in all America, south of Halifax, for the rendezvous of a large fleet of heavy ships, the country around being plentifully timbered and watered."[5] Despite Romans's enthusiasm, the beautiful bay and its environs never became an important part of the British Empire. With the onset of the American Revolution in 1776, British activity in the Gulf region was sharply curtailed, quashing Lord Hillsborough's dreams. During the Revolutionary War, northern Florida became a temporary haven for several thousand Tory Loyalists, but none of them settled near Tampa Bay. In any event, under the Treaty of Paris, Britain ceded Florida back to Spain in exchange for the Bahamas, and the defeated British withdrew from Florida in 1783 leaving few vestiges of their occupation.

The ups and downs of imperial fortunes were major events in London, New York, and Madrid, but they had little impact on the Pinellas Peninsula. A much more significant development locally was the changing nature of the Creek Confederation. Near the close of the first Spanish period, perhaps as early as 1750, many Florida Creeks began to go their own way, distancing themselves from the Confederation and often merging with fugitive black slaves from Georgia and South Carolina. As these renegade Creeks and ex-slaves became a separate people, the Spanish began to refer to them as *cimarrónes*, or "wild roamers." The Indian pronunciation often came out as "Simalones," which was anglicized to "Seminoles" by the British.

Most of the early Seminoles lived in the Alachua and Tallahassee-Miccosukee regions of northern Florida, but a few bands filtered farther south. When Celi visited Tampa Bay in 1757, he encountered a small number of musket-bearing Indians that almost certainly were Seminoles. During the eighteenth century the local Seminole population was probably concentrated on the east side of Tampa Bay, but there were small settlements on the Pinellas side, including a village near the western edge of the peninsula, in an area

Another view of Shell Mound Park, circa 1920. Courtesy St. Petersburg Historical Society

now known appropriately as Seminole. The Seminoles of Pinellas left few traces of their culture or economy, which suggests that they were never very numerous. They were an agricultural people, devoted to the cultivation of corn and beans, but we can only speculate about the specific rituals and mores of their society. Living in the shadow of a lost Indian civilization must have given them cause for reflection and wonder, but what they thought of the relics and mounds of the Tocobaga was never recorded.

During the second Spanish period (1783-1821), Florida was only nominally under Spanish control. From the Cascades to the Argentine Pampas, Spain's New World empire was crumbling, and Florida was no exception. Nevertheless, the Spanish Crown did make a few fleeting attempts to extend its sovereignty beyond the walls of St. Augustine and Pensacola. In the fall of 1783, less than a month after the signing of the Treaty of Paris, Capt. José Antonio de Evia made an extensive reconnaissance voyage along the Gulf coast, stopping twice in Tampa Bay. On his second visit, Evia encountered a mounted Indian hunting party made up of Yuchis, Tallapoosas, and Choctaws. The Indians had come south in search of pelts which could be traded to British merchants in northern Florida. After a little prodding, the Indians insisted that they would welcome trade with Spanish merchants, a fact which Evia

duly reported to his superiors in Havana.

Despite this encouraging experience, ten years passed before the beleaguered Spanish returned to Tampa Bay. In 1793, Capt. Vicente Folch y Juan was sent to the bay to negotiate a trading relationship with the local Indians, who were presumed to be Lower Creeks or Seminoles. Spanish officials hoped to construct a trading post and fort that would preempt American settlement in the area and challenge the trading monopoly of English-speaking merchants. After surveying the shoreline of the bay, which he found overgrown with mangroves and sea grapes, Folch y Juan visited two Indian villages, Cascavela and Anattylaica. According to the Spanish captain, the natives of both villages greeted the idea of a local Spanish trading post with enthusiasm. Thus, he proposed the establishment of a large Spanish settlement in the area. In the end, Spain did establish a small garrison of soldiers and traders on the eastern side of the bay, but the post proved unsuccessful and was abandoned after a few months.

The reasons for the trading post's failure are unclear, but the Spanish experienced similar disappointments all across Florida during these years. To their considerable embarrassment, the dominant force in Spanish Florida continued to be the Scottish trading firm of Panton, Leslie, and Company. Paralleling the settlement patterns of Lower Creeks

A marker in Abercrombie Park, near Boca Ciega Bay, locates the site of another shell mound.
Courtesy St. Petersburg Times

and Seminoles, Panton, Leslie maintained approximately a dozen trading posts in northern and central Florida. However, its southernmost post was at Volusia, near Lake George, more than a hundred miles northeast of Point Pinellas. Thus, the Indians of Tampa Bay and the lower Gulf coast were generally left to themselves. Despite intermittent contact with the British traders to the north, they were set apart from the mainstream of Seminole culture.

In fact, prior to the general amalgamation that followed the First Seminole War (1817-1821), most of the Indians in the Tampa Bay area were not, strictly speaking, Seminoles. Although Americans often classified them as Seminoles, they were actually "Spanish Indians," a conglomeration of Upper Creeks, Cuban fishermen, mestizos, fugitive black slaves, and perhaps a few surviving Tocobaga and Calusa. Probably numbering fewer than a thousand all told, the Spanish Indians inhabited the Gulf coast from Charlotte Harbor to Anclote Bay. Speaking an eclectic dialect that combined everything from Yuchi to

Spanish to several West African languages, they lived off the sea and had little contact with the Seminoles of the interior. Most of the Spanish Indians lived south of the Manatee River, but when the fishing conditions were right, more than a few could be found on the Pinellas barrier islands.

For three-quarters of a century the Spanish Indians of the Gulf coast lived on the fringes of Florida history, isolated and independent, with little to concern them but the vagaries of wind, water, and fish. They took no part in the colonial wars that would ultimately bring their way of life to an end. During the War of 1812, the Creeks and the Seminoles divided into pro-British and pro-American factions. For General Andrew Jackson and other Americans who coveted Spanish Florida, the wartime activities of the pro-British Indians, known as the Red Sticks, served as a convenient justification for invading the area, which was regarded as an unfortunate refuge for fugitive slaves. When Jackson pursued the Red Sticks deep into Florida territory in 1814, he triggered a series of events that would lead to the First Seminole War and the Adams-Onís Treaty of 1819. Unable to protect its embattled colony, Spain agreed to cede East Florida to the United States and to renounce its claims to West Florida, which had already been seized by the Americans. In 1821, after two years of procedural delays, the American annexation of Florida became official. For better or worse, three centuries of Spanish involvement in *La Florida* had come to an inglorious end.

Following the annexation, thousands of American settlers poured into Florida, although only a handful strayed south of St. Augustine. For the time being, central and southern Florida were left to the Indians and a few adventurous traders and pirates. Under the Treaty of Moultrie Creek, signed in 1823, the Seminoles of central Florida agreed to restrict their settlements to a narrow strip of land running from the Green Swamp to Charlotte Harbor. Consequently, in an attempt to monitor and control the Seminoles' activities, the United States Army erected a fort near the mouth of the Hillsborough River in January 1824. Named for its commander, Col. George Mercer Brooke, the fort was part military outpost and part frontier trading center. Drawn by the opportunities for trade, the Seminoles soon established several villages within a day's walk of Fort Brooke. The largest of these settlements were Thonotosassa, Eaufaula, and Angola—all on the eastern side of Tampa Bay. A few Seminoles lived on the Pinellas side, but the fact that the peninsula was well beyond the boundaries of the reservation created by the Treaty of Moultrie Creek kept the number small. When the Indian agent John R. Bell visited the area in 1821, he discovered a small maritime Indian settlement on the western edge of the peninsula. The inhabitants of the village, which was known as *Tate-ta-la-hosta-ka*, or "Watermelon Town," may well have been Spanish Indians. But, whatever their derivation or subculture, the Indians of *Tate-ta-la-hosta-ka* were too few to concern American officials during the 1820s.

To the soldiers at Fort Brooke, the Pinellas Peninsula—commonly known as Fishermen's Point—was essentially a hunting and fishing ground, a place where they could stalk deer and wild boars, or perhaps fish and swim in the shallows. It was a beautiful, unspoiled land, an arcadia that could not last in a society driven by dreams of expansion and progress. For the Seminoles and Spanish Indians of Pinellas, the onset of the Second Seminole War in 1835 was the beginning of the end. Goaded by the insatiable demands of white settlers and land speculators, the American government ordered the complete removal of Florida's Indian population. The resulting war lasted seven long years, costing the Americans $20 million and several thousand casualties. By the time it was over, the Indians of Tampa Bay, like their counterparts elsewhere, had either been killed or driven from their land. Those with dark skins, presumed to be fugitive slaves or the descendants of slaves, were sold into bondage. Some of the survivors escaped into the Green Swamp or the Everglades, but most were removed to Oklahoma. Twenty years after the departure of the Spanish, the Indians of Florida were all but extinct. Florida was now on the eve of statehood, with no human impediments (the mosquitoes and the humidity were another matter) to slow the advance of white settlement.

It would be many years before the onrush reached Fishermen's Point, but from the mid-1830s on, a trickle of white settlers found their way to the area. During the final years before removal, the Indians of Pinellas shared the peninsula with at least six white settlers. A Spaniard by the name of Antonio Máximo Hernández operated a fishing rancho near the southern tip of the peninsula, in the area now known as Maximo Point. Hernández often served as a fishing guide for the soldiers at Fort Brooke, sometimes taking them to Egmont Key in search of turtle eggs. After aiding the United States Army during the Second Seminole War, he was rewarded with a special land grant in 1842. Two other Spanish fishermen, Joe Silva and Juan Levique (also known as John Levick), lived on the eastern shore of Boca Ciega Bay, while on the opposite side of the peninsula William Papy fished the waters of the bayou that now bears his name. Finally, there were the peninsula's two most prominent pioneers,

Capt. William Bunce and Dr. Odet Philippe.

A native of Baltimore, Captain Bunce was a coastal trader who operated out of Key West during the late 1820s and early 1830s. In 1834, after a brief stint as a customs collector for the Key West District (which included the Tampa Bay area), he established a large fish rancho near the mouth of the Manatee River. Employing approximately 150 Spanish Indians, Cubans, and Seminoles, he carried on a lucrative trade with the fish markets of Havana. Unfortunately, Bunce's Indians, as they were called, were soon caught in a crossfire of mistrust and misidentification. During the early stages of the Second Seminole War, American officials informed Bunce that his Indian workers would be required to move to an island reservation. When he refused to cooperate, insisting that his Indians posed no threat to American interests, federal gunboats shelled his rancho, burning it to the ground. Undaunted, Bunce retreated north to Palm Island (Cabbage Key), where he resumed his fishing operations. For a time, the officials at Fort Brooke winked at this defiance, knowing that Bunce was a popular figure among local civilians; in 1838 he was even selected as one of Hillsborough County's delegates to a territorial constitutional convention. But, in October 1840, as the frustrations of the war mounted, federal gunboats once again destroyed Bunce's rancho. Emotionally and financially shattered, Bunce himself did not live to see the end of the war.

As exciting as they were, William Bunce's tragic experiences were no match for the dramatic saga of Odet Philippe. A larger-than-life character with a penchant for hyperbole, Philippe was part adventurer and part charlatan. Among other claims, he professed to be a French nobleman, a classmate and friend of Napoleon's, and a high-ranking medical officer in the French navy. During the Battle of Trafalgar in 1805, he allegedly was captured by the British who took him to England as a prisoner of war. Paroled to the Bahamas, he made his way to South Carolina, and later to Florida, before being waylaid by an ailing pirate crew in need of medical attention. After bringing the pirates back to health, he was rewarded with a treasure chest full of gold and a map directing him to a homestead site on the western shore of Old Tampa Bay. Although this romantic tale has often been repeated as fact, there is little evidence to support Philippe's extravagant claims. In all likelihood, he used these legendary exploits as a smokescreen for his real-life activities as a smuggler and slave trader.

Born in Lyon, France, in 1788, Philippe surfaced in Charleston after the War of 1812 and remained there for at least a decade working as a cigar maker. During the 1830s, he divided his time between New River (Fort Lauderdale) and Key West, where he became involved in a number of entrepreneurial ventures. His far-flung business interests, which almost certainly included slave trading, took him to Charleston and Havana, and ultimately to Fort Brooke.

Sometime between 1837 and 1842, Philippe moved his base of operations to Tampa Bay, constructing a plantation house on the former site of the Tocobaga capital, in the area now known as Safety Harbor. Although the exact timing of Philippe's arrival at Safety Harbor is unknown, his official land claim dates from the Armed Occupation Act of 1842, which opened the Indian lands of central and southern Florida to homesteading. Any settler who agreed to build a house, clear at least five acres, plant crops, and live on his property for five years was granted 160 acres of free land. The law was designed to attract new settlers to the region, but it also allowed existing squatters such as Philippe, Hernández, Levick, and Silva to gain clear title to their land. Even though the overall response to the new law was disappointing—on the Pinellas Peninsula only twenty-five claims were filed in 1842-1843, and most of those were never consummated by actual settlement—Philippe and a few others took full advantage of this opportunity. Surrounded by his four daughters and a few slaves, Philippe soon settled into the life of a small planter. Calling his plantation St. Helena, in honor of Napoleon's final refuge, he raised everything from cattle to cotton and successfully developed the area's first citrus grove. Providing fresh fruit and vegetables to

the commissary at Fort Brooke brought him a
steady income and a measure of influence, and
St. Helena became a popular way station for
soldiers traveling between the main fort and
Fort Harrison, a recuperative outpost established on the northwestern coast of the Pinellas
Peninsula in 1841.

Fort Harrison was abandoned at the close
of the Second Seminole War, but Fort Brooke
and the nearby town of Tampa remained. With
the Pinellas side of the bay still raw frontier,
Philippe spent much of his time in Tampa,
where he maintained an eclectic array of business interests, including an oyster bar, a
ten-pin alley, and a one-man cigar-making
operation. Although small and unincorporated,
early Tampa was a lively community that
attracted its share of adventurers, pioneers,
and others searching for opportunity, particularly during the Mexican War (1846-1848),
when Fort Brooke served as a staging ground
for American troops. The war brought new
settlers and public notice to the region,
prompting the federal government to order a
land survey as a prelude to large-scale
settlement.

Small parcels of the Pinellas Peninsula
had been surveyed in 1844 and 1846, but the
first extensive survey was conducted by
George D. Watson, Jr., in the spring and summer of 1848. Working with three assistants,
Watson measured and charted most of present-
day St. Petersburg, including the shoreline
from Pinellas Point to the northern reaches of
Boca Ciega Bay. At the same time, workmen
were putting the finishing touches on the
Egmont Key Lighthouse, a seven-thousand-

dollar structure designed to ensure safe entry
into Tampa Bay. At long last, the peninsula
was truly becoming a part of the known world.
For better or worse, these attempts to sys-
tematize and control the natural environment—to turn land into real estate and coastline into sea lane—marked the beginning of
Pinellas's modern history.

The natural era may have been on the
way out, but it did not go quietly. The coming
together of natural and institutional history
was punctuated by an awesome reminder of
human vulnerability. As if to serve warning to
future developers, speculators, and technol-
ogists of pavement and landfill, the proverbial
storm of the century literally struck the
peninsula in the fall of 1848. After two days of
intermittent gales and freakish atmospheric
conditions, hurricane-force winds roared into
Tampa Bay on Monday morning, September
25. Although the storm's peak winds (ninety to
a hundred miles per hour) and barometric low
(28.18 inches) did not equal those of other Gulf
storms, both earlier and later, the accompanying tidal surge was the highest ever recorded in
the area. This unusual surge was related to the
direction and pace of the storm, which seemed
to hug the coastline as it moved northward
from the Florida Keys. As the eye of the storm
approached the Pinellas Peninsula, the normally placid waters of the Gulf were pushed into
Tampa Bay. Once the eye had passed, the wind
direction suddenly reversed, and within a few
hours' time, a towering wall of water had raced
from Egmont Key to the head of Tampa Bay
and back again, inundating everything in its
path. At one point, most of the Pinellas Penin-

sula was under water, as the waves reached the treetops in low-lying areas.

The results were devastating, even though the loss of life was minimal by modern standards. All of the buildings at Fort Brooke were heavily damaged, while much of Tampa simply washed away. Ships were tossed about like matchsticks—a schooner bearing the Fort Brooke payroll came to rest several hundred yards inland—and piers and wharves crumbled into the bay. On Egmont Key towering waves cracked the foundation of the new lighthouse, driving keeper Marvel Edwards, and his wife and five children, into the sea. The terrified family rode out the storm clinging to the sides of a small skiff that they tethered to a palm tree. Although the entire family survived, Edwards was so unnerved by the ordeal that he resigned his post. The storm was even too much for Antonio Máximo Hernández, who had weathered many a long blow during his long career as a fishing guide. Although Hernández emerged from the storm with his

life, his celebrated fish rancho at Frenchman's Creek was completely destroyed. Salvaging a few soggy remnants of his property, he solemnly booked a one-way passage to Havana, from which he never returned.

At the other end of the peninsula, the master of St. Helena, Odet Philippe, proved to be more resilient, despite the loss of his house and most of his citrus grove. The residents of the plantation saved themselves by scurrying to the top of a Tocobaga mound, although they had a few anxious moments when a section of the mound collapsed and washed into the bay. After the storm, Philippe replanted his grove and wisely relocated his house on higher ground. But he never forgot the tidal wave that almost drowned him. Twenty years later, on the eve of his death, the old Frenchman was still embellishing tales of the "great gale of '48."[7]

For Philippe, as for most of those who survived the storm, the true measure of its force was its long-term impact on the natural

This advertisement appeared in the Tourist News *in 1924. Courtesy St. Petersburg Historical Society*

This Indian canoe from the late eighteenth or early nineteenth century was recovered from the bottom of Crescent Lake in 1924. The eighteen-foot long cypress canoe is now in the possession of the St. Petersburg Historical Society. Courtesy St. Petersburg Times

environment. By the time the wind and water subsided, large sections of the local landscape were unrecognizable. Islands were sliced in two, high ground was turned into marshland, and channels and inlets appeared where none had existed before. The entire configuration of the barrier islands was changed, plants and animals were forced to adapt to new surroundings, and whole forests were either uprooted or destroyed by salt-water contamination. Almost nothing was left unaltered, as John Levick and Joe Silva, who were en route from New Orleans when the storm hit, discovered. When they returned to the Pinellas Peninsula in early October, the two turtlers gaped at an unfamiliar shoreline and sailed into Boca Ciega Bay through a channel (John's Pass, named for Levick) that had not been there a week earlier. They soon learned that most of their possessions, including much of their land, had washed away during the storm. Poorer, but wiser, they rebuilt their homesteads on higher ground and lived out their lives on the bay.

Chapter Two

The Pinellas Frontier

1849-1885

Mrs. Sarah Bethell, wife of John Bethell, sitting on the front porch of the Pinellas Village (Big Bayou) post office, circa 1900. For nearly a decade, from 1876 to 1885, the Bethell cottage was the only post office on the lower Pinellas Peninsula. Mrs. Bethell replaced her daughter Mary as postmistress in 1894 and served until 1907, the year the Pinellas Village post office was closed. Courtesy St. Petersburg Historical Society

The natural regeneration of the Pinellas Peninsula following the great hurricane of 1848 must have been an intriguing sight: seabirds adjusting to new nesting areas; shellfish coming to rest on pristine sandbars; animals foraging in the decomposing underbrush; new stands of oak and pine and sawgrass vying for space and sunlight; and so on. Unfortunately, this complex drama, with its countless subplots of adaptation and survival, can only be reconstructed in the realm of imagination, or perhaps in a limited way through an archaeologist's cunning. With the exception of Joe Silva, John Levick, and the small band at St. Helena plantation, no humans were present to witness nature's regenerative artistry. Máximo Hernández, William Bunce, the Spanish Indians of Cabbage Key, and the Seminoles of Watermelon Town were all gone, and for a brief moment the natural world of the peninsula was left to itself. While the rest of the nation was busy helping President Zachary Taylor divide up the spoils of the Mexican War, the Pinellas frontier was catching its breath, so to speak, as if to brace itself for the inevitable onrush of modern civilization.

For better or worse, civilization of a sort had already reached the eastern shore of Tampa Bay. After the storm cleared away the rickety shacks of the original settlement of Tampa Town, it was rebuilt on a much grander scale. With new streets and buildings, and with a population approaching a thousand, the town took on an air of permanence and respectability that had been lacking in its rough-and-tumble early years. According to an 1856 survey, the new Tampa boasted two hotels, two schools, one church, an increasingly busy land office, one bakery, one silversmith, a Masonic lodge, and seven lawyers. It also had an energetic corps of local boosters, led by Capt. James McKay, a Scottish-born entrepreneur who first arrived in Tampa in 1846. An inveterate promoter who tried everything from coastal trading to citrus farming, McKay extended Tampa's participation in the first Florida boom by initiating a lucrative cattle trade with Cuba in 1858.

By twentieth-century standards, the Florida boom of the 1850s was hardly a boom at all. Nevertheless, it represented a major turning point in the lives of those who had committed themselves to this isolated and unheralded appendage of the Deep South. Between 1845, the year Florida gained statehood, and 1860, Florida's population more than doubled, as the state welcomed a steady stream of immigrants, mainly from nearby Georgia and South Carolina. On the eve of secession, Florida still had fewer inhabitants (140,424) than the city of Baltimore. But the state's demographic pulse was definitely quickening, and some Floridians were even beginning to dream of an emerging empire in the sun.

Antebellum Florida's most celebrated dreamer was Senator David Levy Yulee, a transplanted West Indian Jew who persuaded the state legislature to finance a cross-state railway. Yulee's original plan of 1851 called for a main road from Fernandina to Tampa Bay, with a spur line running north to Cedar Keys. But unfortunately for the boosters of Tampa Bay, political and economic pressures eventually forced Yulee to alter the route. When it was finally completed in 1858, the narrow-gauge Florida Railroad consisted of a single line from Fernandina to Cedar Keys. Nevertheless, for a time, Yulee's original plan inspired hopes and renewed interest in the bay area. At the senator's request, a team of United States Navy surveyors, commanded by Lt. C. H. Berryman, took more than thirty thousand soundings in the bay during the spring and summer of 1854. Berryman's primary mission was to find the best site for a seaside railroad depot where deep-draft sailing vessels could load and unload their cargoes. After several weeks of reconnaissance, he selected a prime location on the southeastern shore of the Pinellas Peninsula. On that spot, which was later known as Paul's Landing, the expedition's carpenter, William Paul, hastily constructed a small hamlet, complete with temporary barracks, a short pier, and a smokehouse. Such were the simple origins of St. Petersburg's downtown waterfront.

In late August, Lieutenant Berryman and the survey team abandoned their makeshift camp, but three months later, following his discharge from the navy, William Paul re-

Captain Abel Miranda and his wife Eliza, circa 1870. The Mirandas settled at Big Bayou in 1857. Courtesy St. Petersburg Historical Society

turned to the site in a two-masted schooner, accompanied by his wife and son, and all of his possessions, including fifty orange seedlings. He remained there for three years, supporting his family by fishing in the bay, and patiently waiting for his orange trees to mature. Tragically, his ambitious plans for a commercial citrus grove had to be scratched in 1857 when his wife became seriously ill. Forced to head north in search of a competent doctor, the despondent carpenter sold his home and outbuildings to Abel Miranda for thirty-five dollars. The land, of course, was not his to sell. Technically, Paul was a squatter, even though for a time he was quite literally the master of all that he surveyed.

By the mid-1850s, the upper Pinellas

Peninsula had attracted several clusters of settlers, including the large McMullen clan. But the lower peninsula remained raw frontier. As late as 1856, Paul's only neighbor was James R. Hay, an itinerant cattle drover who had settled two miles inland, near present-day Lakeview Avenue. Living alone in a one-room shack, Hay made a good living tending the herds of several Tampa cattlemen.

In 1858, Hay resettled near Clam Bayou, on Boca Ciega Bay, and three years later, after the outbreak of the Civil War, he left the peninsula altogether. But fortunately for Abel Miranda, he was around long enough to help relocate William Paul's ill-fated homestead. Miranda was a native of St. Augustine and a descendant of the Minorcan colonists who had settled on Florida's east coast in the late eighteenth century. A talented fisherman and tracker, he had served as an irregular army scout during the Third Seminole War (1856-1858). Released from the service in early 1857, he decided to settle at Big Bayou, where he had discovered a fresh-water spring during the war. Leaving his wife Eliza and an infant son in Tampa, he spent several months clearing a large plot of land, where he hoped to establish a fish rancho that would rival the earlier efforts of William Bunce and Máximo Hernández. Luckily, he arrived just in time to take advantage of William Paul's impending departure. With Hay's help, he was able to dismantle Paul's buildings, float the parts down the bay to Big Bayou, and eventually reassemble them—an amazing feat by any standard. Within three years, Miranda's recycled homestead was processing more than enough mullet to support his family, including his wife's two younger brothers, John and William Bethell, who had migrated to Big Bayou from Key West in 1859. Before long the Bethell brothers moved out to establish their own mullet ranch at Little Bayou. But they remained close to their strong-willed brother-in-law, a larger-than-life character who was destined to become "the Rebel terror of Tampa Bay."[1]

The lower Pinellas frontier had no slaves to emancipate and no "fire-eater" politics to raise its ire, but the Civil War came to the area just the same. Although the peninsula was never a major theater of military operations, it did play an indirect role in the Union's campaign to blockade Florida's Gulf coast, which was a potentially important source of salt and beef for the Confederate army. Beginning in the fall of 1861, a small fleet of Union blockaders was stationed at Egmont Key, at the entrance to Tampa Bay. The port of Tampa, like most of Florida, was rabidly pro-Confederate, and the blockaders were given the almost impossible task of sealing off the bay. Egmont Key also served as a refuge for the local Unionist minority, which included James Hay, who fled to the island at the beginning of the war, after selling his Clam Bayou homestead to William Coons for twenty-five dollars and a silver watch. For a time some Unionists

tried to remain on the mainland, but sooner or later they were either killed or driven out by the local Confederate Homeguard.

In one such incident, a well-known Unionist, Scott Whitehurst, was shot and killed in an ambush near Pinellas Point. Rightly or wrongly, the Union commander at Egmont Key blamed the murder on Abel Miranda and vowed to bring him to justice. Miranda claimed that Whitehurst was a cattle thief who was supplying the Yankees at Egmont Key with stolen Rebel beef, but the commander was unmoved. In the end, Miranda avoided capture, but in February 1862, a naval raiding party burned and looted his entire estate. According to John Bethell, who watched in horror from a nearby Indian mound, the Union raiders not only torched Miranda's home and destroyed his orange grove, but also killed or maimed most of his livestock. The entire experience only deepened Miranda's commitment to the Confederate cause. After removing his family to Tampa, which remained in Confederate hands until 1864, he extracted a heavy toll of revenge from the local Union forces, primarily as a blockade runner. Following the surrender at Appomattox, Miranda returned to the Pinellas Peninsula, but he never rebuilt his fish rancho at Big Bayou. Instead, he moved two miles inland, where, he claimed, no Yankee gunboat could ever bother him again. Unrepentant and unreconstructed, he lived on the peninsula until his death in 1900.

At the end of the Civil War, the only settlers still living on the lower Pinellas Peninsula were William Coons, the enterprising fisherman who had purchased James Hay's Clam Bayou property in 1861, and his wife. Abel and Eliza Miranda returned to the peninsula in early 1866, followed by John and Sarah Bethell in 1867; and a year later they were joined by a handful of new settlers, including Sarah Bethell's uncle, Vincent Leonardi. But, even with this trickle of immigration, the area remained a semideserted backwater, a half-forgotten frontier that played no significant role in the drama of Reconstruction. While Florida's political leaders were squabbling over railroad bonds and the implications of black citizenship, and while marauding Klansmen were trying to break the will of Scalawags and Carpetbaggers, the pioneers of lower Pinellas were preoccupied with the problems of survival and subsistence.

Of course, very few Floridians actually experienced the "Black Reconstruction" that later dominated the mythology of the New South. To the dismay of the state's seventy thousand freedmen, Radical Reconstruction in Florida was never very radical. Although Florida's Reconstruction lasted for twelve years, far longer than in most areas of the South, the state's ruling coalition of white Republicans presided over a conservative program of limited social change and racial adjustment. When the era was finally brought to a close by the infamous Compromise of 1877—the backroom deal that put Rutherford B. Hayes in the White House in exchange for a formal end to the Reconstruction experiment— the freedmen of Florida were left with little but unfulfilled dreams and broken promises. While they generally retained the right to vote, Florida blacks were seldom able to acquire their own land, or to sidestep the social and educational restrictions of a white supremacist society.

One of the rare exceptions to this bleak reality was John Donaldson, the first black man to settle on the lower Pinellas Peninsula after the war. An ex-slave who had lived in Alabama, Donaldson migrated to the area in 1868 as an employee of Louis Bell, Jr., a white homesteader originally from the Florida panhandle. The Bell household also included Anna Germain, a mulatto housekeeper who later became John Donaldson's wife and the mother of his eleven children. The Donaldsons lived and worked with the Bells for several years, but they eventually struck out on their own, purchasing a forty-acre farm located one mile northwest of Lake Maggiore (then known as Salt Lake). Although illiterate, John Donaldson was a man of many talents and won the grudging admiration of almost everyone who knew him. Working as a truck farmer, drayman, timber cutter, and general jack-of-all-trades, he exercised considerable independence and earned a comfortable living for his large family.

Writing in 1914, John Bethell remembered Donaldson as "a man universally respected and one who really kept pace with his white neighbors."[2] Donaldson's success can be attributed, in part, to his own resourcefulness. But he also benefited from the physical isolation and racial homogeneity that characterized the Pinellas frontier: out on the fringes of settlement there was very little organized social life, and thus little reason for whites to be overly concerned with the dictates of caste and class—particularly when the local black community consisted of a single family. The tolerance and respect accorded John Donaldson would not be extended to later black settlers, no matter how talented or resourceful they were.

St. Petersburg's pioneer era was relatively brief, surviving little more than a generation, from the mid-1850s to the late 1880s. But while it lasted—before the coming of the railroad, and before the technological wizardry of Thomas Edison and Henry Ford seemingly changed everything, allowing metropolitan values and institutions to extend their reach into the remotest of areas—this special period spawned lives of quiet courage and rustic simplicity that later Americans would find unimaginable. The pioneers who migrated to the lower Pinellas Peninsula came for a variety of reasons. Some were drawn by the simple promise of cheap land, others were chasing extravagant dreams of wealth and upward mobility, and still others were responding to the lure of the wilderness. But, in one way or another, nearly all of them reflected the restless temperament and enterprising spirit that dominated late nineteenth-century America. As the moral enthusiasms of the Civil War and Reconstruction gave way to the expansive energies of the Gilded Age, the pioneering frontiersman loomed larger than ever in the American consciousness, especially in undeveloped areas like Florida, where the frontier experience had not yet been reduced to an historical artifact suitable for caricature in dime novels.

Despite being the second largest state (58,600 square miles) east of the Mississippi River, Florida ranked thirty-fourth out of

John Bethell as a young Confederate soldier, 1862. Bethell served in Company K of the Seventh Florida Regiment from 1862 to 1865. Courtesy Pinellas County Historical Society

The Bethell homestead and wharf at Pinellas Village, on the shore of Big Bayou, 1893. Courtesy St. Petersburg Times

thirty-seven states in population (269,493) in 1880. Only Oregon, Nevada, and Delaware had fewer inhabitants. Vast areas of the state lay unsettled, particularly in central and southern Florida, and one had to travel to the Rocky Mountain territories to find lower density rates. Florida's overall population density (4.9 persons per square mile) was well below the average for the nation (16.9) and the South Atlantic region (28.3), and it was the only state east of the Mississippi with fewer than 21 persons per square mile. It is little wonder that one Northern visitor in 1872 reported, only half facetiously, that "Florida was nine-tenths water, and the other tenth swamp," or that Senator John Holmes of Maine declared that it would not be much of "a loss to the United States were the whole peninsula of Florida to sink into the Gulf of Mexico."[3]

Such harsh judgments probably would have been confirmed by a visit to the lower Pinellas Peninsula, which was sparsely settled even by Florida standards. With no more than thirty families at any one time during the 1870s, lower Pinellas lagged far behind the Manatee River area to the south and the Safety Harbor-Clearwater area to the north, not to

mention the town of Tampa (population 720 in 1880) across the bay. Nevertheless, the sprinkling of homesteaders on the lower peninsula gave the area a semblance of settlement that, at the very least, punctuated the wilderness. In addition to the Miranda-Bethell-Leonardi clan, which dominated the area west of Big Bayou, the early settlers included James Barnett, a Confederate veteran who settled on the future site of Disston City (Gulfport) in 1868; John L. Branch, a citrus farmer who came to the lower peninsula in 1869; Ambrose Tompkins, an English sailor who made his way to the area in 1870 after serving with the Union Navy during the Civil War; William Benton, a farmer who established a large homestead near Big Bayou in 1872; and Richard Strada, Timothy Kimball, Rafeno Emanuel, and Joseph and Ben Puig, all of whom came to Boca Ciega Bay from New Orleans in 1874. These men were all permanent settlers, pioneers who, along with their wives and children, helped to lay the foundation of early St. Petersburg society. But, as such, they were anything but representative of the mass of settlers who migrated to the area during the two decades following the Civil War.

For every pioneer who came and stayed,

there were three or four who came and went in quick succession, proving that a life of hardship among the mosquitoes and the alligators was not for everyone. Some could not adjust to the mind-numbing isolation of frontier life, while others could not abide the humid climate and malarial hazards of Florida's semitropical lowlands. But for most of Pinellas's early pioneers the chief problem was economic failure, or more specifically, the inability to make money. Subsistence and self-sufficiency were well within the means of most early settlers, but, in the context of a national culture devoted to the gospel of upward mobility, very few were satisfied with mere survival. Whatever their expectations, settlers quickly discovered that lower Pinellas was not a likely place to turn a profit, much less to strike it rich. Despite an abundance of rainfall, an un-

usually long growing season, a seemingly inexhaustible supply of fish, and plenty of grazing land, the jingle of coins was rarely heard on the Pinellas frontier, especially during the nationwide depression of 1873-1878. Local pioneers tried everything from sugar cane to sheep, from grapefruit to mullet. But in an age without pesticides or herbicides, or refrigeration, insects and weeds and other problems inherent in a semitropical environment made successful farming extremely difficult, regardless of the choice of crop.

Of course, even when crops were bountiful, there was little likelihood of getting them to market. The local population alone was too small to support commercial truck farming, ranching, or fishing; and access to more distant markets was haphazard at best. The nearest rail depot was at Cedar Keys, ninety miles to the north, and the narrow mudpaths that masqueraded as roads were almost useless for commercial purposes. The best hope was the coastal shipping trade, but the shippers involved invariably organized their routes to suit the needs of the farmers and stockmen of more settled areas such as Tampa and Pensacola. The occasional schooner from Cuba or Key West (the only city in Florida that lacked an agricultural hinterland) that docked at Big Bayou was a welcome sight, but it did little to alleviate the general problem of isolation. Thus, prior to the completion of the Orange Belt Railroad in 1888, getting commodities to market was a game of chance that allowed for few winners. Far too often, stocks of fish went uneaten, crops rotted in the fields, and oranges and grapefruit were left on the trees to wither in the sun. In such circumstances, even the hardiest pioneers sometimes gave up.

Some early settlers were land speculators who never had any intention of establishing permanent homesteads. But, whether the primary reason for leaving was unsuccessful farming or successful speculation, the end result was a rapid turnover in population and land titles. The saga of the Hackney-Perry property is a case in point. Between 1869 and 1872, Dr. James Sarvent Hackney purchased 424 acres of land running from Booker Creek to Bayboro Harbor. A relatively wealthy man for his time, Dr. Hackney poured all of his energy and resources into his Pinellas homestead. After building a comfortable home and draining several acres of wetland, he planted more than a hundred citrus trees and brought in large herds of cattle and hogs. In early 1873, he was joined by the Perry brothers, William and Oliver, who had acquired 80 acres of land nearby. Within a few months, the Perrys seemingly had settled in, having planted sugar cane, sweet potatoes, pumpkins, and corn. However, when W. F. Spurlin came along in late 1873 and offered to buy Hackney and the Perrys out for a total of forty-four hundred dollars, all three men jumped at the chance. Spurlin, who obviously harbored dreams of an agricultural empire, also brought 120 additional acres from the state. But within three years he too was

gone. After suffering through two unprofitable harvests, he sold out to John Constantine Williams of Detroit for three thousand dollars—almost fifteen hundred dollars less than he had paid for the property in 1873. This was the origin of the famous Williams tract, which ultimately played a pivotal role in the early development of St. Petersburg.

The silk-hatted stranger who bought out W. F. Spurlin represented a new element on the lower Pinellas frontier. At last, the area had attracted a dreamer whose resources matched his ambitions. John Constantine Williams, with piercing eyes and long-flowing beard, had the look and manner of an Old Testament patriarch. Born in Detroit in 1817, Williams was the scion of one of frontier Michigan's leading families. His father, John R. Williams, was the first mayor of Detroit, elected in 1824. Reelected three times, the elder Williams went on to make a small fortune in real estate speculation. After his father's death in 1854, John Constantine Williams further enlarged the family's real estate empire, while simultaneously parlaying his influence into a modestly successful political career. Despite this success, a bad case of asthma and a quixotic temperament ultimately led him to Florida, where he hoped to find an ideal town site. In 1875, he visited Jacksonville, Tampa, and Cedar Keys, plus dozens of smaller communities in between, before finally stumbling upon the Pinellas Peninsula.

What attracted him to the area north of Big Bayou, other than happenstance and W. F. Spurlin's eagerness to sell, is unclear. But Williams was convinced that he had found the town site that he had been looking for. In addition to the Spurlin property, he purchased nine hundred acres of largely adjoining state land. Thus, his total Pinellas holdings came to more than sixteen hundred acres, dwarfing the properties of Abel Miranda, John Bethell, or anyone else living on the lower peninsula at that time. According to John Bethell, local residents welcomed Williams, but at times they must have wondered whether any of their new neighbor's dreams would ever be realized. Returning to Detroit in January 1876, Williams allowed his sprawling Pinellas lands to lie vacant for more than three years. After purchasing several additional tracts in 1878, he finally returned to the peninsula in early 1879, accompanied by his wife and children and a young nephew.

Upon his return, Williams was pleased to discover that the area had undergone subtle but significant changes since his first visit in 1875. The cluster of farms at Big Bayou was now officially known as Pinellas Village. Although still unincorporated, the village had acquired its own post office in 1876. Most important, there were a number of new settlers, including citrus farmers William P. Neeld, Jacob Baum, and Thomas Miranda. Another newcomer was an enterprising merchant, R. E. Neeld, who opened a small general store—lower Pinellas's first—in 1878. Neeld's entire inventory was reportedly worth less than two hundred dollars, consisting of little more than nails, matches, and gunpowder, plus a few barrels of coffee, sugar and flour. During Williams's absence, Neeld had also constructed a sturdy wharf to replace the rickety structure that John Bethell had built many years earlier. Bethell's old dream of turning Big Bayou into a major harbor was still unfulfilled, but the number of visitors from Tampa and elsewhere was increasing yearly. Thus, long before the age of million-dollar piers and inverted pyramids, Neeld's new wharf served as an important symbol of local progress.

The changes at Big Bayou reflected the rising expectations of the nation as a whole. In the years between 1875 and 1879, the depression lifted, Reconstruction came to an end, and American democracy celebrated its centennial by narrowly surviving the constitutional crisis of the Hayes-Tilden contest. At the same time, the quickening pace of the Industrial Revolution seemed to be on the verge of changing everything. However, as John Williams soon discovered, one reality that had not changed was the difficulty of farming on the edge of the Florida frontier.

Williams wanted to prove to himself, and to the thousands of prospective settlers who (he hoped) were waiting in the wings, that the Pinellas Peninsula could support commercial farming. After moving into the house that Dr. James Sarvent Hackney had built a decade earlier, Williams experimented with forty acres of prime land. Planting everything from potatoes to sugar cane, he drove himself and his family to the limit. Unfortunately, like Hackney and Spurlin before him, Williams encountered one frustration after another. Bad weather, insects, undependable shippers— everything seemed to conspire against him. After two years of frustrating struggle, the sixty-two-year-old gentleman farmer had little to show for his efforts but a lighter wallet and a bruised ego. By 1881, Williams and his family were back in Detroit, their Florida dream having turned into a nightmare. Sadly, this disillusioning experience weakened an already shaky marriage, and in November 1881 Williams and his wife were granted a divorce. A few months later Williams suffered a disabling stroke, but within a year he was on the rebound, marrying a young Canadian-born widow, Sarah Craven Judge. Nevertheless, it would be several years before the General, as he was known locally, would feel feisty enough to tackle the wilds of lower Pinellas again.

In the interim, local settlers turned their attention to an even more intriguing character, Hamilton Disston. A wealthy Philadelphian in his mid-thirties, Disston had inherited a saw manufacturing company from his English-born father in 1878. Disston first came to Florida in search of tarpon, but soon became taken with the idea of a tropical empire. While his knowledge of the Florida landscape was limited, his timing was perfect. Having overextended itself in railroad promotion, the Florida state government in 1881 was literally on the verge of bankruptcy when Disston appeared on the scene. With the help of a British syndicate, the young saw magnate deposited $1 million in the state treasury in exchange for four million acres of allegedly marginal wetlands. Almost overnight, the state returned to solvency, and Hamilton Disston became the largest landowner in the United States. The state agency overseeing the sale, the Internal Improvement Fund, was only empowered to sell low-lying swampland. But, in actuality, Disston was given title to several large tracts of high land,

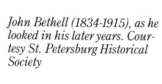

John Bethell (1834-1915), as he looked in his later years. Courtesy St. Petersburg Historical Society

including more than 150,000 acres on the Pinellas Peninsula.

In southwestern Florida, where most of his domain was indeed swampland, Disston envisioned an intricate network of canals that would open the area to settlement and staple agriculture, especially sugar cane farming. But he had even grander plans for the high ground of Pinellas. There he hoped to create a model city that would serve as the unofficial capital of his empire. At first, it appeared that Disston's city would be constructed on a tract of land at the northern end of the peninsula, near Anclote Bay. In early 1883, Disston's agents, led by the former governor of Arizona Territory, Anson Safford, descended upon the tiny hamlet of Tarpon Springs, armed with transits and blueprints. Eighteen months later, the new Tarpon Springs boasted two hotels, a commercial pier, and a stage line to Tampa. Disston was delighted and encouraged his friends and relatives in the North to invest in his blossoming community. Several well-heeled visitors, including Disston's younger brother Jacob, took the bait and built winter homes at Tarpon Springs. But Disston himself soon came to the conclusion that the Tarpon Springs site was better suited to tourism than to serious urban development. By the summer of 1884, his attention had shifted southward to the land adjoining the southern reaches of Boca Ciega Bay.

The man most responsible for Disston's change in plans was an enterprising citrus farmer by the name of William B. Miranda. A nephew of the Confederate fire-eater Abel Miranda, he had lived on the lower peninsula since the mid-1870s. In the fall of 1883, while serving as Disston's guide on a tour of lower Pinellas properties, Miranda eagerly directed the land baron to the waterfront property of Joseph Torres, a Spaniard who had come to the area by way of New Orleans in 1876. Miranda touted the Torres tract, which was almost surrounded by Disston's own holdings, as an ideal town site. After several months of prodding from both Miranda and Torres, Disston became convinced that he had found the perfect location for his capital city. After hiring Miranda as his local agent, he formed a new corporation, the Disston City Land Company, to expand and consolidate his lower Pinellas holdings.

Miranda and Torres were ecstatic over the prospect of a little development, but they soon discovered that Disston's visions were far grander than any they had ever imagined. The city plat filed by Disston in the summer of 1884 encompassed more than twenty-five square miles and called for streets one hundred feet wide, not to mention an even wider boulevard running along the waterfront. The only local property left outside the projected city limits was the land owned by John Williams, plus a small tract near Big Bayou.

The actual community that began to take shape in 1885 was considerably less grand than the plat's projections, but it still eclipsed anything that had been seen on the lower peninsula since the destruction of the Tocobaga in the early eighteenth century. By the fall of 1885, Disston City boasted a population of more than one hundred, three stores, a post office, and the twenty-six-room Waldorf Hotel. There was also a large commercial warehouse and a long wharf which accommodated the *Mary Disston*, a steamer that carried passengers and freight to and from Tampa and Cedar Keys. For a time, Disston City even had its own newspaper, the *Sea Breeze*, edited by William J. McPherson and G. W. Bennett. A bimonthly first published in May 1886, the *Sea Breeze* dared its readers to find "another locality on all the coast of Florida that will take the lead of Point Pinellas."[4]

Disston City's greatest booster was, of course, Hamilton Disston himself, who mounted an ambitious advertising campaign to trumpet the success of his emerging metropolis. From Chicago to London, potential settlers and investors were bombarded with handbills and newspaper advertisements, all extolling the virtues of America's next great city. Foreshadowing a legion of twentieth-century sand merchants, Disston extolled the Florida dream, promising a tropical Camelot where all the winters were frostless and only the gentlest of sea breezes were allowed. Although many buyers never actually made it to Disston City, the sale of lots by mail was brisk, especially in England, where "orange fever" was a common malady in the late nineteenth century. By 1886 several dozen English colonists had settled in or near Disston City, and it was rumored that thousands of others would soon follow. One English settler, Arthur Norwood, opened

Disston City's first school in 1885, and another, William Wood, managed the Waldorf Hotel.

For the long-suffering pioneers of Pinellas Village, the Disston City boom meant new neighbors, rising land prices, and plenty of construction work, especially after Canadian lumberman George King set up a sawmill near Mule Branch in the spring of 1884. And not all of the action was at Disston City. The much-publicized activities of the Disston City Land Company quickened the pace of settlement all across the peninsula. At Pinellas Village, the local population leaped past fifty, the number of stores increased from one to half a dozen, and an entrepreneur from Connecticut, Thomas Sterling, opened a twelve-room hotel to accommodate the growing number of excursionists and drummers visiting the lower peninsula. All over the peninsula new hamlets were suddenly appearing. In the area south of Clam Bayou, Joseph and Ben Puig, who had migrated to the peninsula from New Orleans a decade earlier, went so far as to plat their own town, which they named New Cadiz. In the end, the Puig brothers acquired a post office and even convinced George King to move his sawmill to New Cadiz, but the prospective town did not develop further.

The Puigs' attempt to profit by Hamilton Disston's activity ended in disappointment, but even Disston had his problems. With all his land and resources, he had failed to provide Disston City with the one advantage that it needed to succeed—a railway connection to the outside world. And he knew it. Even though his reputation as a developer was closely associated with dredges and canal building, he was becoming increasingly conscious of the limitations of water transport. Sooner or later, like all late nineteenth-century empire builders, he would have to entrust his fortune to the iron horse. Indeed, during the mid-1880s, Disston had only to look across Tampa Bay to see the "power of the road" in action.

As late as 1882, Tampa was, as one visitor put it, "a sleepy, shabby Southern town."[5] It was a town without a railroad, and some said, a town without a future. Then Henry B. Plant decided to extend his railway system from Kissimmee to Tampa, boasting that he would

John Donaldson, the first black man to settle on the lower Pinellas Peninsula after the Civil War. Born on an Alabama plantation in 1849, Donaldson migrated to the peninsula with his employer Louis Bell, Jr. in 1868. This photograph was taken around the turn of the century. Courtesy Pinellas County Historical Society

Hamilton Disston (1844-1896), the great land baron of Florida's Gilded Age. Courtesy St. Petersburg Times

George King's sawmill at New Cadiz, circa 1885. Courtesy St. Petersburg Historical Society

put Tampa on the map. The state railway charter Plant acquired in May 1883 offered him 13,840 acres of and for every mile of track laid, but only if the rail link could be completed by January 24, 1884. Constructing seventy-five miles of track in seven months seemed almost impossible, but when Plant's work crews finished the link on January 22, a full sixty-three hours before the deadline, skeptics became believers. The human cost borne by Plant's exhausted workers was considerable, but the new railroad's impact on Tampa was everything Plant had said it would be. By 1885, Tampa's population had risen to 2,376, more than three times what it had been in 1880. And, as Plant had promised, this was only the beginning. In 1886, Plant and his associates convinced Don Vicente Martinez Ybor and Ignacio Haya to move their cigar factories from Key West to Tampa. Between 1887 and 1890, Plant built a rail connection to Black Point on Old Tampa Bay, where he proceeded to construct the Port of Tampa (which benefited greatly from the simultaneous development of the local citrus and phosphate industries). From there the Plant Steamship Line would reach out to Key West, Havana, and beyond.

Already the uncrowned king of Tampa, Henry Plant had every intention of expanding his domain from one end of the Gulf coast to the other. The only man who had any chance of stopping him, it seemed, was Hamilton Disston. But to do so, Disston would have to put together a railway empire of his own. Despite Disston's determination, the prospects for such a development were questionable. Disston's land purchases had already stretched his finances to the limit, and Plant was not about to relax and let a rival empire builder beat him. Convinced that the lower Gulf coast could support only one metropolis, Plant did everything he could to ensure that the center of growth and development remained on the eastern side of Tampa Bay. If he had his way, Disston City would fail, and the Pinellas Peninsula would remain a refuge for weekend excursionists, mullet fishermen, and a few foolhardy citrus farmers.

The Sea Breeze, *edited at Disston City by William J. McPherson and G. W. Bennett, was the first newspaper to be published on the lower Pinellas Peninsula. A bimonthly,* The Sea Breeze *was published from May 1886 to mid-1887. Courtesy St. Petersburg Historical Society*

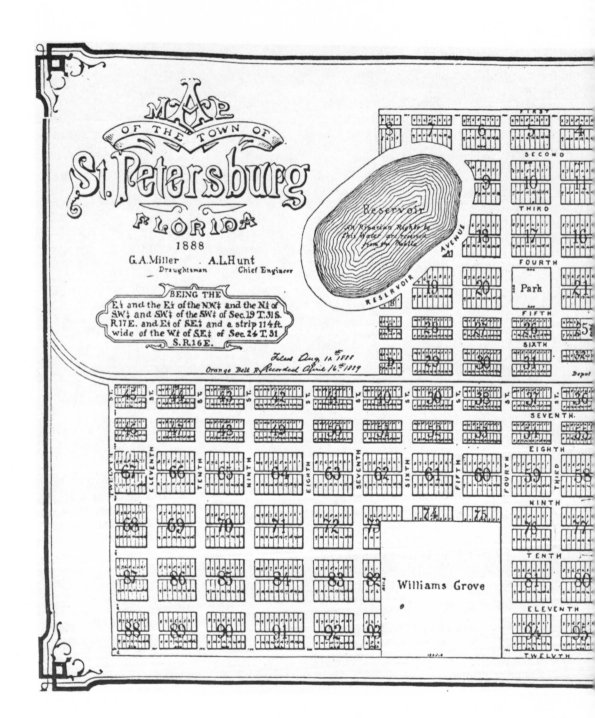

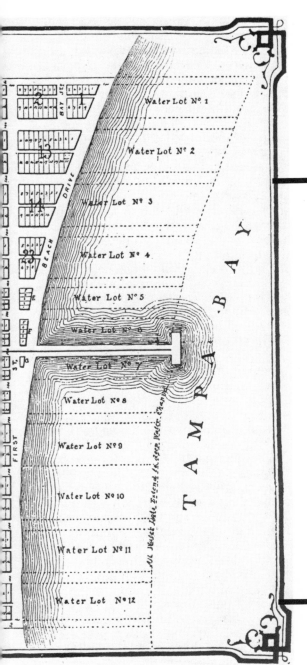

Chapter Three

The Orange Belt Era

1886-1896

The original town plat of St. Petersburg was completed in August 1888. Courtesy St. Petersburg Historical Society

The year 1886 was a momentous one in American history. Within the space of twelve months, the nation witnessed the Haymarket tragedy in Chicago, the stalking and capture of the renegade Apache leader Geronimo, the unveiling of the Statue of Liberty, the creation of the American Federation of Labor, and a series of savage winter storms which killed millions of cattle on the open range, effectively ending the golden age of the Western cowboy. With all these events, few people outside of central Florida paid much attention to the escalating rivalry between Hamilton Disston and Henry Plant. But among local citizens, the Disston-Plant railway war was a major event. Much more than the personal honor and wealth of two plutocrats was at stake. As Disston and Plant juggled ledger books and engaged in backroom wheeling and dealing, local settlers watched and waited, hoping that the final outcome would brighten their individual prospects, or at least not darken them forever.

To add to the drama, the struggle between Disston and Plant ultimately became intertwined with the soaring ambitions of a third would-be empire builder—a remarkable Russian immigrant by the name of Pyotr Alexeyevitch Dementyev. Born in Novgorod province, two hundred miles southeast of St. Petersburg, Russia, in 1850, Dementyev was a well-educated and liberal-minded aristocrat who spent most of his early years in St. Petersburg and Tver, where his family owned a sprawling estate. For a time he served as a captain in the Imperial Guard, but eventually he became an outspoken critic of the Czarist regime. Although Dementyev's dissent stopped far short of revolutionary violence, the general repression following the 1881 assassination of Czar Alexander II drove him to the United States, where he changed his name to Peter Demens. After a brief stay in New York, Demens made his way to east central Florida, where he entered the lumber business. By 1883, he was the owner of a large sawmill at Longwood, ten miles southwest of Sanford. Buoyed by a flurry of railroad construction, he made a good living producing railroad ties and clapboard siding for railroad stations.

In 1885, Demens signed what appeared to be a lucrative contract to supply railroad ties to the Orange Belt Railway, which was being built from the lower St. Johns River to Lake Apopka. But after several months of cutting and delivering ties, Demens discovered that the owners of the Orange Belt had no money to pay him. Undaunted, he arranged to take over the Orange Belt's charter, and with the help of three financial partners—Joseph Henschen, Henry Sweetapple, and A. M. Taylor—he completed the link to Lake Apopka in November 1886. The new town at the end of the link was named Oakland, although a disappointed Demens made it clear that he would have preferred the name "St. Petersburg," in honor of his home city. Whatever its name, the new railroad town represented a minor miracle. Several times during the course of the project the precarious financial condition of Demens and his partners had almost brought construction of the railway to a permanent halt. Thus, nearly everyone was surprised when Demens pushed for an amended Orange Belt charter that called for a 120-mile extension to the Pinellas Peninsula. Under the new charter, the Orange Belt was empowered to sell seven hundred thousand dollars worth of railway bonds, but early efforts to attract investors produced meager results. No one, it seemed, was eager to invest in a railway to the wilds of Pinellas—no one, that is, but Hamilton Disston.

Despite the derisive skepticism of Henry Plant and others, Disston remained convinced that the Pinellas Peninsula was on the verge of large-scale development. Indeed, Disston's faith in the peninsula's future had been boosted by an unlikely but important source. In April 1885, at the annual convention of the American Medical Association, which was being held in New Orleans, a Baltimore physician by the name of W. C. Van Bibber delivered a provocative paper entitled, "Peninsular and Sub-Peninsular Air and Climates." Eleven years earlier, a noted British doctor, B. W. Richardson, had challenged the medical profession to find the perfect location for "Health City," an ideal community with a climate that would maximize health and longevity. To the surprise and amusement of his colleagues in New

Orleans, Dr. Van Bibber claimed that, after a decade of searching, he finally had found such a location just across the Gulf.

Where should such a City be built? Overlooking the deep Gulf of Mexico, with the broad waters of a beautiful bay nearly surrounding it, with but little now upon its soil but the primal forest, there is a large sub-peninsula, Point Pinellas, waiting the hand of improvement, as the larger peninsula from which it juts did but a few years ago. It lies in latitude 27 degrees and 42 minutes, and contains, with its adjoining keys, about 160,000 acres of land. No marsh surrounds its shores or rests upon is surface; the sweep of its beach is broad and graceful, stretching many miles, and may be improved to an imposing extent. Its average winter temperature is 72 degrees; that its climate is peculiar, its natural products show; that its air is healthy, the ruddy appearance of its few inhabitants attest. Those who have carefully surveyed the entire State, and have personally investigated this sub-peninsula and its surroundings, think that it offers the best climate in Florida. Here should be built such a city as Dr. Richardson has outlined.[1]

The fact that Dr. Van Bibber had already purchased a parcel of land near Maximo Point led some observers to question his objectivity, but such quibbles were of little concern to the patriarch of Disston City. Disston welcomed Van Bibber's Health City report as a complement to his own plans for Disston City, although he was aware that neither dream would be realized without the help of a railroad. Stymied at every turn by Henry Plant's widening influence, and under fire from associates who were unmoved by Van Bibber's hyperbolic projections, Disston became increasingly nervous as 1886 drew to a close. By early December, he was desperate enough to pay a visit to the Oakland office of Peter Demens, the eccentric and financially strapped Russian who had patched together the Orange Belt line. Demens was not exactly E. H. Harriman, and a narrow-gauge railway with wood-burning locomotives chugging along at fifteen miles an hours was not what Disston had envisioned as his dream city's lifeline to the outside world, but at that moment he was a man with few options. Like it or not, Peter Demens and the Orange Belt were his best hope.

To Demens's amazement, Disston offered him more than sixty thousand acres of land, plus a promise to lobby the state legislature for additional land grants. All Disston wanted in return was the rapid completion of the Orange Belt extension. This was truly an offer that could not be refused. Although it would be several weeks before a single rail was laid, Disston's proposal gave the Orange Belt instant respectability. Armed with Disston's endorsement, Demens began to get encouragement from the same New York and Philadelphia bond merchants who had snubbed him in the past. His expectations soaring, Demens decided to build the Orange Belt all the way to Mullet Key, a plan that would require the construction of expensive bridges and causeways. What is more, he asked Disston to underwrite the extra expense by donating an additional fifty thousand acres of land to the Orange Belt's coffers. Not surprisingly, this display of gall did not sit well with the board of directors of Disston's Florida Land and Improvement Company. When the board met on December 18, Demens's request for additional acreage was denied. The directors did not realize that their decision would lead to the defeat of their hopes for Disston City.

Acceptance of Demens's proposal would have essentially guaranteed a railway connection for Disston City, but Disston and the board were confident that they could get what they wanted from Demens without paying an exorbitant price. They apparently discounted the possibility that the Orange Belt could be routed to another part of the peninsula. Why would anyone build a railroad to Pinellas that stopped short of the Gulf, or that bypassed the boomtown of Disston City? Despite being rebuffed by Disston's board, Demens still hoped to build the Orange Belt all the way to Mullet Key. Nevertheless, the unsettled financial situation forced him to search for an alternative site for the Orange Belt's western

A photographic portrait of the Williams family, circa 1880. John Constantine Williams, Sr., is seated in the front row (far right). The photograph has been altered to include Williams's second wife Sarah (back row, third from the left), whom he married in 1882. Courtesy Manhattan Hotel and the St. Petersburg Historical Society

John Constantine Williams, Sr., (1817-1892), was a wealthy gentleman farmer from Detroit, Michigan, who played an instrumental role in the founding of St. Petersburg in 1888. Courtesy Pinellas County Historical Society

terminus. Initially, there was undoubtedly an element of bluff in Demens's casting about for an alternative terminus; by introducing the threat of competition, he hoped to pressure the board into reconsidering its rejection of his request for an additional fifty thousand acres. But the bluff soon turned into reality, setting off a chain of events that forever altered the contours of the peninsula's development.

The search for an alternative terminus led Demens's partner, Henry Sweetapple, to the parlor of John and Sarah Williams. Following the farming fiasco of 1881, John Williams had returned to his native Detroit. But it was not long before the asthma-ridden developer once again succumbed to the lure of the tropics. By 1886, he was back in Florida, living with his second wife in a Tampa mansion. Although Williams retained all of his lower Pinellas land holdings, his interest in the Pinellas side of the bay had waned considerably. Nevertheless, it did not take much prodding from Sweetapple to revive the dream of building a town on his Pinellas property. The fact that Henry Sweetapple and Sarah Williams were both Canadians also smoothed the negotiating process. An intelligent, cultured woman with a disarming

manner, Sarah Williams took the lead throughout the negotiations. Without her involvement, the fateful agreement signed on January 24, 1887, might never have come to pass. The agreement provided for a railway route that would pass through Williams's property on its way to Tampa Bay. In return, Williams agreed to give the Orange Belt 250 acres of prime waterfront land. The land transfer was to occur only after the Orange Belt completed both the railway and a wharf that reached far enough into the bay to accommodate ships drawing twelve feet of water.

The deal between Williams and the Orange Belt seemed to please everyone but Hamilton Disston. But even Disston was not particularly concerned at this point. He knew that Demens and Sweetapple still had their eyes on Mullet Key and that they still regarded the Williams tract as a fallback to be used only if the Orange Belt's financial condition remained precarious. Unfortunately for Disston, the funds that would have taken the Orange Belt to Mullet Key, Disston City, or anywhere else on the Gulf never materialized. The Mullet Key destination turned out to be a pipe dream, and in the end the utmost Demens could

Sarah Williams Armistead, at age sixty. The widow of John Constantine Williams, Sr., and Mayor James Armistead, she was a leading figure in the Woman's Town Improvement Association and the Women's Christian Temperance Union. She died in December 1917. Courtesy St. Petersburg Historical Society

manage was to extend his railway as far as the Williams tract.

From the first call for workers in January 1887 to the laying of the last rail in the spring of 1889, the Orange Belt was plagued with one problem after another. Torrential rains, delayed steel shipments, defective equipment, cost overruns, and a chronic lack of funds stretched Peter Demens's emotional and material resources to the breaking point. On several occasions he was literally besieged by impatient creditors or angry workers demanding their pay. In February 1887, a timely loan of a hundred thousand dollars from H. O. Armour and Company of Philadelphia saved the project from an early collapse. But by mid-spring, Demens's financial woes were worse than ever. The situation reached a crisis in August, when the Orange Belt's difficulties were compounded by a severe yellow fever epidemic in Tampa. As the graders and track layers approached the stricken city, panic set in, and only Demens's iron will, supplemented by a generous stock of strong liquor, prevented a mass desertion.

Conditions deteriorated even more in early September, when several irate creditors chained and padlocked the Orange Belt's locomotives to the rails. All this was too much for Henry Sweetapple, who, after witnessing the chaining, dropped dead of stroke. The death of the Orange Belt's treasurer momentarily shook Demens's normally unflappable demeanor, but somehow he rounded up enough money to gain the release of his locomotives. Nevertheless, on October 1 he faced an even greater crisis when more than a hundred

Peter Demens, born Pyotr Alex-eyevitch Dementyev (1850-1919), was the Russian-born railroad promoter who brought the Orange Belt Railroad to the Pinellas Peninsula in 1888. Courtesy St. Petersburg Historical Society

workers, most of whom were Italian immigrants, surrounded the Orange Belt office in Oakland and demanded three weeks of unpaid wages. Some members of the mob threatened to lynch Demens if he did not come up with the wages by eight o'clock that night, and only a last-minute intervention by several of the Russian's well-heeled friends saved him from bodily harm. Two days later, Demens was elated when a long-overdue shipment of steel rails arrived by schooner. But elation turned to despondency when the schooner's captain refused to unload the rails without first receiving a cash payment. It took Demens almost a week to raise the money, and the construction of the Orange Belt fell even further behind schedule.

The Orange Belt's financial situation improved somewhat during the final months of 1887, but the major force that kept the project going was Demens's fanatical determination to complete the railroad or die in the trying. The "damned Russian" seemed to be everywhere, badgering friends and brokers for loans one minute, and driving his work crews to the limit the next. Demens's furious pace was dictated not only by his personal drive but also by a December 31, 1887 deadline. Thousands of acres of land grants would be lost if the tracks of the Orange Belt failed to reach the Pinellas Peninsula by the end of the year. In the end, Demens missed the dreaded deadline by more than a year, but he was saved from disaster by Hamilton Disston's willingness to grant an extension. Even though Demens and his partners forfeited twenty-five thousand acres of state land, the retention of the Disston grants was enough to keep the Orange Belt solvent. Disston's apparent generosity was somewhat self-serving, since he still held out some hope that the Orange Belt could be rerouted to Disston City. Moreover, from his perspective, all was not lost even if the Orange Belt ended at the Williams tract. With property holdings all over the Pinellas area, Disston reasoned that a railroad to the wrong side of the peninsula was better than no railroad at all.

Disston's ambivalence notwithstanding, the tracks of the Orange Belt pushed southward from Tarpon Springs and Clearwater during the spring of 1888. Supplementing his work force with several hundred black laborers, Demens pounded his way to the western edge of the Williams tract by April 30. Reaching this long-awaited milestone was cause for celebration, but the end of the tracks (at the junction of Ninth Street and First Avenue South) was still a full mile from the bay. Even so, Demens wisely called a temporary halt to construction. His work crews were exhausted, and he needed every bit of leverage he could muster in his continuing negotiations with John Williams. The two men were still trying to work out the details of their joint responsibility for developing the town site, and Demens wagered that a tantalizing delay might wring some concessions from his wary collaborator. To the Russian's dismay, this delaying strategy backfired—Williams stubbornly refused to turn over the deed for the Orange Belt's half of the town until the railroad linked up with the wharf that Demens had promised to build. Fortunately, neither man was foolish enough to let this dispute destroy what they had accomplished.

Temporarily burying their differences, Demens and Williams publicly shared the glory when the first train pulled into the Ninth Street terminus on June 8, 1888. As a small crowd of bemused settlers and proud railway workers looked on, the locomotive known as the *Mattie* puffed and belched its way to the end of the line. Behind it were an empty freight car and a passenger coach bearing a single passenger, a salesman from Savannah who had come to hawk his wares. There was no depot to accommodate the new town's first visitor, just a shaky wooden platform that led to a dusty street. But this temporary embarrassment did not lessen the significance of the event. Against all odds, the age of the iron horse had finally made it to the lower Pinellas

Peninsula.

The shoe salesman left the next day, obviously unimpressed by the ramshackle community that surrounded the Ninth Street terminus. All he saw were railroad workers and struggling citrus farmers, not the kind of people who were likely to be interested in calfskin boots or patent-leather Oxfords. There were no real streets or sidewalks, and even the name of the place seemed to be in doubt. Before boarding the train in Oakland, he had been told that the final stop was "St. Petersburg." Yet when he got to the end of the line, several people welcomed him to "Wardsville," which was understandable since the only notable building in sight was E. R. and Ella Ward's combination general store and post office.

In truth, the official name was St. Petersburg. Like "Paul's Landing" and "Pinellas Village," "Wardsville" was about to become an historical footnote. Although probably inevitable, Wardsville's removal from the map was unintentionally hastened by postmistress Ella Ward. Several months before the tracks reached Ninth Street, she traveled to the Orange Belt headquarters in Oakland to discuss the official designation of her new post office. Peter Demens was out of the office when she arrived, but one of Demens's partners, the Swedish immigrant Joseph Henschen, assured Mrs. Ward that the railroad's Pinellas terminus could have no other name but St. Petersburg. Although he knew that the Wards were content with "Wardsville" and that John Williams had his heart set on "Williamsville," Henschen insisted that the community should be named after the birthplace of Peter Demens. Besides if the place ever began to develop into a major city, which Henschen admitted was highly unlikely, an inspiring name would prove useful. "So I told Mrs. Ward we'd call it St. Petersburg," Henschen recalled many years later, "And St. Petersburg it became. I signed a petition, got four or five others to sign it, and we sent it to Washington where it was approved by the post office department."[2] Local folklore would later substitute apocryphal stories about the naming of the city: one version has Demens winning a coin toss, and another has John Williams picking the pro-

St. Petersburg's Russian-style Orange Belt depot, circa 1889. Located near the corner of First Avenue South and Second Street (the future site of the Atlantic Coast Line depot), the Orange Belt depot was completed in December 1888. The Orange Belt's company offices can be seen in the background. Photograph by J. R. Tewksbury, courtesy St. Petersburg Historical Society

verbial short straw. But, in all likelihood, it was Henschen's petition, not the luck of the draw, that put a little bit of Russia in the Florida gazetteer.

Naming a railroad hamlet after one of the largest cities in Europe seemed comical to some, but Peter Demens was determined to have the last laugh. On June 14, less than a week after the *Mattie's* inaugural run, Demens rolled into town in his private railway car to confer with John Williams. Following a wary handshake, the two men agreed to split the cost of hacking back the palmettoes and pines to make way for the town's proposed streets. They also collaborated on an ambitious town plan that called for streets a hundred feet wide and a large central park. To encourage development, Demens promised to extend the Orange Belt's tracks eastward to Second Street as soon as possible. Moreover, he promised to build a depot and a grand hotel that would symbolize St. Petersburg's potential. Although Demens and the Orange Belt would bear the cost of building the hotel, it would be named the Detroit, in honor of Williams's home city. Considering the Orange Belt's shaky finances, Williams must have questioned Demens's ability to deliver. But by the end of the year, Demens, aided by a small army of carpenters and day laborers, had made good on all of his promises. To the amazement of almost everyone, the railhead at Second Street was flanked by a beautiful Russian-style depot and an even more impressive forty-room hotel. Three and a half stories high, with a seventy-foot tower that afforded a magnificent view of the bay, the Detroit quickly became the pride of the lower peninsula.

Despite all this activity, John Williams steadfastly refused to grant the Orange Belt its half of the town site prior to the completion of the wharf. This truculence infuriated Demens. Without a formal transfer of title, the Orange Belt Investment Company could not sell any lots without first getting Williams's consent. Consequently, only two lots were sold prior to the wharf's completion in February 1889. In the interim, E. R. Ward and Jacob Baum decided to create a subdivision of their own south of Mirror Lake. With lot prices ranging from twenty to sixty dollars, the Ward and Baum tract filled up rapidly, much to the consternation of Williams and L. Y. Jenness, the Orange Belt's land agent.

At this point, the greatest concentration of settlement was near Ninth Street. But once the wharf was finished, the center of activity moved eastward toward the bay. Eager to sell lots, Williams and Jenness allowed their customers as much as nine years to pay for their

Another view of the Orange Belt depot, 1889. Courtesy St. Petersburg Historical Society

land. However, they did require all houses to have painted exteriors and brick or stone foundations. In this way, they hoped to dissociate St. Petersburg from the motley collection of shacks that had grown up around Ninth Street. For several years, there was a sharp division, and some rivalry, between the uptown section around Ninth Street and the downtown section surrounding the depot and the Detroit Hotel. Development along Central Avenue eventually blurred this distinction.

At a somewhat slower pace, the area between the railhead and Pinellas Village (Big Bayou) also began to fill in. This trend was encouraged by John and Sarah Williams, who built an elegant home at the corner of Fifth Avenue South and Fourth Street, on the site of the old Hackney homestead. Completed in 1890, the Williams mansion was a lavishly furnished showplace that gave St. Petersburg its first touch of Victorian decadence. The General and his wife had lived on the peninsula since 1887, having fled Tampa during the early days of the yellow fever epidemic. But their initial accommodations were a bit spartan for a family that was accustomed to upper-class luxury. Some local settlers regarded Williams as a Yankee snob who put on airs, but even his sharpest critics acknowledged his power and influence.

During the early 1890s, Williams was not only St. Petersburg's wealthiest citizen; he was also the patriarch of the town's most visible family. His eldest son, John Constantine Williams, Jr. (commonly known as "Tine"), operated a large general store across from the Detroit Hotel. Opened in 1889, it eventually became the busiest and most profitable store on the peninsula. In 1891, Tine helped his father develop Williamsville, a large subdivision south of Booker Creek. A year later, he and his younger brother Barney organized the Crystal Ice Works, a highly successful venture that boosted the local fishing industry. An accomplished boat builder and fisherman, Barney Williams was a fixture on the St. Petersburg waterfront for many years. Not to be outdone, a third brother, J. Mott Williams, owned and operated St. Petersburg's only machine shop. General Williams also had four daughters, plus a fourth son, but during these years they remained in Detroit with his first wife.

Later generations would remember Williams as "the father of St. Petersburg," which is not surprising since much of the original city was carved from the Williams tract.[3] Indeed, Williams himself actively encouraged such characterizations prior to his death in 1892. Perhaps he was justified in doing so, but it is clear that a number of his contemporaries resented his claims of civic paternity. As might be expected, loyal supporters of the Orange Belt often protested that Peter Demens's role in the creation of the town was at least as important as Williams's. Unfortunately, Demens himself did not remain in St. Petersburg long enough to dispute his rival's claims.

During the summer of 1889, barely a year after the Orange Belt had reached the Williams tract, Demens packed up his family and moved to Asheville, North Carolina. He left an embittered man, his dreams of empire shattered by his recent loss of the Orange Belt. During its first year of operation, the Orange Belt had fallen deeper and deeper into debt. By the spring of 1889, the struggling railroad owed a staggering $900,000 to a Philadelphia syndicate led by H. O. Armour. Although Demens made a valiant attempt to prop up the Orange Belt's finances with special tourist excursions and discounted freight contracts, nothing seemed to work. Thus, when the Philadelphia syndicate demanded $55,000 in interest payments on July 1, Demens and his partners had no choice but to sell out at whatever terms they could get. In the end, the Orange Belt's three surviving partners shared a paltry settlement of approximately $25,000. Demens, as the

senior partner, received $14,400; Joseph Henschen received a little less than $9,000; and A. M. Taylor walked away with $2,000.

Despite this disappointment, Demens ultimately recovered. After three years in North Carolina, he moved on to southern California, where he became a successful journalist and businessman. Investing heavily in orange groves, he was eventually comfortable enough to devote most of his time to public commentary on European affairs. As Los Angeles's most vocal Russian emigré, he became a minor celebrity during the years of the Bolshevik revolution and World War I. At one point, he even went to New York to help manage the overseas purchases of Alexander Kerensky's tottering regime, but the fall of Kerensky soon drove him back to Los Angeles, where he died in despondency in 1919.

During his later years, Peter Demens traveled widely. Indeed, on the eve of the first Russian revolution in 1905, he made an extended visit to his native Russia. Yet he never traveled back to Florida. Some suspected that he was too embarrassed to return. Although the completion of the Orange Belt project was a testament to Demens's determination, the actual railroad that resulted from the project was an economic and technological failure. Although the Orange Belt was the largest narrow-gauge railway in the nation, it was also one of the most shabbily constructed lines anywhere. Even those who were captivated by the romance of pioneer railroading cursed the notorious Orange Belt. Uneven gradings, loose rails, broken-down locomotives—everything conspired to make traveling on the Orange Belt a nightmare. The experience of John Churchill, a visitor from Iowa who traveled on the line in 1891, was typical: "The engine used to jump the track about once a week but I never heard of anyone being killed or even seriously injured—the train didn't go fast enough. Wood was used as fuel and in wet weather, when the wood got wet, you could keep up with the train by walking."[4] It is little wonder that local historian Karl Grismer once described the Orange Belt as a "comic strip railroad."[5]

Yet, even with its limitations, the Orange

Belt rapidly transformed St. Petersburg into the commercial hub of the lower peninsula. Almost overnight, shipping and trading activity shifted away from Disston City and Pinellas Village, relocating near the railhead. The impact on Disston City was particularly dramatic, as several local merchants sold their stores and moved to St. Petersburg. At the same time, a number of new settlers followed the Orange Belt to town. The resulting construction provided work for scores of laborers, including many who previously had worked on the railroad. The flurry of activity also prompted George King to move his sawmill from New Cadiz to a site near Booker Creek.

By 1890, St. Petersburg was well on its way to becoming a full-fledged town. In the two years since the coming of the railroad, the local population had risen from fewer than 50 to 273. With two hotels (the Detroit was joined by the thirty-two room Paxton House in 1890), two ice plants, two churches, a public school, and a busy sawmill, St. Petersburg could no longer be dismissed as a figment of John Williams's imagination. Although still an unincorporated village, it had become the largest community on the peninsula. Its streets were little more than rutted dirt paths, and the only sidewalk in town, a creaking wooden structure on Central Avenue, stopped after two hundred

yards. But the fact that the town had any streets at all was a marvel to the old-timers who could remember when the area was a trackless wilderness inhabited by alligators and wild boars.

The coming of the Orange Belt had altered the pace and scale of local life, and nowhere was this more evident than in the changing nature of St. Petersburg's economy. During these years, the life's blood of the local economy was commercial fishing. Despite an abundance of fish, making a living from Tampa Bay, or from the Gulf for that matter, had never been easy. However, once the railroad opened, local fishermen began to come into their own economically. The man most responsible for the development of the local fish trade was Henry W. Hibbs, a North Carolina native who operated a fish warehouse in Tampa for several years before moving his business to St. Petersburg in 1889. Traditionally, most Pinellas fishermen had sold their catches on the wharves of Tampa, an arrangement that was rarely profitable and never very convenient. Thus, when Hibbs

opened a fish house on the Orange Belt pier, many fishermen decided to forgo the traditional trip across the bay. Before long, Hibbs was processing more than a thousand pounds of fish a day, prompting several other fishhouse entrepreneurs to take advantage of the opportunities created by the Orange Belt. With local plants providing ice for packing, St. Petersburg's fish houses were soon shipping huge quantities of mackerel and snapper to cities along the eastern seaboard. By the late 1890s, more than two hundred fishermen and scores of middlemen were involved in a trade that produced as much as three million pounds of fish a year.

Other local industries did not develop as rapidly as the fish trade. Citrus and truck farmers welcomed their newfound access to the outside world. Yet, even with the railroad, commercial farming remained a difficult enterprise, particularly where perishable fruits were concerned. Despite its name, the Orange Belt did not boost the citrus trade as much as it might have. Freight rates were often exorbitant, and the unusually long distance to urban markets made it difficult for Pinellas farmers to compete with farmers in more centrally

located areas. Ironically, the local citrus industry did not really take off until after the great freeze of 1894-1895. While the freeze inflicted minor damage on the Pinellas Peninsula, it nearly destroyed the citrus industry in northern Florida, forcing hundreds of citrus farmers to relocate in more southerly areas, including Pinellas.

The tourist industry, which would later figure so prominently in the city's economy, was even slower to develop, although early efforts to promote tourism were not wanting. Beginning in July 1889, the Orange Belt sponsored seaside tours to exotic and healthful St. Petersburg. Highlighting the Detroit Hotel and Dr. Van Bibber's Health City endorsement, advertisements in Northern newspapers beckoned tourists and invalids to a tropical paradise. Closer to home, the city was billed as a cool refuge from the sweltering heat of inland Florida. At this point, the Gulf beaches were all but inaccessible from the St. Petersburg railhead, but the syndicate that operated the Orange Belt compensated by building a large bathing pavilion, complete with a toboggan slide, adjacent to its downtown pier. The pavilion delighted visitors and local folk alike,

An Orange Belt locomotive, circa 1895. Courtesy St. Petersburg Historical Society

An Orange Belt locomotive loading lumber at George King's sawmill near Booker Creek, circa 1890. King moved his sawmill to St. Petersburg from New Cadiz in 1888 to take advantage of the new railway line. Courtesy St. Petersburg Historical Society

but it alone could not turn St. Petersburg into a major tourist center. Despite good fishing and bright sunshine, early St. Petersburg had difficulty competing with its Atlantic coast rivals. Some visitors were intrigued by the town's primitive character, but too many went away mumbling about dusty streets and oversized mosquitoes. Of course, St. Petersburg itself deserved only part of the blame for its mixed reputation. Whatever else happened, the aggravations encountered on the Orange Belt were usually enough to convince most visitors that they were heading for something less than paradise.

When tourists arrived, they found themselves in a small town that was unsure of its future and a little uncomfortable with its present. The opening of the Orange Belt did more than transform the local economy; it also introduced sharp distinctions of class and culture into a frontier community that had rarely experienced such distinctions. The social and political implications of these divisions were complex, but they often translated into heated battles over "development" and "progress." While many local businessmen were disappointed by St. Petersburg's growth rate, other settlers were concerned that events were moving too fast. Not everyone was pleased by the broad changes that had occurred

in the lower Point since the coming of the railroad. Fancy swimming pavilions were nice, but some old-timers longed for the days when they could swim without worrying about the formality of a bathing suit, or hunt game without walking five miles into the woods.

During the early 1890s, such misgivings crystallized in an effort to prevent municipal incorporation. Most local businessmen favored incorporation, which they felt would raise the community to a higher level of respectability. But the forces of uplift faced strong opposition from settlers who feared that incorporation would result in higher taxes and increased restrictions on personal freedom. Exhibiting the same kind of agrarian pride that infused the Populist movement, some local farmers and fishermen bitterly resented the encroachment of urban values and institutions. They felt that it was bad enough having General Williams and his silk-hatted friends looking down their noses at the common folk. They were even more concerned over the movement to rid the town of saloons and talk of prohibiting livestock owners from letting their cows graze on the town's fields and lawns. Energized by the fear that such restrictions might come to pass, local recalcitrants successfully blocked incorporation for two years. But, in a special town meeting held on February 29,

1892, the pro-incorporation forces finally prevailed. The vote was fifteen to eleven.

Once incorporated, St. Petersburg quickly formed a local government. Within hours of the incorporation vote, the town had elected a mayor, five town councilmen, a clerk, and a marshal. The mayoral election pitted John Constantine Williams, Sr., against David Moffett, an Indiana-born farmer who had moved to St. Petersburg in 1881. The owner of a citrus grove bordering the western shore of Reservoir (Mirror) Lake, Moffett possessed neither the wealth nor the stature of General Williams. But he did have the solid backing of the local temperance forces, and that was enough to carry him to victory by a vote of twenty-one to ten. Moffett's anti-saloon ticket, which included George King and John Constantine Williams, Jr., won every office but city marshal, humiliating the open saloon ticket led by General Williams. One local editor judged the election to be a battle between "wets" and "drys," describing the winners as "conservative, temperate, sturdy property owners, generally understood as the Anti-Saloon faction."[6]

General Williams could not help taking the political loss personally. As a young boy of seven, Williams had watched his father become the first mayor of Detroit. Now, at the age of seventy-five, it was his turn to become the mayor of a town that he had done so much to create, or so he thought. Enraged by the ingratitude of his neighbors—especially that of his eldest son—Williams immediately challenged the legality of the election in court. One of his closest friends, Judge William Benton, granted a temporary injunction that prevented the new town government from taking office. The injunction was eventually overturned, but Moffett and his colleagues refused to wait for the slowly turning wheels of justice to validate their authority.

During the first week of March, the new town council met three times, producing several controversial ordinances. The first ordinance to be approved provided stiff penalties for anyone guilty of indecent exposure, drunkenness, or disorderly conduct; and a second law prohibited stores from doing business on Sunday. Additional ordinances made it illegal for hogs to run wild in the town's streets, outlawed gambling and the discharge of firearms within the town's boundaries, and established license fees for various occupations, including saloon keepers. This last measure pleased local "wets," who had feared that saloons would be banned altogether. The new council even passed a speed law; trains were limited to six miles per hour, and citizens on horseback could be fined or imprisoned if they rode too rapidly through the town's streets. Accordingly, the council empowered the town marshal, W. A. Sloan, to construct a municipal jail. Measuring eight feet by twelve feet, the "town calaboose," as it was called, was tangible evidence that, for better or worse, the forces of law and order had taken charge of St. Petersburg.[7]

General Williams and others questioned the validity of the new ordinances, but in June 1893 the state legislature approved a bill sustaining their legitimacy. The council's critics were crestfallen, although Williams himself did not live to experience this final humiliation. In failing health since his rejection by the voters, Williams died on April 25, 1892. At the end, his estrangement from the town he had helped to found was almost complete. Although his estate was appraised at more than $125,000, Williams's only bequest to the citizens of St. Petersburg was a single lot, valued at $200, to be used as a site for a firemen's hall. Nearly disinheriting his eight children, he bequeathed the major share of his estate to his wife Sarah. An out-of-court settlement ultimately led to a more equitable distribution, but this final fit of pique severely tarnished the late General's reputation.

Despite the death of the founder and the onset of a national economic depression in February 1893, St. Petersburg continued to grow during the mid-1890s. By 1895, the town boasted a municipal band, a public park with a bandstand, an Odd Fellows Chapter, a Masonic Lodge, and two new hotels, the Sixth Avenue House and the Clarenden. There was also a three-story opera house constructed by James A. Armistead, a Bartow hotel owner who had moved to St. Petersburg in September 1894,

The Wardsville-St. Petersburg business district at the intersection of First Avenue South and Ninth Street, 1888. The rails of the recently completed Orange Belt Railroad are just visible in the foreground. From left to right, the seven buildings in the photograph have been identified as (1) the residence and hardware store of J. T. Meador; (2) the residence and bakery of C. Durant; (3) the residence and store of the Bohrer family; (4) a barbershop operated by a black man named Powell; (5) Douglas Jagger's grocery store; (6) unidentified; and (7) the carpentry and contracting business of W. V. Futrell. Courtesy St. Petersburg Historical Society

following his marriage to Sarah Williams. The social center of the town, Armistead's opera house hosted all manner of theatrical productions and doubled as a community meeting hall. Even more amazing, the fledgling town supported no less than four newspapers: the *South Florida Home*, a monthly edited by Young G. Lee; the *Town Talk*, a semiregular publication edited by H. M. Longstreth; the *Sub-Peninsula Sun*, a moralistic journal published by Richard J. Morgan, the pastor of the First Congregational Church; and the *St. Petersburg Times* (originally published in Clearwater at the *West Hillsborough Times*), a weekly edited by J. Ira Gore, a seasoned journalist who previously had edited the *Florida State Journal* in Cedar Keys. By 1897, only the *Sub-Peninsula Sun* and the *St. Petersburg Times* were still in business, but the survival of even two newspapers was an impressive accomplishment for such a small town.

During these years, St. Petersburg did indeed remain small—less than a tenth the size of nearby Tampa. yet, everywhere one looked, there were hopeful signs of development. Following the success of the Park Improvement Association, an organization which turned a downtown field into a fenced public park in 1893, the women of the town

pressed for additional amenities such as improved streets and sidewalks. Although these civic reformers were sometimes disappointed by the level of cooperation that they received from the local citizenry—including the all-male town council—their efforts did not go unrewarded. To cite one example, walking down Central Avenue in 1895 was a far different experience from what it had been four or five years earlier. Not only had the infamous swale of water between Second and Third Streets been filled in, but also the old wooden sidewalks had been replaced by new shell-covered walkways. Unfortunately, this particular bit of progress came at a considerable cost: in an act of desecration, the significance of which no one seemed to appreciate, several local Indian mounds were leveled to provide shells for the new walkways. Later generations would look back and wonder how the early residents of St. Petersburg could have been so insensitive to the dignity of the past. But, at the time, the destruction of the mounds provoked little comment.

Perhaps residents were preoccupied with

The elegant Detroit Hotel was brand-new when this photograph was taken in 1888. Photograph by Eddie Durant, courtesy St. Petersburg Historical Society

the precarious condition of the Orange Belt railroad. The syndicate that had run the railroad since 1889 had never exhibited as much interest in the Orange Belt as local citizens thought it deserved. But following the financial panic of 1893, the syndicate's lukewarm support turned to utter neglect. Consequently, the already troubled railroad went into a financial tailspin that threatened its very existence. Still reeling from the aftereffects of the financial panic, the Orange Belt nearly failed after the severe freeze of 1894-1895. With most of its citrus shipments canceled, the railroad hovered on the brink of bankruptcy until February 1895, when Henry Plant agreed to lease the line for ten years.

Absorption by the Plant system kept the railroad open, but local skeptics feared that the Tampa-based railroad magnate would see to it that St. Petersburg became a minor whistle-stop. In truth, Henry Plant was too busy protecting his empire from the depression to spend much time plotting against St. Petersburg. Still, during the seven years that he

operated the line—which he renamed the Sanford and St. Petersburg Railroad—Plant did little or nothing to encourage development on the Pinellas side of Tampa Bay. Thus, even though the sinister image of Plant was sometimes overdrawn, the nervousness of local boosters was by no means irrational. Henry Plant, the most powerful man on the west coast of Florida, usually got whatever he wanted. And with the departure of Peter Demens and the death of John Williams, there was no one left with the power and audacity to stand up to him.

By 1896, even Plant's old rival Hamilton Disston had passed from the scene. With his Florida land empire fully mortgaged, Disston had no chance to withstand the ravages of the depression. Despondent over the loss of his fortune, he took his own life on April 30, 1896. Although his death was unusually dramatic—he shot himself in the head while sitting in a Philadelphia bathtub—the Disston City dreamer would not be the last person to gamble and lose under the Florida sun.

This ornate bathing pavilion was added to the Orange Belt rail-road pier in 1890. An artesian well provided fresh-water showers, and a toboggan slide was added in 1891. Courtesy St. Petersburg Historical Society

This view of St. Petersburg looks west along the Orange Belt rail-road pier, circa 1894. Courtesy Florida State Archives

St. Petersburg's first school was semipublic, organized by the Congregational Church in 1888. This one-room schoolhouse, located near what is now the corner of Tenth Street and Central Avenue, was in use from 1888 to 1890. Twenty-nine students were enrolled in 1888. Courtesy St. Petersburg Times

Students at St. Petersburg's first school gather for a patriotic pose, circa 1889. Courtesy St. Petersburg Historical Society

St. Bartholomew's Episcopal Church, circa 1890. The first church to be built on the lower Pinellas Peninsula, St. Bartholomew's was completed in late 1887. Courtesy St. Petersburg Historical Society

The First Congregational Church, shortly after it opened in March 1889. Located on the southwestern corner of First Avenue North and Fourth Street, the church was razed in 1916 to make way for the open-air post office. Courtesy St. Petersburg Historical Society

An early view of John and Sarah Williams's Queen Anne-style mansion, located near the corner of Fifth Avenue South and Fourth Street. Constructed in 1890, the Williams home became part of the Manhattan Hotel in 1905. Courtesy St. Petersburg Historical Society

The interior of the Williams mansion featured a beautifully carved staircase and a series of ornate doorways. Courtesy St. Petersburg Historical Society

The estate of R. C. M. Judge, the son of Sarah Judge Williams and the stepson of John Constantine Williams, Sr., 1890. Judge served as his stepfather's clerk during the 1888-1889 negotiations with Peter Demens and Henry Sweetapple over the route of the Orange Belt Railroad. Photograph by J. R. Tewksbury, courtesy St. Petersburg Historical Society

The home of Dr. George Kennedy, near Round Lake, circa 1890. Note the Cracker-style tin porch roof. St. Petersburg's first dentist, Kennedy also served a brief tenure as city postmaster in 1895. Courtesy St. Petersburg Historical Society

The home of Joseph and Kate Pepper, and family, in 1891. Joseph Pepper became St. Petersburg's first town assessor in 1892. The man pushing the carriage is Arthur Norwood, the British-born businessman who brought telephonic communication to St. Petersburg in 1898. The Pepper home was located on Central Avenue (then known as Sixth Avenue), between Eighth and Ninth Streets. Courtesy St. Petersburg Historical Society

This building was constructed by the St. Petersburg Land and Improvement Company in 1888. During the following decade, it was used for a variety of purposes—a land office, saloon, dry goods store, and hotel. When this photograph was taken, circa 1890, the building was being used as the Central Hotel. Courtesy St. Petersburg Historical Society

David Moffett (1842-1921), the first mayor of St. Petersburg (1892-1893), and his wife Janie, circa 1890. Courtesy St. Petersburg Historical Society

This orange grove was located near the present-day intersection of Central Avenue and Seventh Street. The photograph was taken after a freeze, circa 1892. Courtesy Pinellas County Historical Society

The St. Petersburg Graded School, circa 1895. Constructed in 1893, the Graded School included a library, an assembly hall, and seven classrooms. It was located at the southeast corner of Fifth Street and Second Avenue North, the present site of St. Petersburg City Hall. Courtesy Pinellas County Historical Society

Students at the St. Petersburg Graded School celebrate Washington's Birthday in 1899. Courtesy St. Petersburg Historical Society

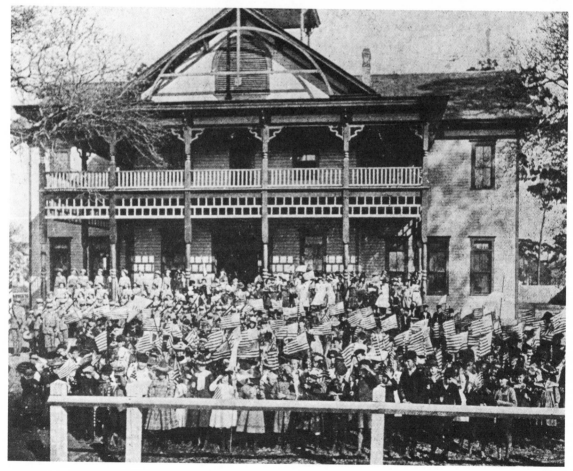

The Sixth Avenue House, located on the northeast corner of Central Avenue (then known as Sixth Avenue) and Sixth Street, was built by J. D. Bates in 1893. This popular small hotel was later remodeled by George King, who renamed it the Lakeview House. In 1902, a new owner, William H. Tippetts, turned it into the Belmont Hotel. Courtesy St. Petersburg Historical Society

A picnic gathering at the corner of Central Avenue (then known as Sixth Avenue) and Fourth Street, circa 1894. Courtesy St. Petersburg Historical Society

Chapter Four

Machines and Gardens

1897-1906

The railroad pier was a popular fishing spot in 1897. Courtesy Stokes Collection, University of South Florida Library, Tampa

Just before his death in 1915, John Bethell, the eighty-year-old sage of Pinellas Village, published a richly textured memoir of his life on the Lower Point. Looking back on the pioneer era with more than a touch of nostalgia, he recalled a world of natural beauty and unrelenting wildness, a world where people reveled in the simple pleasures of independence and self-reliance. In one of the memoir's most striking passages, Bethell described the wildlife that dominated the lower peninsula prior to the Orange Belt era:

There were deer, bear, 'coons, 'possums, rabbits, squirrels, turkeys, geese, ducks, whooping cranes, blue and white cranes, curlew, quail, plover, snipe, etc. Besides these there were panthers and wildcats by the hundreds, and 'gators just as plentiful. All one had to do was to load his gun and go off from his enclosure, so as not to shoot any of his family, and kill a turkey or some other kind of game for dinner . . . . I have stood on my porch and shot turkeys while eating my tomatoes. In duck season I would often kill at my waterfront landing enough to keep my family a day or two. Deer frequently swam across the bayou. I overtook one crossing one day and knocked it in the head with my oar, and my brother killed one with his hatchet . . . . We never in those days killed game for profit or for the fun of it, as has been done in later years, but just what was absolutely necessary for home consumption . . . . Our section was full of game for a long time after the war, and there would be plenty of game now if it had not been for the murderous guns in the hands of brainless pot-hunters that slaughtered everything that had hair and feathers on it. There were plume and song birds of every description that the Creator had placed here to beautify and adorn Man's Paradise, but the lawless marauders just about destroyed everything that came in reach of their powder and lead.[1]

John Bethell's arcadian jeremiad may have been the product of a selective memory,

but his sense of loss was genuine nevertheless. During the last decades of his life, this mid-Victorian gentleman witnessed changes that amazed and baffled him, as the onset of automobiles and electricity set the pace and tone of twentieth-century living. Although all ages involve transition, some, like the period 1885-1915, bring qualitative changes that shake society to its foundations. In these years a series of technological and organizational innovations radically transformed the nature of American life, especially in the nation's larger towns and cities. Urban America was coming into its own, much to the dismay of some rural Americans.

As the locus of power moved to Main Street, the political and social implications of urbanization became increasingly more profound. These new technologies and organizations were conceived and nurtured by urban institutions, and many did not make their way into the countryside until the mid-twentieth century. The cultural distance between town and country would eventually shrink, due to the proliferation of rural electrification, automobiles, and mass media. But, for a time, America was sharply divided into two subcultures: one traditional and agrarian, and the other modern and metropolitan. Expansive and cosmopolitan, metropolitan life featured a whole host of modern amenities: electric lights and streetcar lines, telephone and telegraph service, daily mail deliveries, morning and afternoon newspapers, sophisticated banking and brokerage facilities, hotels and restaurants, indoor plumbing, municipal sewage systems, paved roads, an expanded network of voluntary associations and public institutions, and relatively easy access to the outside world. By contrast, agrarian communities generally lacked almost all of these advantages. Farmers and villagers lived in a face-to-face folk culture where religion, family, and largely unmechanized means of production defined the parameters of life. Despite their involvement in an increasingly integrated national economy, most rural Americans remained aloof from the hustle and bustle of urban culture.

Rural disengagement from urban values and institutions was often ridiculed by "city slickers" who looked down upon back-country "rubes" and "hayseeds." Even though rural folk sometimes countered with epithets of their own, castigating the city as a fount of sin and corruption, urban chauvinists ultimately got the better of the exchange. The main battle-field for this unequal war of words was the small town press, particularly during the William McKinley-William Jennings Bryan presidential campaigns of 1896 and 1900. Unfortunately for Bryan and the agrarians, by the end of the century antirural stereotypes had fueled the insecurities of small town businessmen, prompting them to side with the city and providing a strong impetus for urban growth and development. Whatever their true feelings about their country cousins, small town boosters did not want to be caught on the wrong side of the urban-rural fault line. In St. Petersburg, as elsewhere, the gospel of progress carried the day.

For most American cities, urbanization has been a two-stage process. The first stage—the transition from village to town—was generally made possible by the development of a railroad connection, or in a few cases, a commercial harbor. With a little luck and the help of an agricultural hinterland, a railroad or seaport town could take root and grow. How-ever, the second stage—the transition from town to city—invariably depended upon the development of an industrial-commercial infrastructure. During the past century, very few American communities have become cities without first creating an industrial base.

Significantly, St. Petersburg stands out as one of the few exceptions. Blessed with an abundance of sun and sea, the city's major product has always been itself. Mass culture would eventually make almost all American cities centers of consumption as well as production. But St. Petersburg was consump-tion-oriented from its very beginning. Long before the heyday of Ivy Lee and Madison Avenue, "the Ideal City by the Sea" entrusted its fate to advertising, public relations, and the hard sell.[2] Dr. Van Bibber set the tone in his 1885 paean to beautiful "frostless Pinellas," and the effusion of praise and puffery has not let up since.

St. Petersburg's prosperity was destined to rely on tourism, the service trades, and the spending habits of winter visitors and retirees. But the emergence of this unusual nonproduc-tive economy was by no means a foregone conclusion during the late nineteenth century. Most early boosters believed that the town's future growth was contingent upon the devel-opment of commerce and industry. The normal path to metropolitan status was through a mix of production and distribution, and the notion that a town could become a city without acquir-ing such a mix seemed far-fetched. Most obser-vers simply assumed that the rate of urbaniza-tion depended upon the pace of assembly lines and the volume of freight-car traffic.

The growth of nearby Tampa was a case in point. Although it had been little more than a village at the end of Reconstruction, Tampa was well on its way to becoming an industrial metropolis by the turn of the century. With more than a hundred cigar factories and a booming phosphate industry, the "Queen City of the Gulf" was the envy of Florida's business community.[4] Thus, even though the militancy and ethnic clannishness of Tampa's predomi-nantly Latin work force was cause for concern in some quarters, many St. Petersburg boosters hoped to emulate the city across the bay.

During the 1890s, local leaders concen-trated their energies on developing St. Peters-burg's potential as a commercial port. Once the town became the commercial gateway to the Gulf of Mexico, they reasoned, industrial growth would surely follow. Accordingly the railroad pier at the end of First Avenue South quickly became the pride of the local business community. Built in 1889 as the terminus of the Orange Belt Railroad, the three-thousand-foot-long structure was lined with loading docks and warehouses, although many visitors used it primarily for fishing and swimming. Accommodating everything from small freight-ers to vacationing bathers, the pier served as the hub of the downtown waterfront. Situated just south of the only deep-water channel connecting the downtown shoreline with the open bay, the pier area was vitally important to local boatmen.

In the early years, Orange Belt officials

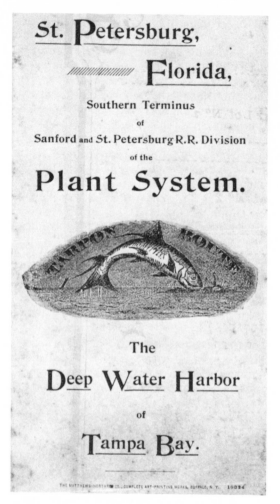

St. Petersburg,

//////////////// Florida,

Southern Terminus
of
Sanford and St. Petersburg R.R. Division
of the

Plant System.

The

Deep Water Harbor

of

Tampa Bay.

THE MATTHEWS-NORTHRUP CO., COMPLETE ART-PRINTING WORKS, BUFFALO, N.Y. 10034

This 1896 brochure was distributed by Henry Plant's Sanford and St. Petersburg Railroad (formerly the Orange Belt). Courtesy St. Petersburg Historical Society

made no attempt to restrict access to the pier. But these freewheeling days came to an abrupt end when Henry Plant took control of the railroad in 1895. Hoping to establish a monopoly for his own steamship line, Plant instituted a twenty-five-dollar docking fee for independent boat operators. If his competitors wanted to continue to use the pier and the nearby channel, they would have to pay for the privilege. The new restrictions were in keeping with the spirit of Gilded Age business practices. But Plant may have had more than profits on his mind. Some suspected that he also wanted to punish St. Petersburg residents for stymieing his efforts to build a grand hotel on the waterfront. Plant had angrily changed the prospective hotel site to Belleair, after several shrewd property owners demanded premium prices for their waterfront land. As a result, there was no love lost between Henry Plant and St. Petersburg; when a fierce storm nearly destroyed the railroad pier in the fall of 1895, some residents viewed the calamity as divine justice.

Plant's machinations severely damaged St. Petersburg's prospects for a major commercial harbor. But local interests did not give up easily. In 1896, one local boat builder, D. F. S. Brantley, built a pier of his own. Located at the foot of Second Avenue North, the narrow Brantley pier stretched fifteen hundred feet into the bay. Standing in seven feet of water, the pier head contained a commercial loading dock joined by wooden rails that ran the length of the pier. To the delight of his customers, and to the amazement of gawking tourists, Brantley operated a small horse-drawn flatcar to carry passengers and freight to the shore. Despite Brantley's ingenuity, the pier proved to be too far from the railroad depot to be a commercial success. Fortunately, the thirty-four-room bathing pavilion that he constructed a thousand feet from shore was a more successful enterprise.

Despite continuing troubles on the waterfront, as the century drew to a close local boosters were heartened by the town's recent progress. According to the special September 1897 "exposition" edition of the *St. Petersburg Times*, the town had kept in step with "the sturdy march of civilization." As the *Times* headline put it, "No Place in Florida Offers Greater Attraction for the Tourist . . . . Broad Avenues, Fine Bicycle Roads, Elegant Hotel Accommodations, Schoolhouses, Churches, Beautiful Residences, Fishing, Boating, etc. Railroad and Steam-boat Accommodations Unsurpassed." The paper went on to boast that the community had recently acquired a bicycle shop, a steam laundry, two dairies, a small cigar factory (M. Castillo and Sons, the producers of "St. Petersburg Smokers"), and a "fibre-factory" that turned palmetto leaves into mattress stuffing. St. Petersburg also had three general stores, two lawyers, and five doctors, but only one undertaker: "Mr. H. P. Bussy does what little there is to do and owns his own hearse and cemetery. He carries a full line of caskets and is fully equipped for embalming." In the best tradition of small town boosterism, Ira Gore, the editor of the *Times*, praised everything from local fishing conditions—"Spanish mackerel . . . are caught by the hundreds daily"—to the quality of Richard Strada's meat market—" well supplied with the best of Florida and Western meats."[5] But Gore was proudest of the town's latest achievement: the opening of a fifty-watt electric power plant at the foot of Central Avenue.

The man responsible for the power plant was Frank Allston Davis, a visionary developer destined to play a major role in the city's history. Born on a Vermont farm in 1850, Davis worked as a teacher, a machinery salesman, and a publisher of county histories before moving to Philadelphia in 1880. During the 1880s, he developed a successful publishing house that specialized in medical textbooks and periodicals, and by the end of the decade, he was well on his way to becoming one of Philadelphia's leading businessmen. However, his life took an unexpected turn in 1890, when a bad case of rheumatism drove him to the Gulf coast of Florida. After one balmy winter in Tarpon Springs, a rejuvenated Davis decided to live out his days in the Florida sun.

Although he was fond of his new home, Davis could not resist trying to bring the town of Tarpon Springs into the modern age. His first project demonstrated the wonders of electrification. With the encouragement and financial backing of Hamilton Disston's younger brother Jacob, he constructed a small power plant at the center of town in 1895. Unfortunately, the plant failed to attract more than a handful of customers. A disappointed Davis publicly blamed the failure on a backward citizenry who preferred oil lamps to electric bulbs, but this only made matters worse. Disgusted, Davis soon gave up on Tarpon Springs and moved his operation to St. Petersburg, where he hoped to find a more progressive environment.

In February 1897, the voters of St. Petersburg granted Davis a municipal utilities franchise, and six months later the power plant was ready for operation. Housed in a rickety wooden building, the tiny plant consisted of "a wood-burning boiler, a steam engine, and a 50-watt dynamo."[6] But somehow this "wonderful collection of junk" produced electricity, and that was enough to impress most of the locals. When the first switch was thrown on August 5, the grateful town marked the event with a day-long celebration. Following an early afternoon bicycle race and a baseball game against archrival Clearwater (the home team won seventeen to eleven), the entire town assembled in the municipal park, which was "beautifully decorated with evergreens, Spanish moss, and bunting, and brilliantly lighted with electricity."[7] Governor Henry Mitchell, Mayor James Armistead, and other dignitaries were on hand to address the throng, and the town band played into the night. After a deafening fireworks display, most of the crowd returned to the darkness, while the town's more fortunate citizens retired to a grand ball at the Detroit Hotel. The birth of the electric age seemed to please almost everyone, and by the end of the year St. Petersburg's thirty-two street lights had become a major source of community pride.

The opening of Frank Davis's power plant inaugurated a series of technological advances that transformed local life at the end of the nineteenth century. In 1898, the town got its first telephone through Arthur Norwood, a British-born merchant who had moved to St. Petersburg from Disston City a decade earlier.

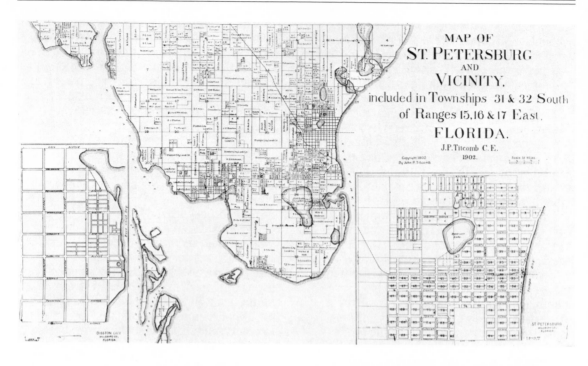

MAP OF
ST. PETERSBURG
AND
VICINITY,
included in Townships 31 & 32 South
of Ranges 15,16 & 17 East,
FLORIDA.
J.P.Titcomb C.E.
Copyright 1902   1902.
By John P. Titcomb.   Scale of Miles

The owner of two stores four blocks apart, Norwood was determined to solve his communication problems with a personal telephone link. After purchasing two antiquated receivers, he convinced A. P. Weller, the manager of Davis's power plant, to string two thousand feet of wire along Central Avenue. The result was a barely audible but nonetheless amazing connection.

Norwood's telephone was a curiosity, but many local residents wanted access to a real telephone system. In 1899, several impatient businessmen patched together a small system that served eighteen subscribers. But the town's first extensive telephone network would not be installed until 1901, when the Bell-affiliated St. Petersburg Telephone Company was formed. The new system proved popular, and in June 1902 a long-distance hookup with Tampa was added, allowing subscribers to call across the bay for twenty-five cents.

For many local residents, the construction of a municipal waterworks system was an even greater sign of change. After local voters approved a ten-thousand-dollar bond issue in May 1899, workmen constructed a water tower at the junction of Fifth Street and Second Avenue North, plus a series of water mains that connected the downtown area with Reservoir (Mirror) Lake. By the end of the year, several hundred downtown residents were enjoying the benefits of a public water supply. Predictably, property owners who lived beyond the reach of the new system grumbled about an unfair tax burden. But, with the gradual extension of the system, such protests became less frequent.

Many local residents were proud of the fact that at the turn of century St. Petersburg was the only town on the peninsula with electric lights, telephones, and public water. But no one was more pleased by these developments than Frank Davis. Even though his power plant failed to make money, he quickly became St. Petersburg's most enthusiastic booster. Convinced that the town had unlimited potential, he launched a promotional campaign that dwarfed any other the area had seen. Taking full advantage of his Philadelphia publishing company, he printed and distributed thousands of broadsides and leaflets, many of which cited Dr. Van Bibber's 1885 Health City report. In virtually every issue of the *Medical Bulletin*, a popular monthly read by thousands of doctors, Davis extolled the health-restoring virtues of St. Petersburg's climate. Doctors were encouraged to send their patients on the next train, or to hop on the train themselves, since no one could fail to benefit from a visit to sunny Pinellas. In 1901, Davis published a 104-page booklet, *Progress and Possibilities of St. Petersburg*, and five years later he followed it with an even splashier booklet entitled *St. Petersburg, the Pleasure City of the South*. A self-styled poet, he also touted his adopted home in a book of verse entitled *Poems of the Pinellas*. For a brief period in 1905, he even published a special journal, *Florida Magazine*, that was devoted almost entirely to the promotion of St. Petersburg.

For almost a decade, the irrepressible Davis acted as a one-man chamber of commerce. Although he did his best to enlist other local businessmen in his promotional causes, he invariably shouldered the burden himself. In 1899, L. Y. Jenness of the St. Petersburg Land and Improvement Company presided over a small group that called itself the Board of Trade. But the short-lived organization never amounted to much. Three years later there was a second attempt to organize a board of trade, but once again the results were disappointing. The new board did appropriate $125 for a promotional brochure to be printed by Davis's publishing company, and ten thousand brochures were actually produced. But the board lost heart in 1903 when the city council refused to approve a $500 appropriation for municipal promotion. Three years of inactivity followed, before a final reorganization

led to the establishment of a permanent board of trade (later known as the Chamber of Commerce) in 1906.

Even though he was often a solitary figure, Davis's enthusiasm for the promotion of St. Petersburg never seemed to flag. Fortunately, his task was made easier by the lifting of the depression in 1898, and by the Spanish-American War. Nearby Tampa was the major staging ground for the American Expeditionary Force, and Mullet Key became the site of Fort De Soto, central Florida's main bulwark against the Spanish navy. As a result, St. Petersburg and the surrounding Pinellas Peninsula became a common stomping ground for soldiers and other personnel awaiting passage to Cuba. Men and women who had never heard of St. Petersburg or the Pinellas Peninsula visited the area, and more than a few returned as settlers after the war.

With this inadvertent help from the war, Davis's dreams of growth and development began to materialize. By the time the 1900 federal census was taken, St. Petersburg's population had risen to 1,575, almost six times the figure of 1890. The census count represented the year-round population, but, as Davis was quick to point out, the local population was much larger during the winter months. Moreover, the area of the town had grown to almost two square miles, more than twice the size of the original 1888 plat. Viewed from the perspective of New York or Philadelphia or even Tampa, St. Petersburg was still little more than an overgrown village masquerading as a town. But local residents were proud of the community's growth nonetheless.

At the beginning of the new century the mood of St. Petersburg was upbeat and expansive. The town was in the midst of a major building boom, and carpenters' hammers could be heard from one end of the community to the other. The buildings under construction in 1900 and 1901 included Edwin H. Tomlinson's Manual Training School, a two-story brick structure that opened in December 1901, and the town's first high school, an equally impressive brick building that opened the following fall. Scores of homes were also under construction, and one of the grandest was Tomlinson's late Victorian "palace" located at the corner of Fourth Street and Second Avenue South.

A Connecticut-born philanthropist who had made a small fortune in mining, Tomlinson had been a winter resident of St. Petersburg since 1891. Known for his generosity as well as his eccentricities, he financed several local institutions, including a student orchestra, St. Peter's Episcopal Church, and a colorful array of flags that became a fixture in the town's annual Washington's Birthday celebrations. He also gained notoriety for the famous but short-lived Tomlinson Tower. While traveling in Italy in 1898, he met Guglielmo Marconi, the inventor of the wireless telegraph. Marconi's work fascinated Tomlinson, particularly after the Italian inventor expressed interest in conducting telegraphic experiments in Florida. Consequently, when Tomlinson's home was completed in early 1901, it sported an enormous 137-foot tower which awaited Marconi's inventive hands. Marconi never came, however, and the ill-fated tower was destroyed by lightning less than six months after its completion.

Tomlinson had better luck with the Fountain of Youth, a sulfuric artesian well located at the foot of Fourth Avenue South. With Tomlinson and others testifying to its restorative powers, the well became an enduring tourist attraction—despite its foul smell. On the nearby waterfront, Tomlinson built a long wharf with a cottage on the end. Known as the Fountain of Youth Pier, the wharf extended just far enough, some neighbors suspected, to take the eccentric builder beyond the range of the fountain's odors. The local gentry did not always approve of the

exotic creations concocted by St. Petersburg's wealthiest citizen, but even his sharpest critics acknowledged that his enthusiasms sometimes yielded practical results. When the town welcomed its first automobile—an Orient that sputtered along newly paved Central Avenue at six miles an hour—the driver and proud owner was Ed Tomlinson. The year was 1905, the same year that he designed and built an ingenious open-air post office. Tomlinson's unique post office became a city landmark, and its 1917 replacement, a large masonry structure, retained the open-air design.

Tomlinson was an unforgettable character who left his imprint on the local community. But the man who had the greatest impact on early twentieth-century St. Petersburg was William L. Straub, a remarkable journalist who exerted his influence without the benefit of wealth or Barnumesque showmanship. For almost four decades, from 1901 to 1939, Straub served as the crusading editor of the *St. Petersburg Times*, a financially troubled but increasingly influential city newspaper. Straub transformed a struggling four-page weekly into a major metropolitan daily, and in the process helped to turn a small town into a city.

Born in Dowagiac, Michigan, in 1867, Straub survived a difficult childhood, including a serious hunting accident. The accident left him partially crippled, and for the remainder of his life he was forced to walk with a crutch and a cane. At the age of seventeen, he moved to Dakota Territory, where he worked for a series of small-town newspapers. By the mid-1890s, he had become one of North Dakota's best-known journalists, due in part to his considerable skill as a cartoonist. As the associate editor of the Grand Forks *Daily Herald*, he campaigned for protectionism, the gold standard, and William McKinley in a state that was sorely tempted by the Bryanist crusade of 1896. In 1897, a life-threatening bronchial condition interrupted Straub's career, forcing him to seek a more salubrious climate. After a brief stay in Texas, and an even briefer stop in Tampa—to which he took an instant dislike—the ailing editor finally found an acceptable new home in 1899. St. Petersburg, he recalled many years later, was "just the place" he and his family had been looking for, a community with "clear waters," a "bright beach," and "cleanliness everywhere," a wholesome town where you could get "breakfast like mother used to make."[8]

During his first two years in town, Straub spent most of his time fishing and growing pineapples (according to local editor Ira Gore, the growing of pineapples was the fastest-growing and most profitable industry on the peninsula during the late 1890s). But, in July 1901, he returned to journalism as the editor and part-owner of the *St. Petersburg Times*. Straub and two partners bought the paper from the widow of Ira Gore for thirteen hundred dollars. Since Gore's death in 1900, the *Times'* stature had been slipping, but Straub's pen soon brought new life to the troubled paper.

Almost from the moment he took over the *Times*, Straub was a major force in local affairs. The soft-spoken stranger with the steely gray eyes and the wire-rimmed glasses turned out to be the self-appointed guardian of the community's future. An inveterate booster, Straub filled his pages with rhapsodic descriptions of "St. Petersburg-by-the-sea, the growing city of Florida." For several years, his weekly column "St. Petersburg has . . ." offered readers a heavy dose of self-congratulatory rhetoric. In May 1902, for example, he boasted that St. Petersburg had, among other assets, two thousand inhabitants, eighty-four businesses, eight churches, schools "not exceeded anywhere," a volunteer fire department, an opera house, "one of the best auditorium buildings in the South," and "a surrounding country dotted with the finest orange, grape, tangerine and other citrons [*sic*], fruit groves, pineapple plantations, truck farms and gardens in Florida—and plenty of room for more."[9]

Despite his penchant for boosterism, Straub was also a tireless reformer who exuded the activist spirit of the Progressive Era. Week after week, he penned editorials and cartoons that either tried to goad or flatter the community into broadening its horizons. Although he sometimes commented on national or international affairs, most of his writing focused on issues closer to home. His civic activism touched every facet of local life, usually with favorable results. Publicly and privately, he campaigned for Prohibition, better roads and sidewalks, a more ambitious public school system, more humane penal institutions, morality and local self-determination in government, and public ownership of the waterfront.

Straub sometimes wielded an acerbic pen, and sooner or later almost all local office-holders felt the sting of his lampooning artistry. Yet he had an even greater talent for mediation and compromise, prompting one local historian to dub him the "gentle crusader."[10] For example, in August 1902, after the failure of the town's only bank, he helped to restore order in a community on the brink of anarchy. Although he expressed sympathy for the hundreds of depositors who had lost their life savings, he made a stirring appeal to reason that may have saved the defunct bank's officers from vigilante justice (unfortunately, he would later demonstrate that his willingness to defend the rights of unpopular defendants did not extend to the black community). A year later, he played a similar mediating role when the town council surreptitiously obtained municipal incorporation from the state legislature. This *fait accompli* strategy did not sit well with many local citizens, including Straub, but once incorporation was a reality he did everything he could to convince his readers that the town was ready to become a city. As a city, St. Petersburg could forge ahead with large-scale bond issues and expanded municipal services, two goals that were dear to Straub's heart. With the *Times* lauding the new St. Petersburg city hall and the new city police force, which consisted of four officers and a chief, city status soon became an accepted fact of local life.

Straub was a man of many enthusiasms. But the issue that aroused his greatest passion was the continuing controversy over the development of the downtown waterfront. At the time that Straub came on the scene, the controversy centered around the pier operated by the Sanford and St. Petersburg Railroad. Following Henry Plant's death in 1899, relations between local businessmen and the Plant

System temporarily improved. But opposition to the railroad pier's near-monopolistic control over local commerce eventually led to renewed conflict. The situation reached a crisis during the winter of 1901-1902 when George King and John Chase, the owners of the *Anthea*, a seventy-foot passenger steamer, decided to deepen the channel between the open bay and their Central Avenue dock. Fearing that a new channel would weaken their position, the directors of the Plant System obtained an injunction that temporarily blocked the proposed deepening. This action enraged the local business community, which countered with a plan to terminate the railroad pier's monopoly. Led by A. P. Avery, one of Straub's partners,

the businessmen decided to dredge a T-shaped channel that would open the shoreline between Central Avenue and First Avenue North to deep-draft vessels. Completed in late 1902, the Little Coe Channel (B. E. Coe did the dredging) was viewed as the first step in the creation of a port of St. Petersburg that could compete with the port of Tampa across the bay.

Even before the completion of the Little Coe Channel, the prospects for a new port were boosted by an unexpected development. In April 1902, the Plant System was dismantled, and the Sanford and St. Petersburg Railroad became part of the Atlantic Coast Line. Although no one knew how the Atlantic Coast Line merger would affect St. Petersburg,

Straub editorialized that, considering the town's past difficulties with the Plant System, the change could not help but be "beneficial"[11] He was right, although several years passed before the Atlantic Coast Line provided the level of service that local residents thought they deserved.

To the surprise of many of his readers, Straub was less happy about the digging of the Little Coe Channel. Although he wanted St. Petersburg to expand its port facilities, he was worried that expansion would destroy the natural beauty of the downtown waterfront. Would St. Petersburg continue to attract desirable tourists and settlers if the waterfront area were turned into a full-fledged harbor? Already littered with unkempt docks and smelly fish houses, not to mention a belching power plant, the once-quaint waterfront had become somewhat seedy and was becoming more cluttered and unsightly each year. For Straub, a talented painter, the ugliness alone was discouraging, but in his view the value of the waterfront transcended aesthetics. Like many progressive reformers, he considered public parks as a prerequisite for community order and well-being. In the tradition of Frederick Law Olmsted and Horace Cleveland, he reasoned that the inner city needed beautiful green spaces to compensate for the accelerated pace and unnatural character of urban life. Of course, in a self-styled tropical paradise like St. Petersburg, there was the added necessity of protecting the environment that sustained the local tourist trade.

To Straub, the obvious solution was to preserve the downtown waterfront as a public park, while finding an alternative site for the port of St. Petersburg. Public debate over the waterfront park began in July 1902, after the Board of Trade approved a resolution calling for a public bayfront park between Second and Fifth Avenue North. Straub backed the resolution with a barrage of enthusiastic editorials, but the first real breakthrough did not come until December 1905, when J. M. Lewis unveiled a comprehensive plan to turn virtually the entire downtown waterfront into a park. Lewis's plan became a major issue in the 1906 city elections, with the public waterfront faction eventually winning a majority of the seats on the city council. Straub and his allies also tightened their control over the Board of Trade, which soon adopted the strategy of buying up private waterfront properties and holding them in trust until the city council could afford to turn them into parkland.

The second part of Straub's solution—the acquisition of an alternative harbor site—took longer to develop and might never have occurred without C. A. Harvey, an ex-lumberman from Jesup, Georgia, who migrated to St. Petersburg in 1903. Harvey's involvement in the harbor controversy grew out of his desire to develop a residential subdivision on a stretch of landfill north of Big Bayou and south of downtown. Since his plan to reclaim "Fiddlers' Paradise," a sprawling mudflat that marked the confluence of Salt and Booker Creeks, required the dredging of the Bayboro inlet, he decided to include a deep-water harbor in his subdivision. Initially, this ambitious project was greeted with rude skepticism by almost everyone, including Straub. But when Harvey actually chartered the Bayboro Investment Company in June 1906, many of the city's leading citizens invested in the project. Bayboro Harbor would not become a reality for many years—and the harbor would never fulfill all of Harvey's expectations—but its potential existence was enough to sustain the public waterfront boosters.

During several years of false starts and broken promises, the Board of Trade threatened several times to develop the parkland without the benefit of public ownership, but the first waterfront deeds were finally signed over to the city in January 1909. An additional seventeen months of delay followed before the long-awaited dredging of the public waterfront finally commenced in May 1910. Fittingly, the dredge that cleared away the silt and much was renamed the *Blanche* in honor of William Straub's sixteen-year-old daughter. With the work of the *Blanche* and some hasty landscaping, Waterfront Park officially became a public park in December 1910, although it did not look like much until the addition of seawalls and more formal landscaping in 1911. Over the next five years the park was expanded to include several other lots, so that by 1916 St. Petersburg had one of the largest public waterfronts in the nation.

Although later generations would hail the public waterfront as a masterpiece of urban planning, many of Straub's contemporaries were not pleased by the triumph of his naturalist crusade. Not everyone preferred pelicans and palms to stevedores and packing crates. Many taxpayers were angered by the city council's willingness to spend their money on greenery and scenic walks. The total cost of purchasing and improving the public waterfront (up to 1925) came to almost $2 million, a weighty sum for a small tourist town. Straub probably would have paid any price to save the waterfront, arguing that the citizenry was bound to benefit in the end. But many local residents did not share his disregard for the short-term cost, or his enthusiasm for aesthetic gratification.

One of Straub's major adversaries was F. A. Davis, the transplanted Philadelphian who had done so much to put St. Petersburg on the map. Both Straub and Davis were passionately committed to the improvement of the city, and both men were sometimes criticized for being impractical dreamers. Yet they often found themselves at odds with one another. To Straub's dismay, Davis balked at the idea of moving his power plant away from the waterfront. Moreover, from late 1901 on, Davis was involved in a series of transit projects which complicated Straub's plans for a public waterfront. With the backing of Jacob Disston, Davis organized the St. Petersburg and Gulf Railway Company in December 1901, and, despite strong opposition from the *St. Petersburg Times*, he obtained a trolley franchise from the voters two months later. Construction began in November 1902, and the first phase, a line running from the foot of Central Avenue to the junction of Ninth Street and Eleventh Avenue South, opened for business on New Year's Day 1905.

By the following April, the trolley line was open all the way to the site formerly called Disston City. After the demise of Disston City, John F. Chase, a Union veteran who had migrated to Florida in 1895, devised a plan to turn the area into Veteran City, a retirement community for members of the Grand Army of the Republic. Although the veterans never showed up, the Veteran City trolley line became a popular route to the Pass-a-Grille ferry. Passing through long stretches of uninhabited, junglelike countryside, the line provided vacationers with an exotic, if somewhat steamy, excursion.

Davis would eventually help to turn Veteran City into Gulfport, but in 1905 he was more concerned with the other end of the line. In May 1905, he purchased the Brantley Pier, a wobbly nine-year-old wharf located three blocks north of the Atlantic Coast Line Pier. After organizing the Tampa Bay Transportation Company, a corporation dedicated to the development of trade with South America and the Caribbean, he tore down the Brantley Pier and replaced it with the Electric Pier. Three thousand feet long and sixteen feet wide, the Electric Pier was illuminated by hundreds of incandescent

The railroad pier of the Sanford and St. Petersburg (formerly the Orange Belt) Railroad in 1897. Courtesy Stokes Collection, University of South Florida Library, Tampa

bulbs. Local observers were even more amazed when Davis added to this impressive display by extending his trolley line onto the pier itself. Using special trolley cars to shuttle passengers and freight from the pier head to the downtown business district, Davis entered into serious competition with the Atlantic Coast Line Pier. Thrilled with his new creation, Davis soon purchased the *Favorite*, an enormous five-hundred passenger steamer that made periodic runs to Tampa. Much too large for the St. Petersburg-to-Tampa run, the *Favorite* would eventually be replaced by a smaller and more profitable vessel. But, for a time, watching the *Favorite* pull into the Electric Pier was a popular activity for tourists and locals alike.

In the years before World War I, the Electric Pier became a major tourist attraction and a symbol of the new St. Petersburg. But Davis's plan to establish a large-scale commercial port and to turn the city into a major international trade center never materialized, and he soon shifted his attention to real estate and suburban development. While some residents continued to envy the bustling port city across the bay, Straub and his allies were relieved, preferring to wait for the less disruptive development of Bayboro Harbor. In the meantime, the city could progress at a modest pace, living off tourists, winter residents, and settlers who appreciated the unspoiled beauty of Tampa Bay.

Straub's struggle to preserve the waterfront cut against the grain of the American capitalist ethos. Although conservationist sentiment was on the rise during the Progressive Era, many businessmen remained under the influence of Social Darwinism and the "survival of the fittest" doctrine. Since size, strength, and adaptability were thought to be the keys to success, placing conservation or aesthetics ahead of growth seemed to them foolhardy and self-destructive. This attitude was especially prevalent in up-and-coming but insecure communities like St. Petersburg, where the benefits of growth were projected into a rosy future. In the best of all possible worlds, the local business community would have it both ways—a subtropical utopia that could accommodate everything from freighters to egrets. But in the real world—a society where individual success was often contingent upon the surrounding community's economic growth—practical men had little time to worry about displaced egrets. In other words, one way to resolve the dilemma posed by the proverbial "machine in the garden" was simply to plow under the garden.[12] St. Petersburg, almost alone among American cities, would eventually find a way to avoid this ruthless solution. But during the Progressive Era—an age that knew nothing of old-age pensions or interstate highways—the idea that a large city could subsist on tourism and patterns of residential preference seemed farfetched, if not ludicrous. Perhaps a small town could live off its warm climate and swaying palms, but not a city.

Fishing from the railroad pier in 1897. Courtesy Stokes Collection, University of South Florida Library, Tampa

A westward view from the railroad pier, circa 1898, shows the Clarenden Hotel at the right. The building with the smokestack is an ice plant. Courtesy St. Petersburg Historical Society

The interior of James G. Bradshaw's drugstore, circa 1896. Bradshaw (third from left) served as St. Petersburg's mayor from 1913 to 1916. Courtesy St. Petersburg Historical Society

The Clarenden Hotel opened for business in 1894. Located near the waterfront, on the corner of Central Avenue and First Street, the Clarenden was destroyed by fire in December 1899. Courtesy St. Petersburg Historical Society

The Detroit Hotel, circa 1897.
Courtesy Stokes Collection, University of South Florida Library,
Tampa

Suspecting that some of his guests
would like to spend more time on
the Gulf shore, J. H. Forquer, the
manager of the Detroit Hotel,
bult this "floating hotel" at
Pass-a-Grille in 1897. The
floating hotel was destroyed by
fire in the spring of 1899.
Courtesy St. Petersburg Historical Society

This view looks east along Central Avenue (then known as Sixth Avenue) in 1897. Courtesy Stokes Collection, University of South Florida Library, Tampa

The eastern end of Central Avenue, 1898. The Detroit Hotel, with its distinctive minaret-topped gazebo, can be seen in the center. The gazebo was added to the hotel in the late 1890s. Courtesy St. Petersburg Historical Society

St. Peter's Episcopal Church, 1908. Located at the corner of Second Avenue North and Fourth Street, this Gothic Revival church was built in 1899. Courtesy St. Petersburg Historical Society

The historic Durant block, at the northwest corner of Fourth Street and Central Avenue, circa 1898. Built by Charles Durant in the early 1890s, the Durant block became the site of Arthur Norwood's department store in 1897. In 1907, Norwood sold the building to real estate salesman Noel Mitchell, who turned it into "Mitchell's Corner." The real estate firm of Perry Snell and J. C. Hamlett bought the building in 1914. In the late 1920s, the towering Snell Arcade was built on this site. Courtesy St. Petersburg Historical Society

The St. Petersburg Novelty Works (Seventh Street and First Avenue South) was a major source of building supplies at the turn of the century. The owner was Abram C. Pheil, who served the city as mayor in 1912-1913. Courtesy St. Petersburg Historical Society

The A. T. Blocker House and Lodge on Fourth Avenue North, circa 1900. Built during the 1890s, the Blocker house was razed in 1967. Courtesy St. Petersburg Historical Society

An early St. Petersburg family setting forth to church, circa 1900. Photograph by James Hamilton, courtesy Pinellas County Historical Society

James Hamilton, St. Petersburg's first resident professional photographer, lived in St. Petersburg from 1895 to 1906. Courtesy St. Petersburg Historical Society

These well-dressed ladies and gentlemen attended the "Michigan picnic" on Christmas Eve, circa 1900. The City Park (later Williams Park) bandstand in the background was built in 1894 by the Park Improvement Association. Courtesy Pinellas County Historical Society

During the winter of 1900-1901, St. Petersburg's Winter Exposition Hall featured displays of local products and a portrait of President William McKinley. Photograph by James Hamilton, courtesy Florida State Archives

Local children exhibit their dolls during the 1900-1901 Winter Exposition. Courtesy St. Petersburg Historical Society

A parade scene during the 1901 Washington's Birthday celebration. This photograph was taken at the corner of Central Avenue and Fourth Street. The Durant block (center left) and the First Congregational Church (center right) can be seen in the background. Courtesy St. Petersburg Historical Society

This photograph, taken from the top of the electric power plant's smokestack, looks west down Central Avenue in 1902. The tall building on the far left is Edwin H. Tomlinson's "Marconi tower"—a structure designed to facilitate experiments in wireless telegraphy. Courtesy St. Petersburg Historical Society

An 1899 family portrait of newspaper editor William L. Straub, his wife Sarah, and their daughter Blanche. Straub became editor and co-owner of the St. Petersburg Times in 1901. Courtesy William L. Straub Collection, St. Petersburg Historical Society

An aerial view of St. Petersburg in 1903, from a painting by William L. Straub, Courtesy St. Petersburg Times

St. Petersburg Gothic—Man, Woman, and Fish, circa 1900. Courtesy St. Petersburg Historical Society

*Four men and a 355-pound
grouper on a downtown pier,
1901. Courtesy* St. Petersburg
Times

*A young fishing enthusiast, circa
1905. Courtesy Osgood Collection, University of South Florida
Library, Tampa*

A northwest view from the railroad pier in 1903 includes F. A. Davis's electric power plant on the right. Courtesy St. Petersburg Historical Society

The Atlantic Coast Line railroad pier, 1904. Courtesy St. Petersburg Historical Society

The east view along the Atlantic Coast Line railroad pier in 1904 shows the pier's popular bathing pavilion on the right. Courtesy St. Petersburg Historical Society

Swimmers pose on the downtown waterfront, circa 1903. Courtesy St. Petersburg Historical Society

Boatbuilding was a small but significant local industry prior to World War I. Courtesy St. Petersburg Times

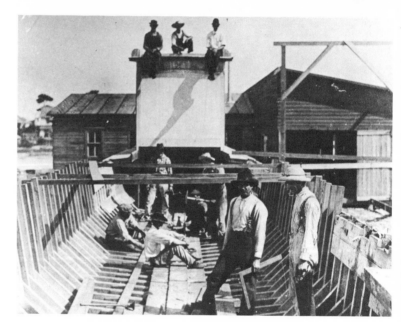

Hattie Dean Blocker (far right), her mother Kate Dean (dressed in black), and a friend pose in front of the Blockers' Queen Anne-style home (145 Fourth Avenue Northeast), circa 1905. Mrs. Blocker and her husband, A. T. "Bert" Blocker, owned the city's largest livery stable. Courtesy St. Petersburg Historical Society

The Paxton House, circa 1904. Built in 1890 by W. W. Coleman, this thirty-two-room hotel was located near the waterfront, on the northwest corner of Central Avenue and First Street. Courtesy St. Petersburg Historical Society

A 15416 Paxton House, St. Petersburg, Fla.

Wicker furniture was definitely in fashion at the Hotel Belmont in 1902. This is a view of the hotel's reception room. Courtesy St. Petersburg Historical Society

The corner of First Avenue North and Second Street, circa 1905, featured large Queen Anne-style homes with multiple porches. The house in the center was a boardinghouse operated by Molly Allen. Courtesy St. Petersburg Historical Society

This advertisement appeared in the 1908 St. Petersburg City Directory. Courtesy St. Petersburg Historical Society

The home of Lillian Livingston, the widow of town councilman B. F. Livingston, was one of St. Petersburg's grandest boarding-houses in 1908. Known as the Manor, this elegant Queen Anne-style structure was located at 127 First Avenue North. Courtesy St. Petersburg Historical Society

Edwin H. Tomlinson (1844-1938), the eccentric mining magnate, became early twentieth-century St. Petersburg's leading philanthropist. Courtesy St. Petersburg Historical Society

The newly organized Cadet Fife and Drum Corps perform in front of the home of Edwin H. Tomlinson in 1902. Tomlinson provided most of the funding for the Corps. Courtesy St. Petersburg Historical Society

A Washington's Birthday celebration, complete with May poles, was held on the grounds of Edwin H. Tomlinson's home circa 1904. Located near the corner of Second Avenue South and Fourth Street, the Tomlinson home, with its distinctive "Marconi tower," was sold to Congressman Joseph Sibley of Pennsylvania in 1905. Prior to a 1901 lightning strike, the tower was much higher. Courtesy St. Petersburg Historical Society

Students work on industrial arts projects at the Manual Training School in 1902. Funded by philanthropist Edwin H. Tomlinson, the Manual Training School opened on December 29, 1901, as an extension of the public school system. Housed in a two-story brick building on Second Avenue North, the school offered courses in manual training, physical culture, and military science. Courtesy St. Petersburg Historical Society

These young naval cadets cut quite a figure during the 1903 Washington's Birthday celebration. Photograph by James Hamilton, courtesy St. Petersburg Historical Society

These St. Petersburg students were known as "the girls of the flag drill" in 1902. Courtesy St. Petersburg Historical Society

The 1902 Washington's Birth-day celebration was a serious affair at the St. Petersburg Normal and Industrial School and Public School, at least for students Bascomb Belcher and Mabel Meares. Courtesy St. Petersburg Historical Society

Working out with Indian clubs was a routine activity for these young students of physical culture. The photograph was taken at the Manual Training School in 1902. Photograph by James Hamilton, courtesy St. Petersburg Historical Society

These tunic-clad girls attended physical culture classes at the Manual Training School in 1902. Courtesy St. Petersburg Historical Society

The St. Petersburg High School baseball team, 1904. Courtesy St. Petersburg Historical Society

Miss Minnie Thompson's class at St. Petersburg High School, circa 1904. Courtesy St. Petersburg Historical Society

The St. Petersburg Graded School band, circa 1905. Courtesy St. Petersburg Historical Society

*The St. Petersburg Fire Depart-
ment, circa 1913. Courtesy
Pinellas County Historical
Society*

*St. Petersburg's volunteer fire
department was replaced by a
paid force in 1907. This photograph was taken shortly after
the 1907 reorganization. Courtesy Pinellas County Historical
Society*

This unusual shell fence, located near the corner of Second Avenue North and First Street, was built by Owen Albright at the turn of the century. One of early St. Petersburg's best-known landmarks, it was destroyed by the hurricane of 1921. Courtesy St. Petersburg Historical Society

Prior to the development of Perry Snell's North Shore subdivision in 1911, this fisherman's shack stood near the present-day corner of Beach Drive and Coffee Pot Boulevard. The photograph was taken circa 1900. Courtesy St. Petersburg Historical Society

This sugar cane mill was located near what is now the intersection of Twenty-sixth Street and Fiftieth Avenue North. The photograph was taken in 1903. Courtesy St. Petersburg Historical Society

St. Petersburg's first electric power plant was constructed by F. A. Davis in 1897. Located at the present site of the St. Petersburg Yacht Club, the plant was torn down in 1915. This photograph was taken in 1905 or 1906, shortly after the opening of the streetcar line. Courtesy St. Petersburg Historical Society

The waterfront between Central Avenue and First Avenue South, as it looked in 1906. A streetcar headed for the recently opened Electric Pier can be seen on the far right. Courtesy St. Petersburg Historical Society

Boating at Big Bayou, circa 1905. Courtesy Osgood Collection, University of South Florida Library, Tampa

A chaperoned beach excursion, circa 1905. Courtesy Osgood Collection, University of South Florida Library, Tampa

Cultivating cactus at Big Bayou, circa 1905. Courtesy Osgood Collection, University of South Florida Library, Tampa

*Seaside cottages at Pass-a-Grille,
circa 1907. The photographer
was looking south from the tower
of the Hotel Bonhomie. Courtesy
Florida State Archives*

Chapter Five

The Sunshine City

1907-1918

Members of the Canadian Society meet at the Tangerine Avenue South home of British-born building contractor Harold Gilbart, circa 1915. Courtesy St. Petersburg Historical Society

St. Petersburg remained a relatively small community as it neared the end of its second decade. In 1907, the local population was still under three thousand, and, aside from a few shipments of fish, lumber, and citrus products, there were no signs of the industrial or commercial growth that normally marked the transition to city status. Yet, with each passing year, the city took on more and more of the characteristics of an urban place. The physical trappings of city life—such as paved streets and electric lights—were the most obvious manifestations of the urbanization process. But the citizens of St. Petersburg also had to deal with new social and cultural forms. Here, as elsewhere, urbanization was accompanied by a formalization of institutions, an inevitable breakdown of communal consensus, a quickened pace, and a growing economic and cultural interdependence with the outside world. In the decade before World War I, St. Petersburg was hardly a metropolis, but the days when everyone in town knew everyone else were over. No longer an intimate village, St. Petersburg was fast becoming a cluster of subcommunities connected by formal institutions.

By 1907 there were several St. Petersburgs. Middle- and upper-class women, blacks, working-class whites, businessmen and real estate promoters, tourists and winter residents—each of these groups constituted a distinct subcommunity. Even though such groups obviously had adjoining and sometimes overlapping interests, boundaries of space, culture, and economics frequently kept them apart. As local life became increasingly complex and stratified, distinctions of class, race, and gender took on new meanings. This complexity was the source of much confusion and disorder, but it also led to the establishment of a more formal social order, as patterns of interaction that previously had been entrusted to custom and tradition were turned over to the institutions of law and politics.

In St. Petersburg, as in most early twentieth-century American communities, middle- and upper-class women lived in a world of their own. Although designed and mandated by men, this special world was one that only women could fully understand or participate in. With few exceptions, their lives were defined and hemmed in by the Victorian cult of domesticity, a curious mixture of restriction and privilege. The ideal late-Victorian woman combined the virtues of patience, modesty, and genteel self-control, and never questioned her supportive role. Her proper place was in the home, caring for the spiritual and material needs of her husband and children. She was too busy nurturing her family to interfere in the public world of men and money. And she had the "good sense" to recognize that she had no aptitude for politics or a professional career. Her interest in education was more social than intellectual, and she learned early that her highest calling was to adorn the male ego, not to challenge it.

The cult of domesticity was a powerful force in St. Petersburg's polite society, but it did not prevent the city's more independent-minded women from playing an active role in community life. In their efforts to find personal fulfillment and social improvement, resolute women often stretched and sometimes violated the limits of Victorian convention. Although they could neither vote nor be elected to public office, the women of St. Petersburg ventured well beyond the confines of the parlor and the kitchen. To the dismay of male traditionalists, their contributions ranged from volunteerism and church work to professional employment and civic activism.

In early twentieth-century St. Petersburg, the world of work was still dominated by men, but working women were far more common than they had been in the nineteenth century. Even though it was still rare for married white women to work outside the home, a surprisingly large number of widows and single women worked as teachers, dressmakers, milliners, nurses, clerks, bookkeepers, and saleswomen. Several local women ran successful boarding houses; Alma Van Landingham managed the local Western Union office; and as early as 1900 the city had two female physicians.

Most of St. Petersburg's working women were black and poor. Employed as laundresses and maids, they shouldered much of the domestic burden in the more affluent sections of the white community. Many black families could not have survived without the income generated by female domestic work, and in some black households the wife was the primary breadwinner. Local whites seldom found themselves in such straits, but voluntary female employment was clearly on the rise in the white community. Although still a novelty, the idea of a respectable woman working outside the home simply because she chose to do so was not nearly as shocking as it had been a generation or two earlier.

Even so, most middle- and upper-class women confined their public activities to volunteerism and church work. From the 1890s onward, local women maintained a number of voluntary associations which influenced the wider community. Several local churches had ladies' aid societies, and by 1910, the Daughters of Rebekah, the Order of the Eastern Star, the Daughters of the Confederacy, the Women's Relief Corps of the Grand Army of the Republic, and the Women's Christian Temperance Union all had active local chapters. Some of these organizations were little more than social clubs, but others, like the WCTU, maintained ambitious programs of reform and outreach. Led by Sarah Armistead, the widow of John Constantine Williams, Sr., and the wife of ex-mayor James Armistead, the local WCTU issued a steady barrage of Prohibitionist propaganda, while keeping a wary eye on the city's two saloons, the Club Buffet and the Sunny South. Armed with a junior affiliate, the Loyal Temperance Legion, and a weekly column in the *St. Petersburg Times*, the ladies of the WCTU were definitely an influential force. When the voters of Pinellas County outlawed saloons in a July 1913 referendum, the unenfranchised but irrepressible women of the WCTU were one of the reasons why.

Local affiliates of national organizations such as the WCTU gave many St. Petersburg women much-needed opportunities for creative self-expression, but the city's most important women's organization was a unique homegrown creation, the Woman's Town Improvement Association. Founded in May 1901, the WTIA was an outgrowth of a local park im-

provement association which dated back to 1888. Dedicated to the beautification of the community and the uplifting of local culture, the WTIA sponsored Arbor Day celebrations, annual flower shows, Lyceum courses, and Chautauqua lectures. Staunch allies of William Straub's public waterfront faction, the women of the WTIA agitated for landscaped parks, sidewalks, band shells, paved streets, and cattle-free lawns. On occasion, the organization embraced a broad social agenda, petitioning for such causes as prison reform, the abolition of the convict lease system, and wildlife preservation. But the WTIA was more likely to be involved in moralistic campaigns aimed at vice and sin. In 1910, the organization enthusiastically endorsed a ministerial effort to rid the community of gamblers, drunkards, and cigarette smokers, as well as an effort to institute a blue law that would prohibit local stores from opening on Sunday. On November 10, after listening to the impassioned arguments of the blue law advocates, the city council directed the city attorney to draw up such a law. But the resultant uproar in the business community forced the council to reverse itself at the next meeting.

Such attempts to return the community to moral rectitude sometimes pitted the women of the WTIA against husbands, fathers, and sons, and perhaps a few daughters as well, but the Victorian gentility of the organization generally prevented all-out conflict. With few exceptions, the members of the WTIA belonged to the city's most prominent families. Black women were excluded from the organization, and white women of modest means rarely became members. Sarah Armistead was active in the WTIA until her death in 1917; the organization's first president was Isabelle Weller, the wife of Arthur P. Weller, F. A. Davis's cousin and the manager of St. Petersburg's electric power plant; and her successor was Sarah Moore Straub, the wife of William Straub. From 1913 to 1929, the WTIA's guiding force was Mary Merrell, the wife of Herman Merrell, a prominent local attorney and real estate promoter. Under her energetic leadership, the WTIA purchased its own building in 1913, an impressive two-story

Editor Lew B. Brown's famous Sunshine Offer, as it was first issued on September 1, 1910. Courtesy Nelson Poynter Collection, Nelson Poynter Library, University of South Florida at St. Petersburg

Lew B. Brown (1861-1944), the editor of the St. Petersburg Evening Independent *from 1908 to 1944. Courtesy Pinellas County Historical Society*

structure which it graciously shared with the Board of Trade. This unusual arrangement disturbed and embarrassed some members of the local male elite, but anyone who lived in the city for any length of time knew that it was not easy to keep up with the "meddling women" of the WTIA.

For some reason—perhaps because the community had such an unusual economic base—early St. Petersburg seemed to attract more than its share of remarkable women. In an age when the medical profession was totally dominated by men, St. Petersburg had a number of female physicians: Dr. Marry Davis, a Pennsylvania native who also ran a local boarding house; Dr. Alvida Arneson, who migrated to the city from Sweden in the 1890s; Dr. Anna Dewey, a widow who practiced homeopathy; and Dr. Adelyne Ellis, who maintained an office in the Pheil Building. Considering its size, the city also had a surplus of women with artistic or literary talent. Dr. Alvida's Arneson's housemate, Florence Goldie, was a New York-born artist, and Annie McRae, the widow of a Methodist minister, wrote most of the Board of Trade's early advertising copy. Bellona Brown Havens, the redoubtable mistress of the St. Petersburg Reading Room and Library, was an accomplished poet and magazine writer, and Katherine Bell Tippetts wrote novels under the pen name Jerome Cable.

During the early twentieth century, the most remarkable woman in St. Petersburg was almost certainly Katherine Tippetts. After growing up in a prominent Maryland family, she married William H. Tippetts, a well-known international newspaper correspondent. In 1902, her husband's failing health brought her to St. Petersburg, and she remained in the city until her death in 1950. Following the death of her husband in 1909, she assumed control of her family's varied business interests, including the management of the Belmont Hotel. Financially successful, she sent two sons to Princeton, a third son to Georgia Institute of Technology, and a daughter to the Florida State College For Women. A talented writer, fluent in five languages, she published scores of essays, short stories, and novels. But she spent most of her time working for the cause of conservation.

In 1909, Tippetts founded the St. Petersburg Audubon Society, which she served as president for thirty-three years. By the 1920s she had gained a national reputation as a conservationist. At one time or another, Tippetts served as president of the Florida Audubon Society, vice-president of the American Forestry Association, a member of the Florida State Reclamation Board, a trustee of both the National Park Association and the National Camp Fire Girls, and the national chairman of the General Federation of Women's Clubs' Committee on Nature Study and Wild Life Refuges. She fought for bird sanctuaries and animal protection legislation, was a major figure in the national "state bird" movement (it was largely through her efforts that the mockingbird was designated Florida's state bird), and played an instrumental role in the establishment of the Florida Fish and Game Commission. In 1922, Tippets ran (unsuccessfully) for a seat in the state legislature—only the second woman in Florida history to do so. In her spare time, she worked for the Chamber of Commerce, served on local hospital and park boards, and organized the city's first Boy Scout troop in 1919. Through it all, she thoroughly amazed and exhausted nearly everyone who came into contact with her.

Katherine Tippetts, Sarah Armistead, and the other prominent women noted above were talented and resourceful individuals who made St. Petersburg a better place in which to live. Nevertheless, they accomplished far less than they might have. With very few exceptions, their visions of reform, like those of their male counterparts, were obstructed by an impenetrable wall of racist ideology. The fact that many of these women had successfully scaled the barriers of sexual prejudice did not seem to give them any special empathy for those men and women who were trapped behind the barriers of racial prejudice. On a personal level, their dealings with black servants and laborers—the only blacks they were likely to encounter—may well have been governed by a generous spirit of kindness and compassion. But, publicly, these women of privilege did little or nothing to challenge an exploitative and degrading system of racial control.

During the early twentieth century, the white South was totally committed to the twin concepts of white supremacy and racial segregation. In St. Petersburg, as in other Southern cities, interaction between blacks and whites was ruthlessly and systematically controlled by a combination of custom and law known as "the color line" or "Jim Crow."[1] Whites who questioned the Jim Crow system were excluded from polite society, and blacks who openly challenged the system were often subjected to physical violence or even death. Although St. Petersburg was not a classic Southern city, its racial mores were generally consistent with the vaunted Southern way of life. By the beginning of World War I, most local whites considered segregation to be immutable and could not imagine a properly ordered society without strictly defined racial barriers. Yet, despite this depth of feeling, the primacy of Jim Crow was a relatively recent phenomenon.

During the frontier era following the Civil War, the dictates of race and racism had little effect on local life. For two decades, from 1868 to 1887, the local black community consisted of a single family. John and Anna Donaldson, the ex-slaves who migrated to the area with Louis Bell, Jr., at the beginning of Reconstruction, lived uneventfully among their white neighbors. The Donaldsons eventually became landowners and reportedly earned a good living from their forty-acre farm. They also raised a large family, and during the mid-1880s they

Fish nets drying on the waterfront, circa 1908, F. A. Davis's Electric Pier can be seen in the background. Courtesy St. Petersburg Historical Society

even sent several of their children to the Disston City School (also known as Prop College) run by Arthur Norwood, the same Englishman who would later give St. Petersburg its first telephone. According to historian Walter Fuller, who interviewed one of the Donaldson children many years later, no one objected to this token school integration; indeed, "nobody thought a thing about it."[2] Thus, even though the Donaldsons undoubtedly encountered racial prejudice from time to time, the Pinellas frontier seems to have been a relatively tolerant place.

This situation began to change in 1888, when the community experienced its first real influx of black settlers. More than a hundred black laborers worked on the final stages of the Orange Belt's construction, and after the railroad was completed in 1889, a dozen or so stayed on. Joined by their families, these early black pioneers created a small subcommunity along Fourth Avenue South known as Pepper Town. Taking advantage of St. Petersburg's rapid growth, they found work as day laborers, domestics, artisans, and fishermen. As the town expanded during the 1890s, additional black settlers drifted in. A few worked on the waterfront as stevedores, and others were recruited by labor agents to work in local hotels. Most of these new black settlers lived in or near a cluster of shacks owned by Leon B.

Cooper, a local white merchant. Located on Ninth Street, just south of the railroad tracks, this second black subcommunity was commonly known as Cooper's Quarters. There were other blacks, usually unmarried men, sprinkled throughout the community, and there was at least one interracial couple living on the edge of town. But the basic pattern of residential segregation was in place well before the turn of the century. Over time, as white residential areas expanded outward from downtown, the black community moved westward. But the boundaries of black settlement remained easily identifiable and nearly inviolate.

In 1910, blacks accounted for 26.6 percent of St. Petersburg's 4,127 inhabitants. Predictably, this striking figure was never included in the city's promotional leaflets. "St. Petersburg does not have a particularly large colored population," city planner John Nolen insisted in the 1920s, "but like all southern cities it has its colored section."[3] This carefully calculated understatement may have fooled a few tourists, but people who actually lived in St. Petersburg knew that the local black community had a significant and growing presence in the city. No amount of rhetoric could hide the fact that black labor was a crucial element of the local economy. Most of the women who washed the clothes and cleaned the houses, and most of the men who carried the tourists'

bags, paved the streets, dug the sewer lines, collected the garbage, cleaned the fish, and constructed the city's houses were black. Without the blood, sweat, and tears expended by people of color, St. Petersburg would not have been the up-and-coming city that local whites praised so loudly. Most whites would not have had it any other way. But the existence of an expanding black community presented white supremacists with a dilemma: how could they exploit black labor without creating a biracial community? As slaves and masters, blacks and whites had lived together in "distant intimacy," but in a free society the simultaneous exploitation and exclusion of an "inferior" race was a much more difficult enterprise.[4]

In St. Petersburg, as in the rest of the South, the preferred solution to this dilemma was a comprehensive system of Jim Crow laws superimposed on a sanctified code of racial etiquette. Under the Jim Crow regime, blacks were only admitted to the white world at prescribed times for prescribed reasons. Blacks were there when whites wanted them, but otherwise they lived in a separate community. During the day, blacks and whites often mingled in the streets and sometimes worked

Favorite Line steamers, the Pokanoket, (center) and the Favorite (right), are docked at the Electric Pier in 1913. A streetcar can be seen on the far left. Courtesy St. Petersburg Historical Society

side by side, but after nightfall blacks were required to return to their own world. This nocturnal separation was mandatory, even for whites; in January 1920, the St. Petersburg police department vowed to arrest "all white men found in the Negro section late at night regardless of their age or social distinction."[5]

St. Petersburg blacks lived in their own neighborhoods, attended their own churches and schools, swam at their own beaches, drank at their own bars, and were laid to rest in their own graveyards. Without exception, local institutions were separate and unequal. In everything from education to employment, blacks occupied the proverbial bottom rail of St. Petersburg society. Since tax support for black schools was begrudging and woefully inadequate, the black school term was barely half the length of the white term, and black teachers were paid far less than their white counterparts. This institutionalized injustice ensured that many local blacks would remain uneducated and impoverished, but most whites regarded this state of affairs as proper and natural.

Since the vast majority of local blacks worked as unskilled or semiskilled laborers, poverty was an ever-present fact of life in black St. Petersburg. Although unemployment was rare, wages were low. Some families had only the barest necessities, and many black homes were little more than tumbledown shacks. However, not all local blacks lived in desperate poverty. Some owned their own homes and businesses, and a few edged their way into the middle class. In 1920, the local black labor force included eighteen teachers, ten grocery store owners, seven barbers, seven tailors, six ministers, four insurance agents, four restaurant owners, two doctors, one dentist, and one hospital superintendent. Collectively, these middle-class occupations accounted for 6.7 percent of the local black working population. Even though many of these individuals had more modest incomes than their titles or occupations would suggest, they represented a nascent black bourgeoisie.

St. Petersburg's small but growing middle-class black economy was wholly internal and almost invisible to local whites. Blacks with money to spend had to be extremely careful, and the fact that some blacks lived better than many poor whites was rarely bandied about. As blacks knew all too well, a failure to live up to racial stereotypes was regarded as an act of betrayal by most whites. Even blacks who could afford better had no choice but to live in one-story bungalows, since any outward display of conspicuous consumption by a member of the inferior race was considered to be a serious breach of racial etiquette. From the white supremacist perspective, blacks were not supposed to own fancy carriages or automobiles, much less drive them through white neighborhoods.

St. Petersburg, like all Southern cities, had its share of mean-spirited racist demagoguery. But, in keeping with the city's genteel image, racial discrimination generally was justified in paternalistic rather than Negrophobic terms. Paternalistic whites prided themselves on knowing what was best for "their Negroes." In enforcing a firm and unforgiving color line, whites allegedly were protecting blacks from themselves. It was an axiom of white supremacist mythology that blacks were inferior, child-like beings who could not handle the responsibilities of freedom without white supervision. During the early twentieth century, this view was constantly being reinforced by popular literature, minstrel shows, and films like D. W. Griffith's *The Birth of a Nation,* which enjoyed a long run at La Plaza Theatre. White paternalism involved periodic acts of benevolence which softened and humanized black-white relationships. But, in the end, such acts served only to sanctify a crippling dependency based on prejudice and self-interest. This inexorable circle of deference and condescension ultimately benefited no one and frequently corrupted both giver and receiver.

Even at its best, paternalistic racism was invariable tinged with contempt. To most whites, the black community was a mysterious world that inspired feelings of fear and loathing. A common repository for white fantasies about sex and violence, it was an endless source of prurient fascination. In contrast to the romantic but mythic world of the "old time darkies," the twentieth-century black community was seen as a den of criminality and lust where primal instincts overwhelmed civilized restraint. Black communities were many and varied, but in the case of St. Petersburg, such images were more revealing about white social psychology than about black social reality. Local blacks undoubtedly produced their share of crime and social deviance. But black society in St. Petersburg was not nearly as pathological and unsophisticated as most whites believed.

Despite the prevalence of poverty, black St. Petersburg was not a community of despair. Even its poorest citizens were frequently sustained by strong kinship networks and a vital Afro-American folk culture based on religion and communal values. Single-parent households were relatively rare, and local blacks did not have to look outside their

The steamship Manatee *was a familiar sight on the St. Petersburg waterfront from 1908 to 1924. This photograph was taken in 1909. Courtesy St. Petersburg Historical Society*

community to find inspiring role models or other sources of individual dignity and self-esteem. Although almost unknown in the white community, Ira Bryant, the principal of St. Petersburg Industrial High School, and the Rev. James B. Lake, the charismatic pastor of the Bethel Baptist Church, were heroic, awe-inspiring figures to local blacks. Moreover, economic hardship and racial condescension did not prevent blacks from developing and taking pride in their own institutions. Several black fraternal organizations met regularly at the Knights of Pythias Hall (there was a separate Knights of Pythias Hall for whites), and, despite being underfunded and under-staffed, Mercy Hospital gave the black community a semblance of medical care. Since city parks and public festivals were generally for whites only, blacks also created their own leisure activities, ranging from musical comedy to baseball. In fact, local black baseball teams were often so impressive that they attracted white spectators, who sat in special segregated bleachers. None of this had much impact on the basic power relationships that divided the city into two separate societies, but at least it took some of the sting out of Jim Crow.

Despite its limitations, the black church was the most important antidote to the poison of Jim Crow ideology. More than any other institution, religion dominated the life of the black community. By 1920, local blacks

supported seven large congregations and numerous smaller storefront sects. As the cornerstone of the community, evangelical Christianity gave the embattled black minority a measure of self-determination and a much-needed outlet for emotion and creativity. St. Petersburg's black churches were comprehensive institutions which provided not only spiritual inspiration and comfort but also social support, cultural enrichment, and entertainment. Not everyone in the black community was religious, but many blacks spent a major portion of their nonworking hours in church activities. At the Mount Olive Primitive Baptist Church, for example, a typical Sunday included no less than four services. Local blacks could choose from a whirl of activities—church picnics, Sunday school classes, and innumerable sermons delivered by charismatic preachers. As a general rule, black preachers were the community's most powerful leaders, often serving as both internal power brokers and external liaisons with the white community. Indeed, in the absence of black public officials, preachers frequently were called upon to fulfill political functions.

Black politics was a sensitive subject in the local white community. During St. Petersburg's early years, it was not uncommon for blacks to vote in local, state, and national elections, or for white politicians to solicit black votes. But, as the black community

The steamship Favorite, *shown in 1912, was brought to St. Petersburg from New York by F. A. Davis in 1906. The five-hundred passenger* Favorite *made daily trips to Tampa and Bradenton. Courtesy St. Petersburg Historical Society*

expanded, black suffrage became increasingly controversial. During the Progressive Era, many local whites enthusiastically embraced the movement for black disfranchisement that was then sweeping the South. After years of complaining about bloc voting and the inappropriateness of allowing the black community to become the balance of power in local elections, several disgruntled Democratic Party leaders demanded an all-white primary in 1913. At the time, approximately five hundred local blacks were registered to vote, and a number of white politicians were openly courting the black vote. This alarmed James G. Bradshaw, the front-running candidate for commissioner of public affairs, who declared that he "wanted to go into public office as the choice of the white voters of the city and would rather not have the office than to rely on the negroes to win."[6] This new policy was wholeheartedly endorsed by Lew B. Brown, the editor of the *St. Petersburg Independent*, who insisted that the white primary was necessary "in order to maintain control of city affairs in the hands of the white people."[7] With Brown's help, Bradshaw got his wish, inaugurating a new era in local politics. Even though an actual "white primary" was not tried again until 1921 and many blacks continued to vote in general elections, widespread intimidation gradually reduced black participation and influence in local Democratic politics—the only politics that mattered in early twentieth-century St. Petersburg.

Blacks were encouraged to distance themselves from the world of politics. But there was no escape from the world of law and order. Although white politicians sometimes stepped into the breach—usually in an effort to prop up sagging electoral campaigns—the task of maintaining white supremacy normally was entrusted to the legal justice system. From the dominant white perspective, this system was necessary for the preservation of civic peace and a properly constituted social order. But from the black perspective, the long arm of the law represented a brutal system of racial control that meted out little justice. In St. Petersburg, as in most Southern cities, the entire legal justice system was biased against blacks. Every aspect—policemen, judges, jurors, attorneys, jail guards, and prison wardens—was totally white. And since legal due process requirements often conflicted with the system's transcendent purpose, the rights of black defendants, as well as the rights of black victims, were routinely ignored. When crime involved a black victim, the police often refused to respond, but when the victim was white, the police reaction was invariably swift and harsh. Black movement was restricted by the enforcement of racially specific curfew laws, and periodic "vagrancy" sweeps cleared the streets of "undesirable" blacks needed to fill out road-gang quotas. All in all, the white system of "justice" worked efficiently and ruthlessly—for whites.

The legal justice system sustained the

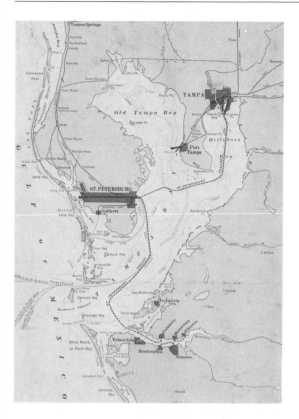

A steamship and railway map of the Tampa Bay region, circa 1914. Courtesy St. Petersburg Historical Society

step aside. Making no attempt to hide their identity, several vigilantes climbed a ladder to Thomas's second-story cell and "shot him to pieces."[9] When even this did not satisfy the mob's thirst for vengeance, the jail doors were broken down so that other members of the crowd could mutilate and kick the body. Even though the identity of Thomas's assailants was well known, no one was ever brought to trial for this heinous crime. The press reaction was muted, and the white community went back to its celebration of the Christmas season as if nothing had happened. The chastening effect on the black community can only be imagined.

Nine years later vigilante justice struck again. This time the catalyst was the murder of Edward F. Sherman, a fifty-five-year-old photographer and land developer from Camden, New Jersey. For several years Sherman had operated a photography studio on Central Avenue, but in 1913 his interests turned to real estate promotion. Having purchased an isolated stretch of woodland on John's Pass Road (Thirtieth Avenue North), he was in the midst of developing his property into Wildwood Gardens, which he touted as St. Petersburg's newest suburb, when he was killed by a shotgun blast on the night of November 10, 1914. Described as "two Negroes," Sherman's assailants also robbed and assaulted his wife Mary.[10] Although beaten with a pipe and possible raped, Mary Sherman crawled and staggered through a half-mile of underbrush to get help. By the next morning, sensational newspaper head-lines and spreading rumors had triggered a massive manhunt by armed whites. Literally hundreds of black men were detained and questioned, and in some cases roughed up.

hegemony of the white community. But, on at least two occasions, local white supremacists felt the need to go beyond the rule of law. In 1905, and again in 1914, St. Petersburg wit-nessed brutal lynchings that were sanctioned by a sizable portion, if not a majority, of the local white population. The 1905 incident was triggered by the murder of city police chief James J. Mitchell. On Christmas day, Chief Mitchell arrested a local black man for dis-orderly conduct, but before he and his prisoner reached the city jail Mitchell was knifed to death by John Thomas, allegedly a black "drifter" who had fled from South Carolina to escape a series of criminal charges.[8] Thomas and his friend were immediately apprehended by one of Mitchell's deputies, but within min-utes some local whites were demanding sum-mary justice. Soon after Thomas was jailed, an angry crowd surrounded the jail building. The officers on duty refused to turn Thomas over to the mob, but eventually they were forced to

Early suspicions centered on Ebenezer B. Tobin, who was whisked away to a Clearwater jail by a deputy county sheriff, and John Evans, a black laborer from Dunnellon who had been fired by Sherman three days before the murder.

On November 11, Evans was taken to the hospital where Mary Sherman was recuperating, but she was unable to identify him as one of the assailants. Evans was then released, but the subsequent discovery of blood-spattered clothes in a house where he had recently roomed led a group of vigilantes to recapture him. After hours of torture and extended but unsuccessful attempts to extract a confession, Evans was again taken before Mary Sherman. Once again she refused to identify him as one of her husband's murderers. Nevertheless, he was placed in the city jail, where a mob of fifteen hundred angry whites soon gathered. After threatening to kill the jailer, E. H. Nichols, the mob tore down part of the jail's side wall and dragged Evans into the street. After placing a noose around Evans's neck, the swelling crowd, which included at least half of the city's white population, then marched west down Central Avenue towards the black section of the city. At the corner of Ninth Street and Second Avenue South, the heart of Cooper's Quarters, a rope was thrown over an electric light pole, and Evans was hoisted up above the crowd. Terrified, Evans wrapped his legs around the light pole, but an unidentified white woman in a nearby automobile pried him loose with a fatal shotgun blast. This made the ritual hanging unnecessary, but for nearly ten minutes members of the crowd emptied their weapons into Evans's swaying corpse. As one eyewitness recalled the scene, "Little kids with guns were shootin', and women standing' there shootin' and screamin' and yellin' and—and shootin'. It was the damndest mess you ever heard in your life, you never heard anything like it."[11]

In the early morning hours, after the crowd had dispersed, a policemen retrieved what was left of the body, but much of the city was still in a frenzy the following day. White vigilantes continued to roam the county looking for Evans's accomplices or sympathizers, and there was even talk of burning down the entire black community. Some local blacks vowed to stand and fight, but many others fled in terror. A few escaped by train, and others took to the woods. And still others—179 black women and children—took the afternoon boat to Tampa.

For a time—particularly after he learned that local vigilantes were planning to storm Ebenezer Tobin's Clearwater jail cell—Governor Park Trammell considered sending in the state militia to restore order. But military intervention ultimately proved unnecessary, as calm returned to the community that billed itself as the "cleanest, cheeriest, most comfortable little city in the south."[12] By the end of November, a local coroner's jury had determined that John Evans had died at the hands of "unknown" persons, and most of St. Petersburg's black refugees had long since drifted back into the city. The wounds were reopened the following September, when Ebenezer Tobin was put on trial for murder. His conviction and subsequent execution (Pinellas County's first legal hanging) in late October 1915 brought to a close the most gruesome and shameful episode in St. Petersburg's history.

Neither the guilt nor the innocence of John Evans and Ebenezer Tobin can now be determined because neither man was given a fair, impartial trial. Many of their contemporaries were convinced that Evans and Tobin did murder Edward Sherman, but both men steadfastly professed their innocence, and Mary Sherman twice could not identify Evans as one of the attackers. Despite this confusion, the meaning of their deaths could hardly be clearer—or more disturbing. The torture and lynching of John Evans—one of sixty-nine black men lynched in the United States in 1914—was much more than a spontaneous act of vengeance committed by ignorant, bloodthirsty rednecks. On the contrary, the mob action culminated from a web of permissiveness, encouragement and secret sanctions from highly placed citizens and public officials.

Not only did a number of highly respected citizens participate in the lynch mob, but also substantial circumstantial evidence strongly suggests that several public officials

These "nature" photographs were taken near Mullet Key (left) and Maximo Point, circa 1910. Courtesy St. Petersburg Historical Society

helped to plan the lynching. Police chief A. J. Easters and his officers made little effort to protect Evans from the mob; in fact, at several points they apparently encouraged the vigilante spirit that was sweeping the community. Even more ominously, on the afternoon before the lynching the local coroner's jury held a secret meeting which may have laid the groundwork for the terror that was to follow. Among St. Petersburg's image-conscious leaders, it was widely believed that swift retribution for the assault on the Shermans was the best way to restore the city's tarnished reputation. As Jon Wilson, the leading historian of the affair, has suggested, the winter tourist season was approaching and "neither killers on the loose nor armed bands of men prowling the county would be attractive to the refined northerners that St. Petersburg hoped to impress."[13] The suspicion that the lynching was accomplished with the connivance of local leaders was confirmed by a published interview with J. P. Walsh, a friend and partner of Sherman's who came to St. Petersburg from Camden, New Jersey, to investigate the murder. Walsh assured the *Camden Courier* that Evans had been tried and convicted by a secret committee composed of fifteen of St. Petersburg's most respected citizens. The fact that this kind of behavior was acceptable to Walsh, or even conceivable, much less a reality, reveals an abuse of authority and privilege that was as barbaric as the frenzy of the lynch mob itself.

The local press also contributed to the mounting hysteria by implicitly condoning mob violence. Although both the *St. Petersburg Times* and the *St. Petersburg Evening Independent* editorialized against lynch law as an abstract principle, their news reports on the affair were consistently inflammatory. Playing up the sexual theme, they suggested that lynching was the inevitable outcome whenever black men sexually assaulted white women. The *Tampa Tribune* and the *Clearwater Sun* issued unequivocal denunciations of the Evans lynching, but the local press did not agree. Even William L. Straub, the Michigan native who periodically professed to be "a friend of the negroes," counseled his readers to restrain

their guilt, "for the whole world knows that the same brute under the same circumstances would have met the same fate in any one of their towns."[14] Lew B. Brown, the editor of the *Evening Independent*, also offered no apologies to the local black community, although he was quick to point out that John Evans was an outsider. "It should be remembered," Brown wrote, "that John Evans was not a St. Petersburg negro; he came here only a few weeks ago from Dunnellon. It is usually the negroes who stray in here and stay only a short while who commit crimes. The bulk of the St. Petersburg negroes are honest, straightwalking people who are industrious and well-behaved."[15] In a similar vein, Straub reprinted an editorial from the *Ocala Star* which argued that Evans was "a bad character" who had been convicted of grand larceny by the Marion County Superior Court. "It was probably safe," the editorial went on, "to lynch him on general principles whether he was guilty of the crime he was accused of or not."[16] In the age of Jim Crow, this was as much contrition and reconciliation as blacks could hope for.

The presence of a large black population and the harsh character of local race relations gave St. Petersburg a Southern flavor. But this was something that the city fathers did not like to advertise. Local publicists took great pains to dissociate St. Petersburg from the languishing cities of the Deep South. "St. Petersburg can scarcely be called a typical Southern town," the editor of the 1912 city directory insisted, "except in respect of natural environment. The residents are from every state in the Union and from other countries beside."[17] In truth, during the period 1888-1918, the city's population was almost evenly divided between Southerners and non-Southerners. However, not everyone who visited or lived in the city was aware of this regional balance, since it was sometimes obscured by the economic superiority and greater visibility of non-Southerners. While the local working class, both black and white, was largely Southern-born, the local elite was dominated by Northern and British transplants. As the broad sample of early business and civic leaders in Table 1 demonstrates, the origins of

St. Petersburg's upper crust were not what one would expect in a Southern city.

Table 1
Nativity of St. Petersburg's Business and Civic Leaders, 1888-1918

State or Country	Number of Leaders N=76
Indiana	7
Pennsylvania	7
Florida	5
New York	4
Great Britain	4
North Carolina	4
Canada	3
Maine	3
Iowa	3
New Jersey	3
Illinois	3
Tennessee	3
Maryland	3
Michigan	3
Georgia	3
Massachusetts	2
New Hampshire	2
West Virginia	2
Rhode Island	1
Ohio	1
Vermont	1
Wisconsin	1
Connecticut	1
Russia	1
Denmark	1
Virginia	1
Mississippi	1
Alabama	1
Arkansas	1
Kentucky	1

SOURCE: Compiled from data in Karl H. Grismer, *History of St. Petersburg* (St. Petersburg: Tourist News Publishing Company, 1924), pp. 217-295.

A half-century before the Sunbelt phenomenon altered the regional configuration of American life, St. Petersburg experienced the coming together of Northern and Southern cultures. This experience ultimately led to a considerable amount of syncretism, as the city became a melting pot of regional cultures. But, in the early years, the perseverance of regional mores and loyalties was striking. The white "Cracker" culture of fishermen, railroad workers, draymen, and other Southern natives was clearly distinguishable from the "Yankee" culture that dominated the downtown business community. Accentuated by class divisions, Southern patterns of cuisine, language, dress, kinship, and historical memory stood out in stark contrast to the cultural patterns of non-Southern transplants. Whether they were regarded as quaint or uncouth, the Crackers often resented the Yankees' thinly disguised condescension. If necessary, they were willing to swallow their pride and work for Yankee interlopers, but they were not about to be improved by them. This cultural tension was a constant undertone of local life, although open conflict between Yankees and Crackers was relatively rare.

One exception was a near riot in 1911. On the eve of the city's annual Washington's Birthday parade, the local chapter of the Grand Army of the Republic threatened to pull out of the parade if the United Confederate Veterans were allowed to carry the Confederate flag. Although Confederate veterans had carried the flag in previous parades, school superintendent W. R. Trowbridge, the official in charge of the 1911 festivities, acceded to the GAR's demand. Trowbridge's decision caused an uproar among local Southerners, and he had to turn to the police to enforce his banning of the Confederate flag. On Washington's Birthday there were hard feelings all around, and only the advanced age of most of the disputants prevented an all-out donnybrook. In the end, even some Northerners expressed sympathy for the ex-Confederates' plight, and on February 25 Trowbridge was forced to resign. The Confederate stars and bars reappeared in subsequent parades, and the GAR never forced the issue again.

The ex-Confederates' victory in the "little civil war" of 1911 was based, in part, on a humane concern for a band of fragile old soldiers who had already suffered more than their share of humiliations. But it also reflected an

emerging white supremacist consensus. The lost cause of the Confederacy was gaining new respectability, even in the North, and the rising popularity of Jim Crow was one of the reasons why. In race relations, more than in any other area, Southern traditions tended to dominate St. Petersburg's local mores. Encouraged by statewide Jim Crow laws, the city's transplanted Northerners often mimicked Southern white supremacists. Indeed, it was sometimes the Northerners who pushed the hardest for segregation. In many cases, of course, more than mimicry was involved. Unaccustomed to a biracial society that entailed personal contact between blacks and whites, many transplanted Northerners welcomed the restrictive barriers of Jim Crow. In a 1981 interview, Paul Barco, the son of a black bartender who migrated to St. Petersburg in 1905, recalled his father's explanation for the hardening of local segregationist sentiment in the years before World War I:

> My daddy said when he came to this city, if you had to go to a doctor, you went on over to the doctor. He had one waiting room there, he waited on whoever was there. And the people who were in there were rustic [white] people, just like others [who were black]. They were not the polished persons from elsewhere, who probably had never been around a [black] person. But my dad said as these persons began to come down who had the great amounts of finance and they had been exposed to a great deal of literary training, then these people felt that they didn't care to sit in the same room with these [black] people.[18]

Whatever their origin, Jim Crow institutions created more solidarity than divisiveness among local whites. Regional subcultures persisted, but differences of opinion on matters of race were seldom the animating force behind this persistence. In early twentieth-century St. Petersburg, regional differences took on special importance primarily because the local white community lacked the ethnic and religious heterogeneity found in most other American cities. St. Petersburg's native-born white population was overwhelmingly WASPish, and even the city's small foreign-born population was predominantly Anglo-American. Prior to the 1920s, the city attracted few settlers of eastern or southern European origin, and only

*Draymen pose in front of
A. T. Blocker's Livery Stable,
located on Second Street South,
1910. Courtesy St. Petersburg
Historical Society*

a handful of Asians, Jews, and Hispanics. Even Irish Catholics were rare; indeed, the local parish could not even justify a full-time resident priest until 1917. Thus, other than economic class, the regional split between Southerners and non-Southerners was the white community's most obvious internal dividing line.

Despite its ethnic and religious homogeneity, St. Petersburg was a divided city—racially, regionally, and sexually—a community whose internal life was more complicated than outer appearance would suggest. Without the contributions of women, blacks, and Florida Crackers—the three groups who did most of the hard labor that sustained the city's growth—St. Petersburg would have remained an unheralded village. And yet, with the exception of a few privileged upper-middle-class white women, these unsung heroes and heroines of the Florida dream were not allowed to participate in the city's public life. Nor were they allowed to intrude into the carefully crafted image that the city projected to the outside world. During the early twentieth century, virtually all American communities expended some effort to idealize and sanitize their public images. But St. Petersburg was one of the first communities to take such efforts to extremes. Devoted to the concept of selling itself, St. Petersburg entrusted its fate to the twin gods of public relations and advertising. This commitment to image-making was a natural outgrowth of the city's dependence on the art of buying and selling land—or more specifically, its dependence on the grand masters of this art. For better or worse, the city's character was molded by the dream merchants of sun and sand.

The first of these men to arrive was F. A. Davis, the Philadelphia book publisher who provided the community with electric lights, trolleys, and a mountain of publicity. In a whirlwind decade, from 1896 to 1906, Davis's expansive dreams helped to transform a town into a city. Unfortunately, Davis's finances proved to be more fragile than his ambitions, and during the national economic panic of 1907 his Florida empire collapsed. Most of his local holdings—the trolley line, the power plant, and the Electric Pier—were placed in a receivership administered by J. Frank Harrison, a highly respected downtown merchant. Eventually, Harrison turned the management of the Davis utilities over to H. Walter Fuller, an enterprising newcomer who was destined to become a real estate mogul of the first order.

Born in Atlanta, Georgia, in 1865, H. Walter Fuller was the son of Henry Alexander Fuller, a prosperous merchant and Confederate cavalry officer. As a young man, he was a consumptive, and in 1883 he migrated to Florida for health reasons. After several years in Tampa, where he was involved in everything from citrus farming to coastal trading, he eventually settled in Bradenton, where he became a successful road and building contractor. The proud owner of sixty pairs of mules, he helped to construct the military fortifications at Fort De Soto and Egmont Key during the Spanish-American War, and a decade later he turned up in St. Petersburg as the paving contractor for the Maximo Road. Fortunately for Fuller, the Maximo paving contract brought him to St. Petersburg at just the moment that Harrison was casting about for a man who had experience with transit companies.

Fuller was entrusted with Davis's holdings because he had constructed and operated a small electric streetcar system in Bradenton, not because he had a reputation for conservative business management. On the contrary, he was a consummate gambler who always seemed to stretch his resources to the limit. With the financial backing of Jacob Disston, Fuller went on an expansionist binge that dwarfed anything F. A. Davis had ever undertaken. Between 1909 and 1917, he increased the

Some St. Petersburg cowboys, circa 1910. From left to right, Jay B. Starkey, Mortie Vickers, Tom Harrison, and Alphonso Thayer. The Detroit Hotel can be seen in the background. Cattle grazing and driving were common activities in the unincorporated areas surrounding St. Petersburg until the early 1920s. Courtesy Pinellas County Historical Society

length of St. Petersburg's trolley system from seven to twenty-three miles, replaced Davis's antiquated power plant with a larger and more modern facility, acquired several new steamships, and purchased thousands of acres of real estate. After buying up much of the southwestern corner of the peninsula, he extended both Central Avenue and the streetcar line all the way to Boca Ciega Bay. This allowed him to sell lots in previously untapped areas, as he laid the foundation for a massive expansion of the city. In the process, he became a millionaire and triggered the city's first real land boom, which lasted from 1911 to 1914. Fuller's insatiable appetite for land—he created subdivision after subdivision—would lead to bankruptcy and temporary disgrace in 1917. But he had an exciting ride while it lasted.

In terms of scale, Fuller's sprawling real estate empire was in a class by itself, but for sheer flamboyance, the soft-spoken Georgian was no match for Noel A. Mitchell, St. Petersburg's self-styled "Sand Man." Born in Rhode Island, in 1874, Mitchell displayed an early aptitude for salesmanship. By the age of eighteen, he had developed Mitchell's Original Atlantic City Salt Water Taffy, which he pedled at resorts along the New Jersey and New England shore. Mitchell's taffy eventually became a big seller, and after coming to St. Petersburg as a tourist in 1904, he decided to invest his earnings in Florida real estate. By 1907, he was

selling land out of Mitchell's Corner, an increasingly frenetic real estate office located at the junction of Fourth Street and Central Avenue. Specializing in beachfront lots and other properties in the western half of the peninsula, he made a small fortune before the market collapsed during World War I. A master at developing advertising gimmicks, Mitchell used everything from motion pictures to picture postcards placed in taffy boxes to sell his real estate. As a stalwart leader of the local chamber of commerce, he financed public picnics and other publicity stunts and never missed an opportunity to boost himself or the city.

Always one step ahead of the competition, Mitchell inadvertently created a local institution in 1908, when he placed several bright orange benches in front of his real estate office. Printed in bold letters on the back of each bench was: "Mitchell, the Sand Man. The Honest Real Estate Dealer. The Man With a Conscience. He Never Sleeps."[19] The benches proved extremely popular with footweary pedestrians, and before long Mitchell's benches dotted the downtown business district. Competing real estate agents and other merchants soon added promotional benches of their own, producing a chaotic variety of sizes, shapes, and colors. In response to this untrammeled creativity, Mayor Al Lang pushed through a city ordinance in 1916 which required all benches to be a standard size and color. Thereafter, St. Petersburg became "the city of green benches," a tradition that lasted until the 1960s, when a youth-conscious city council tried to change the community's image by banishing the famous green benches from the city's parks and sidewalks.[20]

If H. Walter Fuller and Noel Mitchell were the early masters of mass-oriented real estate promotion, C. Perry Snell was the first high priest of up-scale development. Born in Bowling Green, Kentucky, in 1869, Snell owned and operated a successful Louisville drugstore during the 1890s. In 1899, he married Lillian Allen, a wealthy heiress who bankrolled his growing interest in real estate development. After a brief honeymoon visit to St. Petersburg, the Snells returned to the area on several lengthy vacation trips. In 1904, they made a permanent move to the city, and within a year Snell and several associates had formed the Bay Shore Land Company. Snell's new company soon developed two large subdivisions south of Coffee Pot Bayou, but this was only the beginning of a comprehensive North Shore development that would take more than three decades to complete. In 1906, a Snell-led syndicate purchased the Detroit Hotel and several hundred other properties originally owned by the Orange Belt Railroad's investment company. The Orange Belt purchases allowed him to create several new subdivisions between Mirror and Crescent Lakes. For a while, Snell even owned Crescent Lake itself, although he eventually convinced the city to turn the lakefront into a public park. A staunch advocate of William Straub's Waterfront Park, Snell was instrumental in extending the park northward to Coffee Pot Bayou.

The support that Snell gave to the public waterfront faction involved a measure of self-interest, since a beautiful waterfront park complemented his plan for an elegant residential subdivision. A full decade before Addison Mizner and George Merrick laid the first tile of their "Spanish Castles," Snell was busy trying to attract prestige-conscious buyers who would appreciate beautiful landscaping and fine architecture. Although his glory days as the "master of Mediterranean kitsch" would not come until the 1920s, Snell was experimenting with the art of aesthetic residential development long before the First World War.[21] A determined, if somewhat humorless, man, he spared no expense in luring prospective homeowners to his subdivisions. When critics convinced him that his proposed North Shore development was too isolated, he promptly built a streetcar spur line as far north as Coffee Pot Bayou. And when he could not find enough high-quality statuary in the United States to suit his needs, he took off on a series of European shopping sprees.

With Snell nearly monopolizing the development of the North Shore (by 1911 he owned almost the entire northeastern quadrant of the city), and with Fuller and Mitchell buying up huge portions of the western half of the peninsula, smaller developers had to look elsewhere. Some turned to the west central interior area, while others concentrated on the southside. As a result, several long-neglected areas, including the stretch between downtown and Big Bayou, began to fill up. On the southside, the grandiose plans of C. A. Harvey, the erstwhile developer of Bayboro Harbor, were cut short by his death in 1914. But several other southside developers soon picked up the slack. Charles R. Hall, a former millinery salesman from Philadelphia who began his St. Petersburg real estate activities in 1912 with the development of two west central subdivisions, purchased and cleared a huge parcel of land south of Lake Maggiore that would eventually become Lakewood Estates. Charles Roser, the Ohio-born cookie manufacturer who gained fame as the developer of the Fig Newton, began the development of his famous Roser Park subdivision. After selling out to the National Biscuit Company in 1910, Roser resettled in St. Petersburg and almost immediately turned his attention to real estate promotion. By 1914, he had bought several dozen lots along picturesque Booker Creek, with the intention of creating a small, high-quality residential area. On a more modest scale, he hoped to duplicate what Perry Snell was doing on the North Shore. One of the few local builders to use brick, he ultimately created a unique neighborhood whose odd-

Horses were still a common sight on the streets of St. Petersburg when this photograph was taken in July 1912. Courtesy St. Petersburg Historical Society

shaped lots and creekside hills were a welcome change from the flat grid that dominated the local real estate scene.

Although the presence of men like Charles Roser and Perry Snell gave the local real estate industry a certain air of respectability, the land hucksters of early twentieth-century St. Petersburg had an uneven reputation. In a boom town filled with transients and men on the make, the cast of characters ranged from heroes to confidence men, with most individuals falling somewhere in between. Thus, despite the best efforts of the Chamber of Commerce, not everyone went away a satisfied customer. One disgruntled visitor described St. Petersburg as "a place where the natives work less and have more to show for it than any place on earth." And he added that "this is probably due to the fact that they charge northern suckers exorbitant prices for everything they buy. St. Pete is like neither heaven nor hell, for in both places you need no money and in St. Pete you need it every hour."[22] Nevertheless, whatever else can be said about St. Petersburg's sand merchants, they tended to be good at what they did. The best of them were honest, multitalented individuals who excelled at advertising, public relations, and overall salesmanship. In addition to dominating the economic life of the city, they molded the city's image to fit their purposes, making every

effort to convince the world that they were selling little pieces of paradise.

Fortunately for them, they were not alone in their efforts. At one time or another, nearly everyone in the city—from editors and politicians to trainmen and porters—pitched in. Indeed, anyone who spent more than a few hours in the city could sense that St. Petersburg's life's blood was good publicity. Some local enthusiasts, such as Lew B. Brown, the irrepressible editor of the *St. Petersburg Evening Independent*, devoted their lives to the cause of boosterism. For thirty-five years, Major Brown, as he was commonly called, carried on a public love affair with his adopted city.

Brown was born in the Ozark mountain town of Madison, Arkansas, in 1861. At the age of fourteen he moved to Louisville, Kentucky, where he went to work for Col. Henry Watterson, the celebrated editor of the *Louisville Courier-Journal*. After two decades of working his way up the ladder at the *Courier-Journal*, Brown purchased a small weekly in Taylorsville, Kentucky, in 1895. Ten years later he moved on to the *Harrodsburg Democrat*, and in 1908 he bought the *Evening Independent* from Willis B. Powell. Powell had threatened the local preeminence of William Straub's *St. Petersburg Times* by initiating the city's first daily newspaper in 1907. But Straub soon faced an even stiffer challenge from Lew Brown. A clever publicist who knew how to sell newspapers, Brown used everything from sensationalist headlines to sentimental poetry to get his points across. More often than not, his points directly or indirectly served the interests of local boosterism. His favorite topic was St. Petersburg's balmy climate, which he lauded in verse and prose. One mawkish ode to fair St. Petersburg included the verses:

Thine air is like some rich old wine that
   thrills through every vein;
Thy sunshine falls as gently down as
   some far music's strain;
Thy soft perpetual breezes waft a life-
   balm rich and rare—
Where all the time is Summer and every
   day is fair.

Thy rare poinsettia's crimson flame,
   thy bougain's purple pile,
Thy grand begonia's golden mass, which
   charm, enchant, beguile;
And roses rare and verdure rich the
   thought of cold defy—
Where all the time is Summer and the
   flowers never die.[23]

Brown backed up his rhetoric with a unique promise that turned out to be the city's first great publicity stunt. In September 1910, he tendered his soon-to-be-famous "Sunshine Offer." Declaring St. Petersburg to be the "Sunshine city," he vowed to give away the *Evening Independent* "ABSOLUTELY FREE—WITHOUT COST OR CONDITION—to subscribers and strangers alike . . . . every day the sun doesn't shine on St. Petersburg."[24] The offer attracted national attention, and, fortunately for Brown, the sun generally cooperated. During the seventy-five years that the Sunshine Offer was in effect, the city averaged fewer than five sunshineless days a year.

Lew Brown's competitor, William Straub, was never able to come up with anything quite as spectacular as the Sunshine Offer. However, he was instrumental in removing a dark cloud of sorts—the Pinellas Peninsula's lack of political autonomy. The peninsula had been a part of Hillsborough County since 1834, but

until the 1890s, inclusion in Hillsborough County was tolerable, with the peninsula still an unsettled frontier. But once the area acquired a railroad and began to fill up with settlers—and particularly after St. Petersburg became an incorporated city in 1903—talk of an eventual separation became common. To transform talk to action, Straub turned his editorial page into an engine of political reform. From the moment he took over the *St. Petersburg Times* in 1901, Straub missed few opportunities to snipe at Tampa's deficiencies; and on occasion, he more than hinted at the inappropriateness of the control that grubby, corrupt Tampa exerted over beautiful, wholesome Pinellas. However, his all-out campaign for St. Petersburg's political independence did not begin until 1906.

After learning that J. W. Williamson of Clearwater was planning to present a county separation proposal at the next session of the state legislature, Straub waged a campaign for the proposal throughout the spring and summer of 1906. "The little end of a big county like Hillsborough will never get anything like its due," he wrote in July, "until it levies, collects and expends its own taxes."[25] Straub continued in this vein over the next six months, and on February 20, 1907, the boards of trade of St. Petersburg, Clearwater, and Tarpon Springs responded by forming the County Division Organization, the expressed purpose of which was to petition the legislature for the creation of a new county. Three days later, an ecstatic Straub chimed in with a lengthy editorial entitled, "Pinellas County." Later known as the "Pinellas Declaration of Independence," this eloquent editorial made a strong case for the granting of political autonomy. According to Straub, the division of Pinellas and Hillsborough was warranted by geography, demography, and culture. The two sides of the bay had little in common, and the Pinellas side was tired of being ruled by unsympathetic foreigners from across the bay. Creating an independent Pinellas County was not only the right thing to do form a moral point of view; it was also eminently practical, since Pinellans were presently paying thirty-seven thousand dollars a year in county taxes

In December 1909, a large Central Avenue crowd was on hand to welcome motorists returning from a cross-country outing. Noel Mitchell's real estate office can be seen on the far left. The building on the far right is Edwin H. Tomlinson's original open-air post office. Courtesy St. Petersburg Times

and getting little for it.

Coupled with the formation of the County Division Organization, Straub's editorial triggered a storm of protest in Tampa. Walter Stovall, the editor of the *Tampa Tribune*, judged the separation proposal to be "obnoxious from all standpoints," and asked plaintively, "What child was ever benefited from being taken from the breast of the nourishing mother?"[26] Led by Peter O. Knight, the influential attorney who had negotiated the Seaboard Line railway merger of 1903, the Tampa board of trade roundly condemned Straub as a meddling Yankee interloper who had created a problem where none had existed. Mustering all of its considerable political clout, the Tampa establishment mobilized anti-separation sentiment on both sides of the bay. Not everyone on the Pinellas side was enthusiastic about the creation of a new county, and the Tampans did their best to encourage such misgivings. All across the Peninsula there was concern that political independence would be followed by a substantial tax increase, and in the upper peninsula there was the added worry that St. Petersburg would run the new county to suit its own purposes. Fortunately for the pro-separation forces, the latter objection was quickly defused by Straub, who graciously and shrewdly suggested that Clearwater would be the logical choice for Pinellas's county seat.

Not surprisingly, this suggestion proved to be as unpopular in St. Petersburg as it was popular in Clearwater, but Straub eventually managed to convince many local citizens that sacrificing county seat status was a political necessity and a small price to pay for political independence.

Over the Tampans' strong objections, county separation petitions were circulated and signed in March 1907, and a county separation bill drafted by Straub was presented to the legislature a month later. On May 3, after weeks of legislative wrangling and infighting, the bill finally reached the house floor, where it passed by a vote of twenty-eight to twenty-one. But, because of some last-minute intervention by Peter Knight, the bill was later killed in a reconsideration vote. Knight and other opponents of the Pinellas County bill were jubilant, but the bitter legislative struggle of 1907 was only the first battle in a long political war. Over the next four years, the Pinellas and Hillsborough factions-generally represented by the *St. Petersburg Times* and the *Tampa Tribune*—continued to trade vitriolic barbs. The more Straub and his allies pushed, the more their opponents dug in their heels. Throughout most of this period, Straub's politically powerful adversaries seemed to have the upper hand. But finally, in 1911, after a string of discouraging

defeats—defeats which seem to have lulled the Tampans into a false sense of security—the Pinellas County advocates finally won passage of the separation bill.

In the final wrangle, the Tampans pulled out all stops to discredit the Pinellas County faction, charging that Straub and his associates were radical Yankee socialists who had no respect for Southern traditions. As one renegade St. Petersburg resident who testified on behalf of the Tampans told a legislative committee: "Leave us to be controlled by Tampa, if that is true that we are controlled by them; it is at least a southern city, dominated by southern men, southern traditions, southern ideals and southern sympathies."[27] Despite this and other appeals to sectional loyalty and tradition, the Pinellas County bill passed the house on May 5 and the senate on May 16, and six days later Governor Albert W. Gilchrist signed it into law. The law called for a popular referendum, and on November 14 the peninsula's voters approved the creation of the new county by a wide margin, 1,379 to 505.

With the exception of a brief court skirmish over county boundaries, the November 1911 referendum ended Tampa Bay's rancorous civil war. However, the residents of the Pinellas Peninsula, the external struggle with Tampa was soon replaced by a bitter internal struggle over the placement of the new county

seat. In the final weeks before Pinellas County became a legal entity on January 1, 1912, the upper and lower halves of the peninsula squared off in a mini-civil war of their own. During the long fight for independence, William Straub had ensured the upper peninsula's support by working out a compromise that not only made Clearwater the county seat for twenty years but also gave the upper peninsula three of the county's five commissioners. Even though this arrangement seemed to fly in the face of the peninsula's demographic trends, most of St. Petersburg's business and political leaders reluctantly went along with Straub's compromise.

There was, however, an outspoken and determined renegade faction led by Noel Mitchell. In a last-ditch effort to make St. Petersburg the county seat, Mitchell offered to give the county an entire block of land at the corner of Forty-fifth Street and First Avenue North, where a county courthouse could be built. In a spirit of misplaced optimism, the Sand Man even renamed the surrounding area Mitchell's Courthouse Subdivision. But his grandiose plans were soon preempted by a group of Clearwater loyalists who worked day and night to construct a makeshift upper-county courthouse. The law creating the new county required the governor to appoint the county's first officials, and representatives from St. Petersburg and Clearwater had already sent Governor Gilchrist a proposed slate which gave the upper peninsula the agreed-upon advantage. But the upper peninsula faction refused to take anything for granted until county officials were actually conducting business at the new Clearwater courthouse. While it was under construction, the Clearwater courthouse was guarded around the clock to make sure that it was safe from marauders from the south who allegedly were eager to burn it to the ground. In the end, the courthouse survived, and Clearwater became a permanent county seat. But the hard feelings engendered by the county seat controversy would linger for decades.

Despite its inability to wrest the county seat away from Clearwater, St. Petersburg seemed to revive after the formation of Pinellas County. From 1912 to 1914, the growth of the local economy accelerated, as hundreds of new homes and scores of new businesses and public buildings were built. The new structures included such landmarks as the Municipal Recreation Pier, erected alongside the Electric Pier (which was torn down in 1914); La Plaza Theatre, the Woman's Town Improvement Association meeting hall; the Southland Seminary, which would be converted to a Masonic home in 1918; and Bradford Lawrence's waterfront spa, the city's first modern bathhouse. In keeping with the boom mentality of the time, the first major expansion of the city limits was granted in 1912, and a rash of additional expansion ordinances followed the approval of a new city charter in 1913. Thanks to pressure from C. A. Harvey, Perry Snell, and other subdivision promoters, the city was expanding in all directions. The boom was on, and even F. A. Davis, who had lost almost everything in the 1907 panic, was attempting a comeback with a sprawling subdivision known as Davista. In 1914 alone—ironically, the same year that witnessed the lynching of John Evans—the city experienced the opening of its long-awaited municipal gas plant; the acquisition of a second railroad, the Tampa and Gulf, which was absorbed by the Seaboard Line in 1915; and the laying of a cornerstone for a new Carnegie library.

With all this going on, downtown St. Petersburg was beginning to look and feel more like a city, particularly after the opening of George S. Gandy's monumental La Plaza Theatre in March 1913. A New Jersey native who had once served as Henry Disston's office boy, Gandy was one of Philadelphia's leading building contractors before moving to St. Petersburg in 1903. Gandy came to St. Petersburg to help manage F. A. Davis's electric power plant and streetcar line, but he soon became involved in a number of other projects. Although he eventually would be known as the man who built the first bridge across Tampa Bay, during the World War I era his name was synonymous with La Plaza. Located at the corner of Fifth Street and Central Avenue, this huge Mediterranean Revival-style structure cost more than $150,000 to build. Dwarfing everything in sight, it was reputed to have the largest stage south of Atlanta. Skeptics referred to this oversized creation as "Gandy's White Elephant," but somehow Gandy turned his theater into a paying proposition.[28] La Plaza's grand opening on March 13, 1913, featured an operatic performance of *Il Trovatore*, played by a touring ensemble from the Royal Italian company. Through the years the theater continued to attract major stars and large crowds.

La Plaza gave St. Petersburg's citizens a taste of high culture, and many local boosters yearned for more. For the most part, they were destined to be disappointed. However, on January 1, 1914, they were treated to high culture of a different sort when Tony Jannus, a 24-year-old pilot from Washington, D.C., flew his Benoist airboat across Tampa Bay. Later hailed as the birth of commercial aviation, Jannus's New Year's Day journey was the first scheduled flight of the St. Petersburg-Tampa Airboat Line. The idea of a trans-Tampa Bay airline originated with Percy Fansler, a Jacksonville-based electrical engineer who had approached Lew Brown and Noel Mitchell in December 1913. Having just returned from an air race in New York City commemorating the tenth anniversary of the Wright brothers' first flight, Mitchell was wildly enthusiastic about Fansler's proposal. After gathering together thirteen investors—including himself, Lew Brown, Perry Snell, George Gandy, and Charles Roser—Mitchell made sure that the city of St. Petersburg built a hangar for the airboat line and that a huge throng was on hand for the inaugural flight. The event caused a sensation, as a cheering crowd watched Jannus skim across the bay at a height of fifty feet. After a twenty-three minute flight, which included a brief stop due to engine trouble, Jannus and his only passenger—ex-mayor Abram C. Pheil, who had paid four hundred dollars for the privilege of being first—touched down near the Hillsborough River.

In the weeks that followed, Jannus made two round trips a day, transporting everything from Swift hams to bundles of the *St. Petersburg Times*. By mid-March, the fragile biplane had carried twelve hundred passengers and thousands of pounds of freight without a single major accident. Nevertheless, the novelty of crossing the bay by air soon wore off, and by the first week in May the airboat line had suspended its operations. St. Petersburg's first modern hero, Tony Jannus went on to become a test pilot and trainer for the Glenn Curtiss Company, both in the United States and Russia. In October 1916, at the age of twenty-seven, he was killed when his Curtiss K airboat crashed in the Black Sea.

The closing of the St. Petersburg-Tampa Airboat Line was a blow to the city's pride, but local boosters were able to console themselves with more positive developments during the spring of 1914. This was the season when major league baseball arrived in the city. Although organized amateur baseball had been popular in St. Petersburg since the formation of the St. Petersburg Saints around the turn of the century, barnstorming professionals rarely visited the city prior to 1910. The Cincinnati Reds came to the city in October 1908 to play a single exhibition game against the hometown Saints. But serious efforts to bring major league baseball to St. Petersburg did not begin until 1912, when the Board of Trade tried to entice Miller Huggins's St. Louis Cardinals to hold spring training in the city. This first effort failed, but a year later a local group

calling itself the St. Petersburg Major League and Amusement Company signed a spring training contract with the St. Louis Browns. During February and March of 1914, the Browns and their young manager Branch Rickey trained at a makeshift park near Coffee Pot Bayou. Tourists turned out in force to watch the Browns play, but, in the end, the city's first experience with spring training was, at best, bittersweet. The company sponsoring the Browns' stay ended up a thousand dollars in the red, and the team decided to go elsewhere in 1915. Nevertheless, local baseball enthusiasts remained determined to make St. Petersburg the spring training capital of Florida. Because of the efforts of a newcomer named Al Lang, they did not have to wait long.

During the winter of 1914-1915, Lang arranged for the Philadelphia Phillies to train in the city the following spring. A prominent figure in Pittsburgh baseball circles (he also owned one of the Steel City's largest laundries) prior to his arrival in St. Petersburg in 1910, he made good use of his Pennsylvania connection in the negotiations with the Phillies. The deal worked out by Lang delighted everyone concerned—particularly after the Phillies won fourteen of their first fifteen games during the regular season. The Phillies' fast start and pennant-winning year put the Sunshine City permanently on the baseball map, and before long America's pastime had become St. Petersburg's passion. For the next seventy years—with a few exceptions—the city was host to one and sometimes two major league teams each spring. Although the Phillies trained elsewhere after 1918, the Boston Braves were lured to the city in 1921 with the construction of a new waterfront park. They were joined by Babe Ruth and the New York Yankees in 1925. The Braves stayed until 1937 and the Yankees until 1961.

The coming of the Philadelphia Phillies established Al Lang as a local hero, and in April 1916 he was elected mayor, easily defeating Noel Mitchell and three other candidates. Reelected in 1918, Lang proved to be the city's first aggressively active mayor. During his four years at city hall, he directed an ambitious, if somewhat unusual, reform

A landmark for the city's early motorists was Ramm's Garage, near the corner of Second Street and Second Avenue South, circa 1914. Courtesy St. Petersburg Historical Society

program designed to turn St. Petersburg into a full-fledged city. Although he occasionally pushed for better schools and other public necessities, Lang devoted most of his attention to the physical appearance of the city. In addition to the famous green-bench ordinance, he presided over the paving of brick streets, the building of band shells and seawalls, and the construction of a new open-air post office, which was completed in 1917. He even sponsored "Sign Pulling Down Day" (July 15, 1916) to rid the downtown business district of a motley assortment of overhanging signs which he claimed gave the city a "hick look."[29]

Recognizing the growing importance of the tourist economy, Lang also played a leading role in the creation of an annual city festival designed to increase the flow of winter visitors. Known as the Festival of States, St. Petersburg's toned-down answer to Mardi Gras was the brainchild of Lang and William Neal, a Phillies scout who hoped to spice up his team's spring training season. Grafted onto the city's traditional Washington's Birthday and Mid-Winter Fair celebrations, the Festival of States made its first appearance in March 1917. Featuring a "parade of states," a costume ball, innumerable band concerts, and miles of con-

fetti, the four-day festival was a big success. Nevertheless, preoccupation with American involvement in World War I prevented a repeat performance in 1918, and the festival was not resumed until 1922.

Al Lang's tourist-oriented administration represented an important turning point in the city's economic and political history. From the Lang era onward, the public effort to encourage tourism would be formal and unceasing, in sharp contrast to the sporadic promotional campaigns of earlier years. Prior to 1916, the movement to boost St. Petersburg's tourist trade was dominated by the railroads, F. A. Davis, and a few other enterprising individuals.

Haphazard as it was, this early movement created a base upon which the city publicity agents and chamber of commerce representatives of the future could build. Following the merger of the Plant System and the Atlantic Coast Line in 1905, the railroads' promotional contributions increased dramatically, as railway agents distributed thousands of flyers in the North and occasionally organized special tourist trains. The first string of tourist Pullmans from New York rolled into St. Petersburg in 1909. In 1913 the city welcomed its first tourist train from the Midwest—an ACL special carrying two hundred sun worshippers from Ohio and Indiana. Such efforts became more common, if not routine, after the newly extended Tampa and Gulf Railroad brought in a special passenger train loaded with fifteen hundred visitors in 1914.

The promotional efforts of F. A. Davis, who did so much to boost the city around the turn of the century, were hampered after 1907 by his declining financial situation. But a number of other boosters did their best to pick up the slack. William Straub and Lew Brown filled the pages of the *Times* and the *Evening Independent* with tourist news and upbeat stories depicting the Sunshine City as America's premier vacationland. Dozens of photographers and artists produced an endless array of tourist-oriented postcards. In addition to the traditional shots of local landmarks, pictures of alligators, oversized fish, and attractive young women cavorting on the beach were used to advertise the city's charms. H. Walter Fuller used everything from four-color tourist maps to lantern-slide lectures to sell St. Petersburg—or at least his part of it. Noel Mitchell even hung smelly tarpon from the porch of his real estate office in an effort to attract sport fishermen to the city. Mitchell was probably the city's best-known showman during the pre-1920 era, but for sheer imagination the promotional exploits of Bill Carpenter were in a class by themselves.

Known as the "Alligator Man," Carpenter opened the city's first movie theater, the Royal Palm, in 1905, and later added an adjoining gift shop where he sold live alligators and other tropical curiosities. For years he kept a caged alligator out on the sidewalk in front of his shop—which shipped baby alligators to customers all over the country—and on occasion he amazed visiting tourists with impromptu alligator shows. In 1916, with a little encouragement from the Board of Trade, he decided to take his show on the road—all the way to Seattle. Armed with a pile of promotional brochures and accompanied by his friend Joe Honey and a six-foot alligator named Trouble, Carpenter set out in a new Hudson emblazoned with the words: "To the Sunshine City, St.

Pete, Fla.—We are going, come along."[30] For four months St. Petersburg's amphibian ambassadors wandered the country, mostly in the West, attracting crowds that had never seen a man risk life and limb in a wrestling match with an alligator. The show was almost always a hit, and after Trouble was safely put to sleep with an expert stomach rub, Carpenter and Honey would pass the hat and invite the crowd to visit the Sunshine City. By the time Carpenter returned to St. Petersburg to report his exploits to an amazed and grateful business community, both the Hudson and the alligator were on the verge of collapse. Carpenter went on to become a real estate promoter, living in the city until his death in 1973. But nothing in his later life quite matched the alligator tour of 1916.

Bill Carpenter and Noel Mitchell were flamboyant representatives of a business community that had hitched itself to the rising star of real estate development. Everyone, it seemed, wanted to get in on the action. According to the 1914 city directory, there were no less than eighty-three real estate companies buying and selling land in St. Petersburg, all in a community of fewer than eight thousand inhabitants. The livelihood of those involved in these companies—indeed, the livelihood of the community in general—depended upon a steady flow of land-hungry settlers and tourists. More often than not, the tourist market represented the difference between success and failure. New year-round settlers were of course always welcome, but increasingly the local real estate industry focused on winter residents. Even in these early years, the local population increased by as much as fifty percent in the winter months, and the basic rhythm of local life was already defined by frenetic winters and quiet summers. This seasonal polarity was accentuated by the nature of the local tourist trade, which leaned heavily toward upper middle-class tourists who could afford long winter vacations. Even among those of more modest means—many of whom came to St. Petersburg for health reasons—a three- or four-month stay was not uncommon.

St. Petersburg's visitors not only stayed

Elegance on wheels, 1910. The driver is Paula Ramm Williams, the daughter of Fred Ramm, the co-owner of St. Petersburg's first automobile garage. Courtesy St. Petersburg Historical Society

for long periods of time; they also tended to come back year after year. Unlike more casual tourists, these semipermanent winter residents eventually became a community unto themselves. Local leaders—many of whom first came to the city as winter residents—encouraged their seasonal constituents to treat the city as their own. St. Petersburg was billed as a home away from home, a place where one could join with thousands of compatriots who shared not only a common love of sun and sea but also a common background.

The idea of providing familiarity in the context of an exotic tropical paradise was institutionalized in the city's famous tourist societies. Organized according to state or regional origin, the tourist societies became an integral part of the city's social life, allowing visitors with similar backgrounds "to mingle together and become acquainted."[31] The first such group, the Illinois Society, was formed in January 1902, and it was soon joined by similar societies representing visitors from New England (1902), Michigan (1907), Wisconsin (1908), New York-New Jersey (1909), Southland (1909), Pennsylvania (1913), Canada (1913), Ohio (1913), and Indiana (1914). The tourist societies proved to be extremely popular, even among year-round residents, and in 1914 the city's ten societies formed a confederation called the Presidents' Union, which further

enhanced their collective influence on local affairs. All of this was welcome news to the Board of Trade, which viewed the tourist societies as booster clubs for St. Petersburg's tourist trade. In addition to hosting parties, picnics, and other excursions, the societies actively promoted migration to the city, competing with one another for numerical superiority. The overall result was an enormous increase in the city's national visibility. "Hundreds of first-time tourists come to St. Petersburg each fall," Karl Grismer observed in 1924, "for no other reason than that they have heard so much about the city from the tourist society boosters."[32]

The number of tourists coming to the city during the pre-World War I era was impressive, but there would have been many more if St. Petersburg had not been so isolated. From the 1920s onward, the vast majority of the city's visitors would come by automobile. But in the prewar era—when bad roads and flimsy machines conspired to make long-distance motoring a harrowing adventure—reaching St. Petersburg by automobile was not easy. The first Northern visitor to do so was A. W. Hicks, who took fourteen days to drive down from Detroit in November 1906. But, unfortunately for the local economy, very few motorists were daring enough to follow his example. Those who did found that they had little use for a car

Looking east along Central Avenue, 1913. Courtesy St. Petersburg Historical Society

Central Ave. St Petersburg, Fla.

Copyright 1913 by VanDeventer & Son

after they arrived. Most of the city's streets remained unpaved, gasoline was scarce, and county roads were virtually nonexistent prior to the issuance of county road bonds in 1912. Traveling overland to Tampa by automobile was a major accomplishment, and the round trip could take days to complete. With such conditions, even as late as 1908, St. Petersburg's three thousand-plus inhabitants owned a grand total of only twenty-two automobiles.

In the years immediately preceding World War I, Pinellas County—with an eye on the tourist trade—worked hard to improve its roads, but, with the intrusion of world affairs, the expected economic benefits would not be felt until the 1920s. Just about the time that traveling to St. Petersburg by car became halfway practical, the flow of tourists was sharply reduced by America's entry into World War I. The economic impact on St. Petersburg was immediate and devastating. Despite the best efforts of Mayor Al Lang, the local economy was reeling by late 1917, as many local businessmen were caught with over-

stocked inventories, unwarranted capital improvements, and unsold lots.

One of the hardest hit was H. Walter Fuller, the land baron who had once taken the community to the heights of speculative euphoria and who now took that same community down with him into the depths of economic despondency. In developing several new subdivisions in 1912-1913, he had gambled on the open-ended continuation of the real estate boom that had begun in 1911. After the boom ended in 1914, he managed to survive in the sluggish but not altogether unpromising real estate market of 1914-1917. But, by late 1917—when the flow of American doughboys to France far exceeded the flow of tourists to Florida—he was in deep trouble. After tottering for several months, Fuller's empire collapsed on April 29, 1918. On that day, he entered into voluntary receivership, turning his assets over to Philadelphia banker George C. Allen. As the local business community nervously looked on, Allen tried to reorganize and salvage Fuller's far-flung holdings, which

Looking north along Ninth Street from Seventh Avenue South, 1915. The wooden bridge in the background crossed Booker Creek. The home on the left was owned by the family of tobacco magnate James B. Duke. Courtesy St. Petersburg Historical Society

included "most of St. Petersburg west of Ninth Street, five bay steamers, four smaller boats of the Gulf-Pass-a-Grille line, 15 streetcars, the Pass-a-Grille Beach Hotel, and a small shipyard in Tampa."[33] With the help of Fuller himself, who had more economic lives than a cat, Allen eventually restored most of Fuller's companies to solvency, but not before the community was given a stern lesson in the realities of economic life. The big bull land market, which had emerged as the heart of the local economy, had also proved to be its Achilles heel.

The economic downturn of 1917-1918 shook the community to its foundations, but the citizens of St. Petersburg had even more somber events to ponder during these years. The Great War took the lives of sixteen local soldiers, including two black men, and no doubt everyone in the city was touched in some way by this tragic loss of life. Yet, even in its grief, St. Petersburg remained a divided city. The names of the dead, both black and white, were engraved on a war memorial placed in Williams Park. But, in an act of gratuitous, although perhaps unthinking, disrespect, the sponsoring committee made sure that the word "colored" was affixed to the names of the black dead, providing future generations with a haunting reminder that the city of sunshine was also a city of shadow.

Motorists gathering for a "good roads meet," circa 1918. Automobile rallies like this one were used to dramatize the need for better roads. Courtesy St. Petersburg Historical Society

1910

A parade scene from the 1910 Washington's Birthday celebration. Courtesy St. Petersburg Historical Society

Pinellas County was two months old when this banner was unfurled during the 1912 Washington's Birthday celebration. Courtesy St. Petersburg Historical Society

A parade scene at Fourth Street and Central Avenue during the 1913 Fair and Tourist Week. The woman carrying the flag is Marguerite Blocker. The First Congregational Church can be seen in the background. Courtesy St. Petersburg Historical Society

A parade scene during the 1913 St. Petersburg Fair and Tourist Week. The appearance of this ostrich-drawn cart caused quite a sensation. The St. Petersburg ostrich farm was a local novelty and tourist attraction during the early twentieth century. Courtesy St. Petersburg Historical Society

Flag bearer Marguerite Blocker, St. Petersburg Fair and Tourist Week, March 1913. Courtesy St. Petersburg Historical Society

Young women perform in a pageant during the 1913 St. Petersburg Fair and Tourist Week. The 1911 St. Petersburg High School building can be seen in the background. Courtesy St. Petersburg Historical Society

This decorated car appeared in the first Festival of States parade, held in March 1917. The driver is Arthur L. Johnson, the chairman of the Board of Trade's advertising committee and one of the originators of the Festival of States. Courtesy St. Petersburg Historical Society

The Illinois State Society posed during an outing to Davista in February 1915. Courtesy St. Petersburg Historical Society

North and South meet on a Milne-O'Berry citrus packing label, circa 1920. The theme of sectional reconciliation was an important part of St. Petersburg's local culture during the early twentieth century. Courtesy St. Petersburg Historical Society

The local chapter of the United Confederate Veterans, circa 1910. The young woman in the center is May Bradshaw, the daughter of James G. Bradshaw, who served as mayor from 1913 to 1916. Big Bayou's pioneer settler, John Bethell, is the sixth man from the right. The group is standing in front of the Methodist Episcopal Church, where they held monthly meetings. Courtesy St. Petersburg Historical Society

The local chapter of the United Daughters of the Confederacy, circa 1910. Courtesy St. Petersburg Historical Society

Members of the Woman's Town Improvement Association pose in front of their new meeting hall in 1913. Today the WTIA building is partially obscured by a modern facade, but it still stands at its original location on First Avenue North opposite Williams Park. Courtesy St. Petersburg Times

Katherine Bell Tippetts (1865-1950), conservationist and civic leader. Courtesy St. Petersburg Historical Society

The Sunshine City Band in front of the Williams Park bandstand, circa 1913. Courtesy St. Petersburg Historical Society

A fountain in Williams Park, circa 1913. Courtesy St. Petersburg Historical Society

Members of the Sunshine Pleasure Club play cards in Williams Park in 1915. Courtesy St. Petersburg Historical Society

St. Petersburg's first news-stand—the Hole in the Wall— and its two proprietors, Frank C. and Charles H. West (right), 1911. The stand was located on Central Avenue, between Second and Third streets. Courtesy St. Petersburg Historical Society

Breaking ground for La Plaza Theatre at the corner of Central Avenue and Fifth Street, 1912. Photograph by George S. Gandy, Jr., courtesy St. Petersburg Historical Society

George S. Gandy's La Plaza Theatre, at Central Avenue and Fifth Street, nearing completion in 1913. Courtesy St. Petersburg Historical Society

The corner of Central Avenue and Second Street, 1913. The "Ask Mr. Foster?" travel agency, the Rex Theatre, and Clarence Phillips's real estate agency shared the two-story, brick vernacular Foster and Reynolds building, built in 1909. Courtesy of William Wallace

The Detroit Hotel, as it looked in 1915. The sixty-room brick addition on the right was completed in December 1914. Courtesy St. Petersburg Historical Society

Carriages, automobiles, and streetcars vying for space at the corner of Central Avenue and Fifth Street, circa 1914. The Hotel Poinsettia and La Plaza Theatre (right) can be seen in the background. Courtesy St. Petersburg Historical Society

St. Petersburg's small but growing Catholic population welcomed
the completion of this new church
building in 1913. Known as St.
Mary's, it was located at the
corner of Fourth Street and
Third Avenue South. Courtesy
St. Petersburg Historical Society

Black laborers take a break from
their work on a landfill and seawall project in 1913. The project
transformed the downtown shoreline between Second Avenue
North and Second Avenue South.
Courtesy St. Petersburg Times

Workers build a seawall on the downtown waterfront in 1913. Courtesy St. Petersburg Historical Society

A Benoist airboat on the ramp of the St. Petersburg-Tampa Airboat Line hangar on the North Mole of the Central Yacht Basin in 1914. Courtesy St. Petersburg Historical Society

Tony Jannus takes off on the inaugural flight of the St. Petersburg-Tampa Airboat Line on January 1, 1914. Courtesy St. Petersburg Historical Society

Tony Jannus at the controls of Benoist Airboat No. 43, 1914. Courtesy St. Petersburg Historical Society

Tony Jannus (center) and friends, 1914. Courtesy J. D. Smith Collection, St. Petersburg Historical Society

In 1914, the Tampa and Gulf Coast Railway extended its tracks to St. Petersburg, providing the Atlantic Coast Line with local competition. Courtesy St. Petersburg Historical Society

The Atlantic Coast Line passenger depot, near the corner of First Avenue South and Second Street, shortly after it opened in March 1915. The ACL depot was one of the city's earliest Mediterranean Revival-style buildings. The original 1906 ACL depot, located on the same site, was torn down in the fall of 1914. Courtesy St. Petersburg Historical Society

The Municipal Gas Plant, circa 1918. The plant opened in 1914. Courtesy St. Petersburg Times

Students and teachers stand on the steps of St. Petersburg High School, circa 1910. Built in 1902, the two-story red brick building in the background was originally known as the St. Petersburg Normal and Industrial School. The city's high school students moved to a new building on Fifth Street North in 1911. Courtesy St. Petersburg Historical Society

The St. Petersburg High School girls' basketball team in 1910. Courtesy Pinellas County Historical Society

The St. Petersburg Public Library at Mirror Lake. Construction was made possible by a $17,500 donation from the Andrew Carnegie Corporation. The library boasted twenty-six hundred volumes when it was opened to the public in December 1915. Courtesy St. Petersburg Historical Society

St. Petersburg High School was built in 1911 for twenty-eight thousand dollars. Located on Fifth Street North between First and Second avenues, this imposing neo-Classical structure was the home of St. Petersburg Junior College from 1927 to 1942. Courtesy St. Petersburg Historical Society

The St. Petersburg High School boys' basketball team won the state championship in 1911. Courtesy St. Petersburg Historical Society

Postmaster William L. Straub (front row, sixth from right) and postal employees in 1916. Straub's daughter Blanche is standing directly to his left. Straub served as postmaster from 1916 to 1923. Courtesy St. Petersburg Times

The open-air post office at the corner of Fourth Street and First Avenue North, shortly after its completion in 1917. This unique Mediterranean Revival structure was designed by architect George Stewart after postmaster Roy S. Hanna secured a congressional appropriation of $107,500. Courtesy St. Petersburg Historical Society

Raymond Reed (sitting on the motorcycle) and fellow post office employees, circa 1920. The three-wheeled motorcycle was used for package deliveries. Courtesy St. Petersburg Times

Police chief A. J. Easters (second row center) and the St. Petersburg police department in 1915. Easters served as police chief from 1906 to 1921. The three men in the back row were plain-clothesmen. Courtesy St. Petersburg Historical Society

The mutilated body of lynching victim John Evans was left suspended from a Ninth Street South light pole in November 1914. Courtesy Diane Anderson and the St. Petersburg Historical Society

This advertisement appeared in the St. Petersburg Evening Independent, *February 22, 1908.*

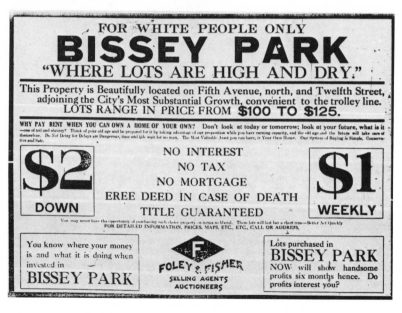

FOR WHITE PEOPLE ONLY

BISSEY PARK

"WHERE LOTS ARE HIGH AND DRY."

This Property is Beautifully located on Fifth Avenue, north, and Twelfth Street, adjoining the City's Most Substantial Growth, convenient to the trolley line. LOTS RANGE IN PRICE FROM **$100 TO $125.**

WHY PAY RENT WHEN YOU CAN OWN A HOME OF YOUR OWN? Don't look at today or tomorrow; look at your future, what is it —one of toil and slavery? Think of your old age and be prepared for it by taking advantage of our proposition while you have earning capacity, and the old age and the future will take care of themselves. Do Not Delay for Delays are Dangerous, time and tide wait for no man. The Most Valuable Asset you can have, is Your Own Home. Our System of Buying is Simple, Conservative and Safe.

$2 DOWN

NO INTEREST
NO TAX
NO MORTGAGE
FREE DEED IN CASE OF DEATH
TITLE GUARANTEED

$1 WEEKLY

You may never have the opportunity of purchasing such choice property on terms so liberal. These lots will last but a short time—Better Act Quickly
FOR DETAILED INFORMATION, PRICES, MAPS, ETC., ETC., CALL OR ADDRESS.

You know where your money is and what it is doing when invested in
BISSEY PARK

FOLEY & FISHER
SELLING AGENTS
AUCTIONEERS

Lots purchased in
BISSEY PARK
NOW will show handsome profits six months hence. Do profits interest you?

Transporting crates of oranges at Eaton's Grove, circa 1917. Courtesy St. Petersburg Historical Society

William and Mary Eaton at Eaton's Grove, circa 1922. Eaton's Grove was located west of Ninth Street near Twenty-first Avenue North. Courtesy St. Petersburg Historical Society

Orange pickers at Eaton's Grove, west of Ninth Street North, 1919. Courtesy St. Petersburg Historical Society

A 1913 postcard view of Noel Mitchell's real estate office—and a "day's catch" of tarpon. Courtesy St. Petersburg Historical Society

Mrs. Mary Eaton, shown about 1888, was the mistress of Eaton's Grove and a founder of the St. Petersburg Memorial Historical Society. Courtesy St. Petersburg Historical Society

A personalized "St. Petersburg fantasy" postcard, circa 1917. Courtesy St. Petersburg Historical Society

Home a Family Pet, Live Alligator,
St. Petersburg, Fla.

A successful alligator hunt, circa 1908. The man holding the rope around the alligator's snout was Bird Latham, the manager of the St. Petersburg Electric Light and Power Company. Courtesy St. Petersburg City News Bureau

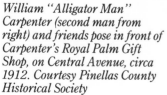

Personalized postcards using "fish story" backdrops were a tourist trade staple in St. Petersburg during the 1910s and 1920s. Courtesy St. Petersburg Historical Society

William "Alligator Man" Carpenter (second man from right) and friends pose in front of Carpenter's Royal Palm Gift Shop, on Central Avenue, circa 1912. Courtesy Pinellas County Historical Society

William "Alligator Man" Carpenter (left) and his friend Joe Honey (right), at the beginning of the 1916 alligator show tour that took them all the way to Seattle. Armed with a pile of St. Petersburg promotional brochures and accompanied by an alligator named Trouble, they spent four months on the road, mostly in the West. Courtesy Pinellas County Historical Society

One man's Florida dream— C. F. Franley's curio room, circa 1915. Courtesy St. Petersburg Historical Society

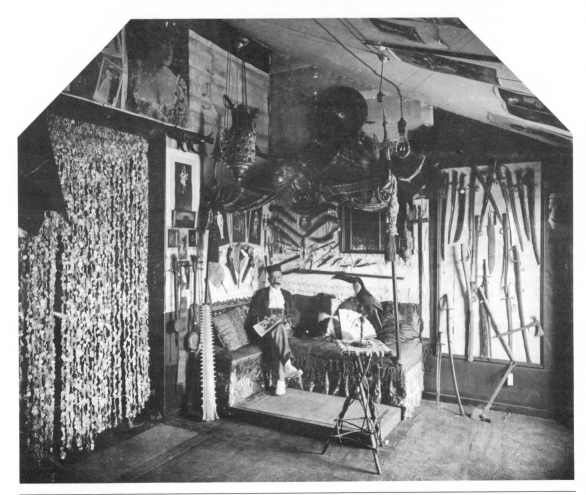

Spectators watch a spring training game between the Philadelphia Phillies and the St. Louis Browns in February 1915. The ballpark, located near Coffee Pot Bayou, was built in 1914, the first and only year that the Browns trained in St. Petersburg. In 1915, and again in 1917 and 1918, the Phillies used the park as their home field during spring training. Courtesy St. Petersburg Historical Society

Mayor Al Lang, circa 1920. Lang served as mayor from 1916 to 1920, and later gained fame as St. Petersburg's unofficial "ambassador of baseball." Courtesy St. Petersburg Times

The elegant Queen Anne-style Springstead residence at 256 Beach Drive, circa 1915. The owner, Chancey W. Springstead, was vice-president of the First National Bank. Courtesy St. Petersburg Historical Society

The North Mole's peaceful shoreline between Second and Third avenues, circa 1913. The Springstead residence on Beach Drive can be seen in the background (center). Courtesy St. Petersburg Historical Society

A tile-roofed pavilion on the southern shore of Coffee Pot Bayou, 1914. Courtesy St. Petersburg Historical Society

Looking southeast from the roof of La Plaza Theatre, 1914. The Sibley (Tomlinson) residence and St. Mary's Catholic Church can be seen on the right. Courtesy St. Petersburg Historical Society

Charles R. Hall's west central subdivision, near the intersection of Central Avenue and Twenty-eighth Street, circa 1915. Courtesy St. Petersburg Historical Society

The Roser Park home of real estate developer Charles M. Roser, circa 1919. Courtesy St. Petersburg Historical Society

Roser Park Drive, circa 1917. Courtesy St. Petersburg Historical Society

*Young girls playing near Booker
Creek, west of Ninth Street,
1918. Courtesy St. Petersburg
Historical Society*

World War I was brought closer to home when this fleet of United States Coast Guard subchasers moored near the St. Petersburg Yacht Club in 1918. Courtesy Earl Jacobs Collection, Nelson Poynter Library, University of South Florida at St. Petersburg

Ensign Albert Whitted at the U.S. Naval flight training school in Pensacola, 1917. St. Petersburg's best-known pilot, Whitted later became an instructor at the Naval flight school. He was killed in a plane crash near Pensacola in 1923. Courtesy St. Petersburg City News Bureau

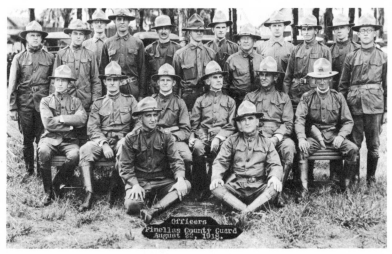

World War I "over here"—the officers of the Pinellas County Guard, August 1918. Lt. Arthur Norwood (front row right), a prominent St. Petersburg businessman, served as battalion quartermaster. Courtesy St. Petersburg Historical Society

Chapter Six

The Boom

1919-1926

The view from the mezzanine deck of the Vinoy Park Hotel, circa 1926. Courtesy Special Collections, University of South Florida Library, Tampa

The vagaries of world war and regional economics set the city back on its heels—but not for long. St. Petersburg was a city that trafficked in optimism, and its leaders were not about to let one bad tourist season disrupt their plans for the future. By the time the armistice was signed in November 1918, the Sunshine City was already on the rebound, despite continuing uneasiness about the city's short-term economic prospects. Everyone seemed confident that the local tourist industry would eventually regain the momentum that it had lost in 1917, but no one knew quite what the winter of 1918-1919 would bring. L. A. Whitney, the secretary of the St. Petersburg Chamber of Commerce, was cautiously optimistic about the upcoming tourist season. But just to make sure that the tourists found their way back to the Sunshine City, he enlisted the services of a young publicity agent named John Lodwick.

Lodwick was a brash but charming twenty-eight-year-old from Cleveland, Ohio, who had drifted into the city during the fall of 1918. A former sportswriter for the *Cleveland Leader* and the *Akron Times*, he immediately gravitated toward the newsroom of the *St. Petersburg Times*, where for several weeks he worked as an unpaid feature writer. His contacts at the *Times* eventually led him to Whitney, who was intrigued by Lodwick's imaginative approach to civic promotion, particularly the suggestion that St. Petersburg could gain fame as a host city for various "world championships." Lodwick waxed eloquent about all the successful publicity campaigns that he had directed back in Ohio, especially those that he had conceived during a two-year stint (1910-1912) as the assistant director of sports and entertainment for the city of Cleveland. But his most important selling point was his willingness to work for whatever pay Whitney thought he deserved. "I'll do the job," Lodwick promised, "and at the end of the season you pay me what you think it has been worth."[1] With little to lose, Whitney accepted the offer—a decision that would have consequences far beyond anything he or anyone else could have imagined in 1918.

The slick-talking hustler from Cleveland turned out to be more than just another ambitious adman. In a city that had more boosters per square acre than any other place on earth—with the possible exception of Miami Beach—Lodwick emerged as the master of masters when it came to public relations. For twenty-three years, first as the press agent for the Chamber of Commerce and later as the city's official publicity director, he proved over and over again that he was as talented as he was unorthodox. Forsaking the traditional method of selling the city—which involved the distribution of brochures and the purchase of newspaper advertisements—he turned to more splashy techniques such as the personal testimonial and the carefully staged publicity stunt. To the delight of the cost-conscious Chamber of Commerce, his techniques were generally less expensive than the traditional approach—and they worked.

In the words of Walter P. Fuller, who watched Lodwick at close range:

> The Lodwick technique was as simple as it was ingenious. Mr. and Mrs. Jones would register at the Chamber from Small Town, Ohio. John's photographer would take their picture. Next day an article would be mailed to the local paper in Small Town with a picture of the Joneses smiling from a bank of palms, or maybe a tarpon leaping in the background, or playing roque or shuffleboard. Except for a "lead" paragraph with the names and the address changed, similar stories by the hundreds went out to other towns all over the U.S.[2]

The Lodwick technique, which would ultimately have countless variations, was at an early stage of development during the winter of 1918-1919. But even at this point it was obvious that he was on to something. The tourist season of 1918-1919 was the most profitable to date, surpassing projections. St. Petersburg's hotels and boarding houses were filled to overflowing throughout much of the winter, allowing the city's merchants to breathe a collective sigh of relief. And the 1919-1920 season proved to be even better. The bust of 1918 had turned out to be nothing more than "an unhappy pause" after all.[3]

This rapid recovery did wonders for the city's self-confidence, and it was all the more impressive because it was set against a backdrop of national unrest. The year 1919 was one of the most turbulent in American history. From Los Angeles to Boston, the daily headlines told a story of mounting disorder and disillusionment. The economic and social plight of dislocated veterans was only the tip of the iceberg, as the nation grappled with seemingly insurmountable problems of postwar adjustment. The areas of conflict ranged from an ongoing and often violent struggle between conservative capitalists and militant labor unions to a bitter controversy over America's proposed entry into the League of Nations. In many cities there was growing resentment toward black workers who had edged their way into the industrial labor force during the war—a resentment that led to some of the worst race riots in American history. Nearly everywhere an uncharitable spirit of ethnic and religious intolerance seemed to be on the rise. The fall of 1919 brought the infamous Palmer raids, which unleashed the full fury of the First Red Scare. With the mass deportation of radicals and other "undesirable" aliens and with the emergence of the second Ku Klux Klan, the nation was capitulating to anti-Bolshevik hysteria and nativistic tribalism. In 1920, the imposition of Prohibition, coupled with Warren G. Harding's pledge to take the nation "back to normalcy," convinced some people that a restoration of order was imminent. But many others continued to wonder if the "nervous generation" would ever calm down.[4]

The stark contrast between the Florida fantasy of St. Petersburg and the grim realities of postwar life elsewhere put the city in an enviable position. Not only did St. Petersburg avoid most of the disorder and divisiveness of the day, but as an avenue of escape the city materially benefited from the problems that plagued the rest of the nation. The real world was a mess in 1919. But, as John Lodwick and other local leaders were quick to point out, the Sunshine City was not the real world. In actuality, of course, it was not that simple. The citizens of St. Petersburg had, at best, a partial

immunity to the problems of postwar America. Nevertheless, the surface reality was close enough to Lodwick's fabled dreamland to allow anyone with an escapist bent to overlook the problems that lay below. With a little imagination—particularly on a beautiful winter day—a visitor from Akron or Pittsburgh could easily convince himself that St. Petersburg was indeed the near-perfect, sun-drenched heaven-on-earth that the sand merchants advertised.

As the decade drew to a close, St. Petersburg's future looked bright. Sensing that it was on the verge of spiraling growth, the business community was full of ambitious plans and economic projections that would have seemed ludicrous two or three years earlier. One of the many local entrepreneurs willing to gamble on the future was W. D. McAdoo, the owner of the northern half of Long Key. The property's previous owner, H. Walter Fuller, had developed grandiose plans for the island and had been on the verge of constructing a bridge to the mainland when his empire collapsed in 1918. Although Fuller's forced withdrawal from the bridge project nullified a hundred-thousand-dollar county bond issue—the county had agreed to split the combined cost of the bridge and a brick road running the length of the island—McAdoo decided to build the bridge on his own. Known as the Pass-a-Grille Bridge, McAdoo's rickety wooden span was opened to the public on February 4, 1919. Although the bridge itself was singularly unimpressive, its existence represented an important turning point in the city's history. For the first time, a major barrier island was easily accessible from the mainland. Traditionally, St. Petersburg residents had paid little attention to the Gulf beaches, opting for the less spectacular but more accessible playground of Tampa Bay. One exception was William L. Straub, who owned a beach cottage on Long Key and who fought for the construction of a public bridge which would link the island with the mainland. The extension of the streetcar line to Boca Ciega Bay and the opening of the Pass-a-Grille ferry in 1914 had already created new interest in Long Key, but serious development awaited the construction of a bridge.

The opening of the Pass-a-Grille Bridge was only the first in a series of postwar road projects that revolutionized local transportation patterns, breaking down the traditional isolation of the peninsula's various communities. The proliferation of Henry Ford's flivvers during the postwar years created an unprecedented demand for roads and bridges, putting local and state officials under increasing pressure to keep up with the new "automobility." A system of narrow, nine-foot-wide brick roads built by the county during the war was already obsolete by the early 1920s, prompting local businessmen and other automobile enthusiasts to step up their campaign for good roads. Fortunately for the local economy, if not always for the landscape, the combined efforts of state, county, and municipal officials soon remedied the situation. During the early and mid-1920s, the city of St. Petersburg spent more than $12 million on road paving, a staggering sum for a community that had been satisfied with roads of rutted dirt or crushed shell fifteen years earlier. In 1923, the county electorate overwhelmingly approved a $2.863 million road bond issue, which led to the construction of the county's first respectable road system. In 1924, the state government built two concrete bridges in Seminole and Safety Harbor, and a year later an additional county bond issue underwrote the construction of an extended network of roads, bridges, and causeways linking the barrier islands with each other and the mainland. Thus, by 1927, traveling around the peninsula by car was no longer the impossible dream that it had been a decade earlier.

As the public support for road and bridge building demonstrated, the upbeat mentality of the time was not confined to the business elite. The local electorate supported virtually very bond issue put before it during the immediate postwar era. Once or twice a year, St. Petersburg's taxpayers were asked to reach into their pockets to pay for new street lights, water mains, sewage lines, or other public improvements, and each time they responded favorably. For example, after the local trolley line went bankrupt in April 1919, the voters overwhelmingly approved a $250,000 bond issue that would enable the city to run the line as a municipal transit system. Six months later they authorized an additional $100,000 in city bonds. Most remarkably, even though city taxes increased dramatically during these years, there were few signs of a tax revolt. Almost everyone, it seemed, was willing to pay for a ride on the boomtime express.

The city's expansive mood was also reflected in the results of the municipal election of 1920. In the year that saw the publication of Sinclair Lewis's *Main Street*, the voters of St. Petersburg filled the city council with an insurance man, a building contractor, a banker, a Ford dealer, a hardware store owner, a retiree from Atlanta, and Virginia Burnside, the first woman to be elected to the council. Burnside, who was reelected twice, served on the city council until 1924 and was not followed by another woman until Daisy K. Edwards won a seat on the council in 1951, twenty-seven years later.

The voters in 1920 also replaced Mayor Al Lang with Noel Mitchell, who finally made it to city hall after several unsuccessful campaigns. Despite his previous losses, Mitchell was a clever campaigner who never failed to put on a show. He was also a shrewd judge of the popular mind, and in 1920 he made a special appeal to female voters, who were actively participating in local politics for the first time. Although the Nineteenth Amendment would not go into effect until August 1920, the women of St. Petersburg had already won the right to vote in a July 1919 referendum. Responding to the pressure applied by Nellie Loehr and the Equal Rights League, a local suffragist group that later became a chapter of the League of Women Voters, the men of the city had approved women's suffrage by the narrow margin of 154 to 148.

Noel Mitchell's stint as mayor would be cut short by scandal after only eighteen months. But, while it lasted, his administration brought a spirit of effervescent optimism to city hall. The embodiment of the go-getter mentality, Mitchell—even more than his predecessor Al Lang—seemed perfectly suited to preside over the first stage of the boom. The Sand Man provided the city with many colorful episodes, but the highlight of the Mitchell era was the creation of Tent City, a municipal campground designed for the "tin can tourists." A new breed of vacationer who came by car and who generally preferred campgrounds to hotels, the tin can tourist earned his nickname by living on canned food which was cooked over open fires or on camp stoves.[5] The idea for a municipal campground was born in late August 1920, when several families of tin can tourists pitched their tents on a city-owned lot (which had served as a squatters' campsite since 1918) at the corner of Eighteenth Street and Second Avenue South. Although the Chamber of Commerce tried to find "proper" accommodations for the families, Mayor Mitchell—sensing that the city's acute shortage of hotel rooms could be turned into a publicity gambit—decided to let the campers remain where they were. In fact, he offered a free campsite to any visiting tourist who cared to pitch a tent at the Eighteenth Street lot. Within two weeks, no less than 120 families were living at Tent City. By the end of the year, there were hundreds more—all grateful guests of the mayor, who began to tout his public campground as a necessary and permanent institution. As he explained in a public letter in early December:

> To meet with the demands of a certain class of our winter visitors, we have gone to the expense of constituting a free public camp site, already known as the "Tent City." Here we provide free water, light, garbage collection, all toilet facilities including shower bath. This Tent City jumped into popularity so suddenly and largely that it is already too small to accommodate all who wish to avail themselves of its offerings, and there is grave talk among some of our far-sighted business men to enlarge it by securing a tract of land sufficiently large and accessible to care for all who may come. When this is done, we will so plat and decorate this site as to make it a veritable park, with entrance archways, winding drives, botanical gardens, playing fountains, and added and enlarged accommodations.[6]

Even without such aesthetic trappings, Tent City was a great success as far as the tin can tourists were concerned. But it was less popular among several members of the city council, who were concerned that St. Petersburg's image might suffer if the city became too closely associated with the tin can tourists. Many local leaders were extremely sensitive about the city's plebeian reputation relative to the Gold Coast of southeastern Florida (a traditional quip claimed that "the St. Petersburg tourist arrived with one shirt and a $20 bill and never changed either all winter"), and they were not amused in December 1920 when the local press reported that one disdainful Northern woman had recently described St. Petersburg as "the place where tourists live in two rooms, eat from tin cans, and sit on benches on the street and pick their teeth."[7] With such criticisms in mind, the council formally abolished Tent City in May 1921, much to Mitchell's dismay. Since the problem of accommodating a swelling tide of tourists remained, the council promised to explore the possibility of setting up a new tent city outside the city limits, but the idea never came to fruition.

Mitchell's noble experiment in sunshine socialism ended, but the tin can legions were not to be denied, as several enterprising individuals soon created private tent cities. Early forerunners of the mobile home parks that would dot the state after World War II, these makeshift vacation communities proved to be immensely popular. During the winter of 1922-1923, Leora Lewis's Tent City, located near Lake Maggiore, did a land-office business renting out campsites for fifty dollars a season. A year later, the newly opened Miller Tent City on Eighteenth Street was jammed with fresh-air enthusiasts who covered the local landscape with a motley but utilitarian assortment of "canvas mansions."[8]

A sure sign of the times, tent cities cropped up all over Florida during the early 1920s. Americans came to the Sunshine State in large numbers during these years—and not all of them came as tourists. The year-round population was also growing rapidly. Florida's population increased by 51.6 percent (from

Looking northwest from the pier head of the Municipal Recreation Pier, circa 1918. Constructed in 1913 at the foot of Second Avenue North, the Municipal Recreation Pier was badly damaged during the hurricane of 1921. It was replaced by the Million Dollar Pier in 1926. Courtesy St. Petersburg Historical Society

968,470 to 1,468,211) during the decade of the 1920s, more than three times the national growth rate of 16.1 percent. In St. Petersburg, the 1910 population of 4,127 had already been tripled to 14,237 by 1920. But this was only the beginning: between 1920 and 1926, the city's population soared to more than 30,000. On an average day a dozen or more new settlers rolled into town, pumping up the fortunes and expectations of delirious real estate salesmen.

Without this influx of permanent settlers, the real estate boom would never have reached the heights that it did. However, the seasonal tourist trade continued to be the bedrock of the local economy. In fact, as Noel Mitchell put it in late 1920, there was a growing recognition that taking care of the tourists was "the chief concern of the Sunshine City."[9] Although there were differences of opinion over how far the local residents should go in their efforts to keep the tourists happy, those who were willing to bend over backward to sustain the incoming stream usually had their way. In July 1921, the *St. Petersburg Times* and other tourist-minded institutions beat back a move to levy a tuition charge on tourists and seasonal residents who sent their children to local public schools. "So many of what have been regarded as 'tourists'," the *Times* assured its readers, "are really winter residents with almost, if not quite as strong an interest and affection for Florida as the place they may still

call 'home.' Thousands are deciding every year to make Florida their permanent home, and our educational institutions are to be credited among our greatest assets."[10]

The *St. Petersburg Times* had good reasons to encourage the influx of tourists and other newcomers. Like many other local businesses, the paper reaped the benefits of boomtime expansion. Led by its enterprising owner Paul Poynter, the *Times* evolved into a major metropolitan daily during the 1920s. Despite serious competition from Lew Brown's *Evening Independent*, the *Times* had been on a sound financial footing since 1912, when Poynter, the thirty-seven-year-old publisher of the *Sullivan* (Indiana) *Democrat*, purchased the paper from William L. Straub for ten thousand dollars. While Straub continued as the *Times*' chief editorial voice (except for the period 1916-1923, when he served as St. Petersburg's postmaster), Poynter ran the business side of the paper. An incurable optimist with an expansionist bent, Poynter was poised and ready when the boom hit in 1921.

During the next five years, Poynter ensured that the *Times*' growth mirrored that of the city. The paper's average daily circulation rose from 3,137 in January 1921 to 10,570 in 1927. At the same time, the size of the issue was multiplied several times over. Consequently, a newspaper that had been produced by a staff of fewer than twenty people as late as

1914 boasted a staff of two hundred in 1925. Since all of these new employees required space, the *Times* built two new buildings during the boom, a three-story brick structure in 1921 and an eight-story office tower five years later. Soaring advertising revenues made this expansion possible. At the height of the boom, in 1925, the *Times* ran 25,159,568 lines of advertising, the vast majority of which involved real estate. The only Florida newspaper to run more was the *Miami Herald*, which set a world record with 42.5 million lines of advertising in 1925. It is little wonder that the *Times* got caught up in the infectious spirit of the boom. "Believe in St. Petersburg and St. Petersburg will believe in you. Let's go!"[11] was its advice to prospective builders in June 1921. Over the next five years, thousands of boosteristic homilies followed. Even after the real estate bubble burst in early 1926, the *Times* refused to acknowledge that the boom was over. "The man who bets against her [St. Petersburg's] progress," a March 1926 editorial intoned, "is taking his chances against the powers of the greatest single force in the universe—the mighty sun, beacon fire of progress, life and light of the world."[12]

The *Times'* rhetorical support for the boom was echoed by dozens of other publications, including the epitome of boomtime journalism, the *Tourist News*. Created by J. Harold Sommers in December 1920, the *Tourist News* promised that it would serve as "the Voice of the Visitor."[13] The first issue set the tone with articles on Tent City, the St. Petersburg Women's Club, the state tourist societies, "Sunshine Sports," "Sunshine Gossip," the Tourist Camera Club, and real estate news. It also included pages and pages of real estate advertisements, an interview with an elderly tourist who had seen Grant and Lee at Appomattox, the first installment of a serial entitled "From Pigs to Pelicans," and an article trumpeting "Millions Spent in Buildings Here." This last article featured a picture of a bungalow that had been built in twenty-one days. "I could have finished in eighteen days except that I needed the workmen elsewhere," the proud contractor boasted.[14] Published as a weekly during the tourist season and as a

Festival of the States Edition 1924
Twenty Cents a Copy

monthly during the summer, the *Tourist News* would print anything that boosted the community or furthered the pursuit of leisure. During its heyday, from 1921 to 1928, it was edited by Karl Grismer, a talented journalist who authored a creditable history of the city in 1924. Before the *News* succumbed to Depression-era economics in 1929, Grismer's slick production had evolved into an almost indispensible accessory to the local boom mentality.

The editors of the *Tourist News* liked nothing better than to wax eloquent about St. Petersburg's golden sunshine and azure blue skies. But, after the autumn of 1921, even they had to admit that the Sunshine City was fallible. On October 25, 1921, the boom under the sun was rudely interrupted by hurricane-force winds and rising water. The worst storm to hit the Pinellas Peninsula since the fabled gale of 1848, the 1921 hurricane frightened and amazed residents and tourists alike, many of whom had never experienced even a minor tropical storm. As all but the most foolhardy huddled indoors, wind gusts reached a hundred miler per hour, and the storm tide rose to six feet above normal, inundating the city's low-lying areas. All across the peninsula windows were shattered and power and telephone lines were blown down, although most of the severe damage occurred on the waterfront, where several small boats were smashed and the municipal pier was badly damaged. On the western edge of the peninsula, the Pass-a-Grille and Seminole bridges were completely destroyed, and for a few anxious hours it was feared that the entire population of low-lying Pass-a-Grille had perished in the storm. Fortunately, the initial report that a major catastrophe had taken place proved false, the loss of life being limited to two unfortunate mainlanders.

In the wake of the hurricane, Mayor Mitchell and other image-conscious leaders did everything they could to downplay the danger posed by this or any other tropical storm. But, to their amazement, such concern for the city's image proved to be unwarranted. Nothing, it seemed, could stop the boom—not even winds of a hundred miles per hour. Indeed, if anything, the hurricane of 1921 propelled the boom to new heights. In the weeks following the storm, the city was swamped with curiosity seekers, most of whom went away convinced that the city had emerged from the hurricane almost unscathed. The weather was beautiful, and the sale of lots was brisker than ever now that St. Petersburg had demonstrated that it was impregnable to the forces of wind and water. This renewed sense of security was based on the reality that the storm had indeed been less than catastrophic, but local leaders encouraged this perception by frantically camouflaging or repairing the damage that had occurred. The Pass-a-Grille Bridge was quickly rebuilt, and Lew Brown of the *Evening Independent* led a successful effort to repair the Municipal Pier, which was reopened in January 1922. By that time, there were few remaining signs of the late unpleasantness, and local businessmen were breathing a little easier. Even so, memories of the storm lingered on, and in late March, when the Festival of States celebration was revived after a five-year hiatus, the devils of wind and rain were formal-

ly exorcised in an elaborately staged ritual called the "Dance of the Sun Worshippers."

St. Petersburg survived the tumultuous autumn of 1921, but Mayor Mitchell's political career did not. The affable mayor was a tower of strength in the aftermath of the storm, cheerleading the city back to buoyant optimism. However, in early November, he hosted a raucous "booze party" at city hall.[15] After the party was raided by the police, local Prohibitionists, who had never been particularly fond of Mitchell, circulated a recall petition charging the mayor with public drunkenness. Despite a public apology from Mitchell, the recall election was held on November 15, and by a vote of 1,374 to 1,033, he was removed from office. Undaunted, he immediately entered the race to succeed himself. Initially, he was opposed by five challengers, but widespread concern that a split opposition vote would ensure his election led to an unofficial "white primary" on December 5. The winner of the primary, Frank Fortune Pulver, went on

Driving to the end of the Municipal Recreation Pier was a popular pastime in the years immediately following World War I. This photograph was taken circa 1920. Courtesy St. Petersburg Historical Society

to defeat Mitchell by a comfortable margin (2,172 to 1,412) in the general election, which was held on Christmas Eve. When Pulver ran for a full term the following April, Mitchell made a half-hearted attempt at a comeback. But on election day, he finished a distant third behind Pulver and George Fitch. Interestingly, 331 of Mitchell's 598 votes came from the black community. Mitchell ran for mayor again in 1924, and he remained active in local real estate circles for a number of years. But he never regained the stature that he had enjoyed prior to the scandal of 1921. Divorced in 1929, he died alone, and almost forgotten, in 1936.

The Sand Man was a hard act to follow, but Frank Pulver, with the help of John Lodwick, became the most colorful mayor in the city's history. During Pulver's two years at city hall, Lodwick invented a number of publicity stunts which caught the attention of the national press. Billed as the "millionaire bachelor mayor," Pulver was periodically dispatched to New York City, where he posed

as the embodiment of the Sunshine City's leisure-oriented culture.[16] Perennially decked out in a snow-white suit, he treated reporters and other onlookers to a series of outrageous stunts, including a celebrated walk down Broadway with a bevy of Florida "beauty queens." On another occasion, Pulver pretended to do battle with the St. Petersburg Purity League, a fictitious organization that allegedly had demanded the appointment of a city bathing suit inspector. According to Pulver's tongue-in-cheek explanation, the respectable women of the city had banded together to protect their husbands "from the wiles of the Sea Vamps."[17] The goal of the Purity League was to make sure that no St. Petersburg "sea vamp" would be allowed on the beach with a bathing suit that covered less than one-half of her body. In an age addicted to ballyhoo and buffoonery, the press welcomed these stunts and begged for more.

With or without the gloss of Lodwick's publicity stunts, Pulver was a remarkable

The St. Petersburg Yacht Club was threatened by rising water during the hurricane of 1921. Courtesy St. Petersburg Historical Society

character whose biography reads like a Horatio Alger novel. Born in Rochester, New York, in 1871, he was the son of working-class parents who could not afford to keep him in school. Apprenticed to a jeweler at the age of fourteen, Pulver later worked as a watchmaker in Elgin, Illinois. He eventually developed a successful chewing gum dispenser, as well as a popular brand of spearmint gum, and sold out to William Wrigley, Jr., in 1913, reportedly for a million dollars. By that time, Pulver had already discovered the charms of St. Petersburg, although he did not make the city his permanent home until 1917. In 1919, he purchased several local properties, including the Detroit Hotel and the Pass-a-Grille bridge, and later acquired the Hollenbeck Hotel. He also became active as a mortgage broker and financier and by 1921 was one of the local business community's most visible figures. Well connected and eminently respectable, Pulver was the perfect choice to succeed the talented but unpredictable Noel Mitchell, or so it seemed in 1921.

In fact, Pulver's administration turned out to be as controversial as it was flamboyant. Lodwick had little difficulty in turning Pulver into a national celebrity, but even he could not make the mayor a popular man at city hall. An impatient, strong-willed man who had little use for political horse-trading, or for that matter, compromise of any kind, Mayor Pulver was embroiled in one feud after another with

various members of the city council. Many of his problems stemmed from his refusal to cater to the whims of militant Prohibitionists, but the combative mayor was often his own worst enemy. For almost two years, he more than held his own in this ongoing struggle—in late 1922, and again in June 1923, he survived spirited recall attempts. But, in August 1923, while Pulver was away on one of his publicity jaunts, the city council staged a municipal coup d'état by implementing a new city charter which reduced the mayor's powers. Drafted by a special committee led by Lew Brown, who was unhappy with Pulver's lax enforcement of Prohibition laws, the new charter was narrowly approved by the voters, 431 to 356. Stipulating that future mayors would be selected from the city council (the councilman receiving the most votes in the city election would automatically become mayor), the new charter ensured that the city council would ultimately prevail in its struggle with the present mayor.

Even so, Pulver fought back as best he could. With the backing of police chief Edward Bindaman, he challenged the legality of the new charter, even though this move added to the chaos at city hall. From October 1923 to March 1924, the city had two police chiefs: Bindaman, who was fired by the city council and then reinstated by Pulver; and James Coslick, who was appointed by the city council but practically ignored by Pulver. After six months of confusion, the courts ruled in favor of Coslick's appointment. By that time Pulver had already been removed from office in a special recall election.

Pulver was replaced by R. S. Pearce, a local druggist who wisely maintained a low profile during his two and a half years as mayor. Pulver never ran for public office again, but for a time he remained active in local affairs as a businessman and publisher. From March 1925 to October 1926, he used a colorful daily tabloid, the *Daily News*, to speak his piece on local issues. But once the *Daily News* folded, he lost most of his influence. Pulver did have one last hurrah during the late 1920s, when he attempted to induce the city to use Weeki Wachee Springs (which he and several partners had purchased) as a public water supply. But, after the city contracted to get its water from the Cosme-Odessa basin in September 1929, he retreated into semiretirement. No longer a millionaire but still a bachelor, Pulver died in St. Petersburg in 1952.

The boom made Frank Pulver a celebrity, but the real star was the city itself, or more specifically, the acres and acres of sun-drenched land that lured tourists, settlers, and investors southward. In St. Petersburg hawking real estate had always been a popular activity, but in the 1920s the art of shuffling deeds became a sanctified obsession. Rivaling the miracle of Miami Beach and the Gold Coast, St. Petersburg's land boom triggered a massive wave of construction which boosted local economic indices to unprecedented levels. As thousands of homes and hundreds of other buildings were constructed, the value of building permits issued by the city increased from $2,801,120 in 1920 to a staggering $24,081,700 in 1925. During this same period, the total valuation of city property went up more than 300 percent, while bank deposits rose from $5,928,171 to $46,167,038. Even after adjustments for inflation were factored in, these were heady figures, and the Chamber of Commerce and the local press proudly cited them at every opportunity. Yet, as impressive as they were, these statistics were somewhat misleading. Despite all the building and real growth, much of the action involved empty lots and temporarily inflated values. The most

popular game in town was not building, but selling. At the peak of the boom, there were more than fifty subdivisions competing in the local real estate market, but many of these subdivisions had more streets that houses. Although the local construction industry kept more than a thousand carpenters, masons, and electricians busy, numerically these workmen were no match for the city's six thousand licensed real estate agents.

In such a situation, competition among real estate agents was fierce, with success often hinging on showmanship or quick-witted one-upsmanship. The most successful salesmen used a team approach which required the hiring of employees known as "binder boys" and "bird dogs." According to Karl Grismer, the longtime editor of the *Tourist News*, the system was as colorful as it was effective:

Most of the salesmen wore knickerbockers, according to the fashion of the day. Hence, they became known as the "knickerbocker boys." They came from all walks of life. Many of them had been peddlers of fake securities—stocks in oil companies never known to have drilled a gusher and companies which dug gold from non-existent gold mines. These fellows stopped at nothing to make sales; they would take the last dollar a widow had and laugh about it. One broker, however, employed no one except retired ministers; ex-ministers, he said, had little trouble in gaining the "confidence" of prospective buyers. To get prospects, the salesmen employed "bird dogs"—men and women who would haunt the green benches, and churches, and tourist clubs, and every other place the tourists congregated, and talk real estate to anyone who would listen. The bird dogs were smooth talkers and they succeeded often in making unwary souls believe they would lose a chance of a life time unless they invested in this or that subdivision. The bird dogs then called the salesmen in—and the sales were clinched. For their efforts, the bird dogs got part of the commissions. Many of the bird dogs were good looking women, young and middle-aged. One woman, thirty-eight years old, was reported to have made $50,000 by three years of talking. . . . During the boom years most of the salesmen made a killing, even after they had paid off their bird dogs. Those who failed to net at least $10,000 a year were considered complete failures. Many made $50,000 a year and more. Few of them, however, saved any money. They lived high, paid fantastic rents for swanky living quarters, and, in many cases, invested all their surplus earnings in real estate. They really practiced what they preached—"buy real estate to become wealthy."[18]

The salesman may have been ruthless, but they had many willing victims. Thousands of ordinary people, many of whom should have known better, were eager to join the mad rush for easy money. Many buyers knew that the "knickerbocker boys" and "bird dogs" were masters of deception and hyperbole, but they did not care. More often than not, they had no intention of building a home on the lot in question. Instead, they were interested in the land as a gambling chip that could be passed on to another buyer at a higher price. In many cases, there were buying land that they had never seen with money that they did not have. As David Nolan, the author of *Fifty Feet in Paradise*, recently pointed out, these speculators knew that "a $500 binder, which would hold down a $10,000 piece of property, could be sold the same day for a profit, and would probably be re-sold dozens of times before the thirty days were up. By then, the $10,000 price might have been kited to $50,000, while everyone along the line took a share of the profits. The original $500 plus profit would be put into other binders, the process repeated, and, within a short time, an impressive paper fortune would result."[19] It was so simple, and as long as land prices continued to rise, no one had anything to worry about. Considering the potential profits involved and the self-indulgent atmosphere that prevailed during the 1920s, it is little wonder that even the cautious sometimes contracted "the Florida disease."

Once it gained momentum, the Florida boom was essentially a self-sustaining phenomenon that fed off the mystique of past successes. But there were certain events that helped to keep the momentum going, that pushed the big bull market on and on. In St. Petersburg, the most important event of this kind was the construction of the long-awaited Gandy Bridge. George Gandy, the Philadelphia contractor who built La Plaza Theatre, had been developing plans for a trans-Tampa Bay bridge since 1910. Working with a syndicate led by H. Walter Fuller, he surveyed the route and even obtained an electric streetcar extension franchise. But, unfortunately, the project had to be temporarily shelved in 1918 when Bernard Baruch's War Emergency Board—which had to approve all large wartime civilian construction projects—turned down Gandy's request for a building permit. A discouraged and financially beleaguered Fuller soon dropped out of the picture, but Gandy refused to give up. By 1922, the gathering boom had given his project new life, partly due to the efforts of Eugene Elliott, an irrepressible real estate promoter from New York. As clever as he was unprincipled, the slick-talking Elliott took the town by storm—and boom-era ethics to a new low. Falsely representing himself as a wealthy financier who had already underwritten much of the project, he convinced hundreds of investors to become Gandy Bridge stockholders. In four months, Elliott and a small army of high-pressure salesmen raised more than $2 million from stock sales, allowing a grateful and somewhat amazed Gandy to begin construction in September 1922.

Building a roadway across Tampa Bay was a major feat of engineering requiring the construction of a concrete bridge two and a half miles long, plus two long causeways totaling three and a half miles in length. Fifteen hundred workmen needed more than two years to complete the project, but when it was finished "Dad" Gandy's $3 million "masterpiece of bridgedom" was a sensation.[20] The opening of the bridge on November 24, 1924, was marked by the largest celebration in the city's history. At least thirty thousand people, including sixteen visiting state gover-

Boats and docks damaged during the October 1921 hurricane. Courtesy St. Petersburg Historical Society

nors, were on hand to watch Florida governor Cary Hardee cut a ceremonial rope of flowers. After presenting Gandy with a huge silver loving cup, Governor Hardee congratulated him for outlasting the "cynics and scoffers" who had ridiculed his effort to span the bay.[21]

Gandy's years of worry and doubt were finally over, as were St. Petersburg's years of not-so-splendid isolation. With the opening of the Gandy Bridge, the motoring distance between St. Petersburg and Tampa was reduced from forty-three to nineteen miles. Thus, even though Gandy's toll bordered on the exorbitant—seventy-five cents for a car and driver plus ten cents for each passenger—the bridge was soon jammed with cars. Not surprisingly, the effect on the cross-bay steamship trade was devastating. But only the steamship owners and employees seemed to notice, as the remainder of the local economy was propelled into an upward spiral of growth and speculation.

More than any other single development, the opening of the Gandy Bridge was responsible for raising the boom to its dizzying apogee of 1925. Real estate prices in the area between the bridge and downtown St. Petersburg skyrocketed, as entrepreneurs scrambled to take advantage of the seemingly inevitable development of previously unpromising properties. As the major entryway into the city, Fourth Street North was soon dotted with new homes and businesses. Indeed, even before its completion, the bridge triggered an explosion of residential development on the northern edge of the city. There were a number of promising new subdivisions, including J. Kennedy Block's Rio Vista and R. H. Sumner's North St. Petersburg. But the most promising of all—on paper—was Eugene Elliott's Florida Riviera.

The heart of Elliott's prospective empire (most of which was under water awaiting the miracle of landfill) was located on Weedon Island, an isolated and overgrown wilderness area that had once been a major center of Indian settlement. The area was named for Dr. Leslie Weedon, a prominent Tampa physician who purchased the island in 1898 and who later built a summer cottage near one of the island's many shell mounds. An amateur archaeologist, Dr. Weedon dreamed of turning the island into a national park. Rebuffed by the Department of Interior, he eventually sold out to Elliott's Boulevard and Bay Land Development Company, setting the stage for one of the Florida boom's most bizarre episodes.

Since no advantage was ever wasted in Elliott's full-bore approach to salesmanship, he did not hesitate to use Weedon Island's Indian past to sell real estate. Convinced that he needed something spectacular to bring attention to his Florida Riviera, he developed an elaborate archaeological hoax designed to attract headlines and home buyers. After planting an assortment of "Indian artifacts" in one of the mounds, he invited J. Walter Fewkes, the director of the Smithsonian Institution's Bureau of American Ethnology, to conduct an archaeological dig on the island. Upon his arrival in Florida in November 1923, Fewkes accompanied Elliott on a boating tour of the lower Gulf coast and was much impressed with the real estate baron's yacht, the *Sunbeam III*. But once he began digging at Elliott's Weedon Island site, Fewkes immediately recognized the pile of bones and trinkets for what it was. Undaunted, Fewkes went on to examine several other mounds and was shocked to discover an intriguing variety of pottery shards and other artifacts. Incredibly, Elliott's crude hoax had led to the discovery of a major untapped archaeological site. To Elliott's amazement and delight, Fewkes and a team of Smithsonian archaeologists were soon touting Weedon Island as a major source of information for scholars of pre-Columbian culture. More convinced than ever that he was sitting on a gold mine of historical romance, Elliott cleared away a palmetto jungle that once encased several of the mounds and renamed the area Narváez Park.

In the end, the Florida Riviera was a dismal failure, but this did not negate Elliott's inadvertent contribution to archaeological science. Long after he went bankrupt in 1926, scholars were still probing the mysteries of the Indian civilization known as Weeden (Fewkes was a first-rate archaeologist but a bad speller) Island culture. Elliott, after accidentally killing his wife in a domestic argument on the steps of their Coffee Pot Bayou mansion, eventually left the city in disgrace. Weedon Island itself had an equally interesting, although less tragic, denouement. After Elliott's departure, the island became the site of a nightclub (J. Kennedy Block's San Remo Club), an airport, and, during the early 1930s, a movie company called Sun Haven Studios (which in 1933 produced three films of dubious merit: *Chloe, Playgirl of Desire*, and *Hired Wife*). Following an aborted attempt to turn the area into a giant floral arboretum in the 1940s, Weedon Island was purchased by the Florida Power Corporation in 1956. Since then a power plant has coexisted with what remains of the mounds. In 1972 Weedon Island was put on the National Register of Historic Places, and subsequently part of the island was turned into a nature reserve, belatedly providing at least some of the Tocobaga ruins with a measure of peace and tranquility.

Although Elliott's plan to expand and improve Weedon Island never came to fruition, many other sections of the city's eastern shoreline went through a radical transformation during the 1920s. All along the bayshore, from Papy's Bayou to Lassing Park, dredging and landfill projects turned shoals into channels and water into land, producing a series of artificial peninsulas that jutted into the bay. In less than a decade, a five-mile stretch of Tampa Bay's natural shoreline was rendered unrecognizable, as the sight and odor of seaweed-covered shallows was replaced by a sanitized man-made "sea walled front yard."[22] This process of reshaping the bayshore had begun prior to World War I with the development of Waterfront Park and the completion of the Meloche fill north of the railroad pier, but the massive landfill projects of the 1920s dwarfed anything that had come before, astounding local fishermen and other old-timers who had grown up on the old waterfront. On the northside, subdivision developers N. J. Upham and Perry Snell created hundreds of acres of new land at Shore Acres and Snell Isle. On the southside, the dredging of Bayboro Harbor, completed in 1925, produced a large landfill that would soon be occupied by Albert Whitted

Airport and a United States Coast Guard station (which made a valiant but futile effort to halt the activities of Gulf coast rum runners). In the downtown area, the developer of the Vinoy Park Hotel added 120 feet of landfill at the foot of Fifth Avenue North, and the St. Petersburg Yacht Club carved out an expanded yacht basin south of the Municipal Pier. Most of the shoreline from Big Bayou to Pinellas Point remained in its natural state, although the southward expansion of Lakewood Estates and the opening of the Bee Line Ferry to Bradenton in 1926 were harbingers of events to come.

The most striking waterfront improvement of this or any other era was the construction of the city's famous Million Dollar Pier. The original Municipal Pier had been built in 1913 just north of F. A. Davis's Electric Pier, which was torn down the following year. Severely damaged during the 1921 hurricane, the Municipal Pier was hastily repaired and reopened, to the relief of tourists and others who used it as a fishing pier and to the delight of motorists who loved to make the bumpy but scenic drive down its plank roadway. However, city engineers soon discovered that the pier's pilings could not last more than a few years. Undaunted, Lew Brown of the *Evening Independent* mounted a drive to raise money for a modern, state-of-the-art recreation pier that would rival Atlantic City's Steel Pier. The idea caught on, and after Brown received three hundred thousand dollars in pledges, the city council proposed a million-dollar bond issue to underwrite a new pier. The bond issue was approved by the voters in May 1925, and construction began in September. Completed in the fall of 1926, the fourteen-hundred-foot-long concrete structure immediately became the city's most popular recreation spot, as well as its most identifiable landmark. The pier was opened to automobile traffic in July 1926, but the official opening took place four months later on Thanksgiving Day, when Mayor Pearce, Senator Park Trammell, and ten thousand beaming spectators attended a rousing celebration on the pier head. Rivaling the grand opening of the Gandy Bridge two years earlier, the day-long celebration was capped off by the Dedication Ball where three

thousand couples danced in the moonlight, many of them undoubtedly wondering if the Florida Dream could ever get any better than this.

The pride of the city, the Million Dollar Pier boasted a municipal swimming area known as Spa Beach, a solarium, a baithouse for fishermen, a two-lane roadway lined with diagonal parking, and a streetcar line that transported passengers to and from a twelve-thousand-square-foot rectangular pier head. On the pier head was a large, two-story Mediterranean Revival Casino building, which included a central atrium where streetcars loaded and unloaded, an open-air ballroom (which was later covered), an observation deck, and, from late 1927 on, the radio studio of WSUN. Along with the Vinoy Park and Soreno Hotels across the water, the Casino building brought inspired architecture and captivating beauty to the downtown waterfront.

Aside from schools, the Casino was one of the few public buildings constructed during the boom. Nearly everything else was private, a fact which ensured that the tastes and predilections of individual developers would have a profound influence on the changing architectural and spatial character of the city. During these years, zoning laws and city planners were relatively new phenomena, and public officials were hesitant to interfere with the plans of private developers. In a city developing as rapidly as St. Petersburg, this lack of planning could have spelled disaster, architecturally as well as socially. But, fortunately, the boomtime architects and builders produced an inordinate number of beautiful buildings, ranging from the Beaux Arts-style Hotel Cordova (1921) to striking Mediterranean Revival creations such as the YMCA building (1925-1926), the Flori de Leon cooperative apartment building (1925), and the Snell Arcade (1926-1929).

Architecturally speaking, St. Petersburg's most important boom-era developer was Perry Snell, the former Kentucky druggist who had been building elegant homes in the northeastern section of the city since 1909. More than any other person, Snell was responsible for St. Petersburg's Mediterranean Revival makeover.

The bandstand in Waterfront Park did not survive the hurricane of 1921. Courtesy St. Petersburg Historical Society

All but abandoning the frame vernacular styles that had dominated the prewar era, he began to build exotic "Spanish castles" in all shapes and sizes. By 1925, Coffee Pot Boulevard, Beach Drive, and adjoining streets were lined with an assortment of stucco-and-tile mansions. The entrance to one subdivision, Granada Terrace, was even embellished with a Stonehenge-like cluster of whitewashed obelisks. Set off by lush tropical foliage and red brick streets, the area later known as Old Northeast was one of boomtime Florida's most stylish neighborhoods. With its mixture of architectural styles, the Old Northeast exuded a charming eclecticism that seemed to please almost everyone.

Ironically, one of the few exceptions was Snell himself. Increasingly absorbed with the Mediterranean Revival motif, Snell dreamed of creating an architecturally consistent subdivision that would showcase the ornate style that he had come to love. Consequently, he embarked on the biggest real estate gamble of his career—the creation of Snell Isle. Dredged out of the muck of Coffee Pot Bayou and Tampa Bay, Snell Isle was conceived as an exclusive tropical paradise. Connected to the Northeast area by a Venetian-style bridge, Snell's dreamland featured broad boulevards, a carefully crafted golf course, a lavish sprinkling of Classical and Renaissance-style statuary, and some of the most opulent "Spanish castles"

in all of Florida. Snell's own home was a three-story Mediterranean Revival extravaganza that dazzled the most sophisticated of visitors; the third story housed his extensive art collection. When Snell Isle opened in October 1925, some of the subdivision's proposed 275 acres were below water at high tide. Nevertheless, early sales were brisk enough to allow a confident Snell to leave on one of his many European art-collecting tours. By the time he returned, the boom was over, which should have ended his grandiose plans. But Snell stubbornly pressed on, refusing to abandon or even to reduce the scale of the Snell Isle project. In the end, the completion of Snell Isle required the sacrifice of almost all of his considerable fortune. But to an orgulous aesthete like Snell, the sacrifice of a memorial like Snell Isle would have carried an even higher cost.

In many ways, the visionary Snell was in a class by himself. However he was not the only northside developer to bring imagination and flair to the up-scale market. Beginning in 1921, John B. Green turned an orange grove west of Ninth Street North into Euclid Place, an exclusive subdivision featuring large stucco-and-tile homes in a variety of styles, from Prairie to Mediterranean and Colonial Revival. Two miles north of Euclid Place, Cade Allen created a much larger and even grander subdivision known as Allendale. A former brick mason from New York who turned to dairy farming after his arrival in St. Petersburg in 1912, Allen built a cluster of high-quality homes on a 160-acre tract of farmland that he purchased in 1922. Drawing upon his background as a mason, he became one of the few developers in Florida to use stone as a building material. The result was a neighborhood distinguished by a curious but striking mixture of Westchester County, New York-style stone mansions and hollow tile-and-stucco "Spanish castles," some looking like fortresses and others like California-style missions. Most of Allen's homes were custom-made to suit the tastes of wealthy Northern clients, but nearly all of his creations combined traditional Yankee styles (sometimes only in the interior) with exotic Mediterranean touches.

The development of Snell Isle, Allendale, and numerous other boomtime subdivisions radically altered the size and shape of the city; between 1921 and 1926, the area of the city expanded from 11.05 to 53.22 square miles. However, some observers—particularly those who could remember what the city was like before the turn of the century—were even more amazed by what was happening downtown. While the city's residential areas were pushing outward into the palm thickets and the mangroves, the downtown skyline was pushing upward. After three decades of horizontal development disturbed only by the Detroit Hotel, Ed Tomlinson's Marconi tower, and Gandy's La Plaza Theatre, the city finally got a taste of verticality in 1922 with the completion of two seven-story buildings: the Sumner Building, an office block constructed at the corner of Central Avenue and Seventh Street; and the eighty-five-room Ponce de Leon Hotel. This was a sign of events to come, but the upward thrust did not become dramatic until the completion of several large hotels in late 1923 and early 1924.

At the beginning of the boom era, the city had a large number of boardinghouses but very few hotels of any size. The largest of these were the Detroit, the Poinsettia, the Floronton, the West Coast Inn, and the Huntington, which catered to the wealthy. Collectively, these hotels provided fewer than five hundred

rooms, which, even with the help of the boardinghouses, was well below the number needed to accommodate the growing throng of winter visitors. The shortage of hotel space contributed to the tent city phenomenon of 1920-1921, which prompted an outcry from city leaders who worried that the city's economic growth was being throttled.

Such fears were soon dispelled by a wave of hotel building. Between 1923 and 1926, ten large hotels were built in or near the city. Seven of these were located in the downtown area. The first to open was the Soreno, a 300-room waterfront hotel designed in a subdued Mediterranean Revival-style by Atlanta architect G. L. Preacher. Billed as St. Petersburg's first million-dollar hotel, the Soreno was owned by Soren Lund, a Danish immigrant who had owned a series of hotels in New York, New Jersey, New Hampshire, and Florida, including the Huntington, which he sold in 1920.[23] The Soreno opened on New Year's Day, 1924, and three days later the city celebrated the opening of the Suwannee Hotel, a 118-room brick vernacular hotel built by John N. Brown, a prominent local politician who was then serving as the clerk of the circuit court. Next came the Pheil Hotel, which had been under construction, off and on, since 1916. Built by Abram Pheil, the ex-mayor who had accompanied Tony Jannus on the famous 1914 Benoist flight, this towering eleven-story structure featured an ornate ground-floor theater that became a local landmark. Unfortunately, Pheil died in November 1922, more than a year before his eccentrically designed but long-awaited building was finished. The fourth downtown hotel to be completed was the Mason, a massive neo-Classical brick structure that overlooked Williams Park and the open-air post office. Designed by F. Jonsberg of Boston, the elegant but oversized Mason went bankrupt within a year of its completion. Reopened in 1926, it was renamed the Princess Martha. By that time, two smaller hotels, the Dennis and the Pennsylvania, had been added to the Williams Park area, giving the city's central park district a new look.

The flurry of downtown hotel construction climaxed in December 1925 with the completion of the lavish Vinoy Park Hotel, a sprawling assemblage of Mediterranean Revival splendor. Owned by Pennsylvania oilman Aymer Vinoy Laughner and designed by Henry L. Taylor, the Vinoy Park was built on a twelve-acre site in the heart of the waterfront park area. The architectural embodiment of the Florida boom, the Vinoy Park had everything: Moorish arches and tile-lined cupolas, elegant Georgian-style ballrooms with leaded glass windows and carved beam ceilings, scores of crystal chandeliers and ornamental urns, and 367 lavishly appointed rooms. A single room went for fifteen dollars a night during the mid-1920s, the highest rate in town, but a bargain considering that the hotel promised to surround its customers with the "quintessence of beauty" including "the blue sea and the sapphire sky and the same profusion of vivid flowers as greeted the earliest Spanish explorers on Florida shores."[24] Just about anyone who could afford it stayed at the Vinoy Park sooner or later: Calvin Coolidge, H. L. Mencken, Babe Ruth—heroes and antiheroes alike—all came to sample the decadent pleasures of St. Petersburg's grand hotel.

The Vinoy Park was probably the most opulent of St. Petersburg's boom-era hotels, but it was rivaled by three elegant Mediterranean Revival creations that graced the western reaches of the peninsula. In the so-called Jungle area, on the eastern shore of Boca Ciega Bay, Walter P. Fuller, the son of H. Walter Fuller, constructed the Jungle Country Club Hotel. Designed by Henry Taylor, the same architect who had worked on the Vinoy, the Jungle Country Club was the centerpiece of Fuller's burgeoning empire. By 1925, he owned La Plaza Theatre, a combination nightclub and shipping center known as the Jungle Prado, the Jungle Golf Course, the Piper-Fuller Airport, and more than a thousand residential lots. Having amassed a fortune of several million dollars, he spent a sizable part of it on his Jungle hotel. Lavishly punctuated with inlaid tile and Spanish-style patios and surrounded by tropical gardens and a meticulously manicured golf course, the Jungle Country Club offered the best of everything. For a time, the hotel even had its own

radio station, WSUN, which delighted patrons with lobby-side broadcasts.

The Jungle Country Club was impressive, but Fuller's friend and associate, Thomas Rowe, was responsible for an even grander example of Mediterranean Revival hostelry—the seaside palace known as the Don CeSar Hotel. When it opened in January 1928, the elegant Don CeSar stood almost alone on the barrier island of Pass-a-Grille. Rising out of the sand like a giant pink apparition, the five-story, 300-plus-room hotel could be seen for miles from all directions. The Don CeSar originally was conceived as part of a high-toned, Spanish-style subdivision, but the Great Depression ended Rowe's grandiose plans. Nevertheless, the majestic Don survived, becoming a favorite haunt of well-heeled vacationers looking for luxurious seclusion. F. Scott Fitzgerald, Clarence Darrow, and a host of other celebrated visitors helped to keep Rowe's shaky empire afloat, as did the New York Yankees, who used the hotel as their spring training headquarters during the early 1930s.

The only other local hotel to rival the pomp and grandeur of the Vinoy Park was the Rolyat, the creation of the boom's consummate high roller, I. M. "Jack" Taylor. A mysterious Gatsby-like figure, Taylor was born (or so he claimed) in New Hampshire in 1876. Although he eventually cultivated an air of WASP-ish exclusivity, he was apparently the son of Eastern European immigrants. Endowed with a quick wit and a keen eye for opportunity, he enjoyed a successful career as an investment banker in Boston and New York, before an ill-fated stock promotion scheme involving a venture called the East Coast Fisheries drove him to Europe. After a three-year exile, during which he managed to elude both angry investors and law enforcement officers, he returned to the United States in search of new opportunities. At some point along the way, he married Evelyn DuPont, an attractive, fun-loving heiress who helped to bankroll her husband's various business ventures. Known as "Handsome Jack," Taylor cut quite a figure, particularly with bejeweled Evelyn on his arm.

Taylor first came to St. Petersburg in late

October 1921, in the wake of the hurricane, and almost immediately began to buy up huge amounts of property in the southwestern quadrant of the peninsula. With his two partners, Fred Aulsbrook and Innes Henry, he purchased all of Davista, a sprawling subdivision that had lain fallow since F. A. Davis's death in 1917. His plan was to turn Davista into a subtropical showplace that would rival the most opulent developments of Florida's Gold Coast. Operating out of a private railroad car—which for a time served as both home and office—Handsome Jack oversaw the creation of an elegant subdivision known as Pasadena-on-the-Gulf. He saw to it that everything in Pasadena, from the landscaping to the curbstones, was of the highest quality. His subdivision had everything—beautiful parks, tree-lined boulevards, Mediterranean Revival mansions, a championship-quality golf course and country club—and he even had plans to add a university before the 1926 bust intervened. Taylor's pride and joy was the elegant Rolyat (*Taylor* spelled backwards) Hotel, a beautiful tile-roofed structure designed by Richard Kiehnel of Miami. When the hotel opened on January 1, 1926, Handsome Jack and beautiful Evelyn hosted a lavish party attended by Babe Ruth, August Heckscher, and scores of other celebrities.

A master showman, Taylor spared no expense in his effort to create an image of high-class luxury, both for himself and his subdivision. At one point, he hired away most of George Merrick's Coral Gables sales crew, and he eventually brought the legendary golf pro Walter Hagen to Pasadena to boost the fortunes of his country club. Everything was done with flair and 1920s-style excess. When Jack and Evelyn were not entertaining guests with caviar and champagne, they were driving around town in their matching Daimler touring cars. The press could not get enough of them, particularly after one shocked real estate salesman spread the rumor (apparently true) that Evelyn had sealed a deal by rolling down her stockings to produce a hidden ten-thousand-dollar bill. In actuality, Taylor's financial backing was shaky at best. But Evelyn's family connections gave him instant financial credi-

bility, and he never missed an opportunity to remind people that he was married to a DuPont. Fortunately for Taylor, the fact that the DuPonts had all but disowned their daughter after her marriage was not widely known.

In his heyday, Taylor never seemed to worry about money, but the appearance of prosperity was all done with mirrors. When the bust came, Handsome Jack was one of the first to go under. In the fall of 1926, he and Evelyn quietly slipped out of town, carefully avoiding unpaid creditors and abandoned employees. A few months later, Taylor reappeared in New York, no longer married to Evelyn, but still the master of the high-rolling confidence game. There is no evidence that he ever returned to St. Petersburg, although no one knows for sure where he ultimately went. Whatever happened to him, Handsome Jack—who lived much of his life one step ahead of the law—undoubtedly would have appreciated the ironic destiny of his beloved Rolyat Hotel, which became the home of the Stetson College of Law in 1954.

Handsome Jack Taylor was never the most popular man in town, but even his sharpest critics acknowledged that he was a formidable figure who, for better or worse, became a symbol of the new St. Petersburg. A romantic, larger-than-life character who exuded youthful vitality, he was the local embodiment of the Roaring Twenties. With men like Taylor in the spotlight, there could be little doubt that St. Petersburg's evolution from a Health City of consumptive invalids to a Sunshine City of energetic vacationers and sportsmen had entered a new stage.

The sporting life was an important element of the city's new youthful image, even though many of its sportsmen were anything but young. St. Petersburg, John Lodwick assured the world, was no longer just a place to rest or convalesce; it was also a playground where individuals could pursue the strenuous life at self-selected levels. Tourists who grew tired of simply basking in the sun could play golf or shuffleboard, go sailing or tarpon fishing, rent a horse at Walter Fuller's riding stable, or even take flying lessons. By 1926, the city boasted an immensely popular shuffleboard and lawn bowling facility near Mirror Lake, a growing fleet of charter fishing boats, a kennel club featuring greyhound racing, four golf courses—including Walter Fuller's Jungle links (formerly the St. Petersburg Country Club), Charles Hall's Lakewood Country Club, and Perry Snell's Coffee Pot course—and a flourishing Yacht club. First organized in 1909, the St. Petersburg Yacht Club constructed a clubhouse and yacht basin in 1916 that quickly became one of the major focal points of the downtown waterfront. A major expansion followed in 1922, and by the end of the decade the club was sponsoring major regattas, including an annual race from St. Petersburg to Havana.

Outdoor sports were an inevitable development in a subtropical seaside resort, but John Lodwick made sure that the local sports scene was tailored to fit the boom era's tourist trade. During the 1920s, St. Petersburg became the self-proclaimed world capital of everything from horseshoes and shuffleboard to checkers and roque. Every year Lodwick and the city would host one or more "world championships," and every year the tourists would come in droves to gape at these contrived, but always entertaining, extravaganzas. Spectator sports were coming of age in American society, and nothing was more popular than a well-staged competition, particularly if heroic champions were involved. Of course, even Lodwick had difficulty turning horseshoe champions into full-fledged folk heroes, in part because the city already attracted many big-name sports celebrities during the winter months. In an era that was taking hero worship to new heights, tourists flocked to see celebrities such as tennis star Helen Wills or golf champions Walter Hagen and Gene Sarazen. In this regard, major league baseball was the biggest attraction, especially after the arrival of Col. Jacob Ruppert's New York Yankees in 1925. Featuring Babe Ruth, the incomparable Sultan of Swat, the Yankees won the World Series in 1923, 1927, and 1928. Every February and March, baseball fans jammed the stands at Crescent Lake Park to catch a glimpse of Ruth (whose fielding practice was once interrupted by a curious alligator) or Lou Gehrig or Tony Lazzeri. The swaggering Ruth, in particular, was the toast of the town, whether he was swatting one out of the park, playing golf with his cronies, carousing at local nightclubs, or simply swapping stories with sportswriters in the lobby of the Princess Martha Hotel.

Ruth's popularity reflected a new mood in the city. Early St. Petersburg had cultivated an image of stolid respectability and family-style wholesomeness, but during the 1920s the city flirted with decadence. Taking full advantage of a new looseness in social mores, the publicity issued by John Lodwick's office made it clear that flaming youth was alive and well in the Sunshine City. Despite the efforts of tee-totaling ministers and other moralistic crusaders, St. Petersburg had more than its share of bootleggers, speakeasies, and nightclubs. Local enforcement of Prohibition laws tended to be extremely lax, and liquor was sold by the truckload within the neighborhood of police headquarters. To the delight of most tourists, city officials made sure that nothing interfered with the pursuit of pleasure. Drunk or sober, those in search of the high life could drive out to the Jungle area to visit Walter Fuller's Gangplank Night Club or dance the night away at the Coliseum. Opened in November 1924, the Coliseum was one of the nation's busiest dance halls. All winter long, devotees of the fox-trot and the Charleston danced to the music of local bands such as the Tom Danks Orchestra or Rex McDonald's Silver Kings. Celebrated big band leaders such as Paul Whiteman, Harry James, and Rudy Vallee also performed at the Coliseum, as did humorist Will Rogers and evangelist Aimee Semple McPherson. The Coliseum was immensely popular, even though one local woman armed with religious pamphlets routinely camped outside the entrance to warn patrons that they were about to enter a den of sin.

Entertainment-minded tourists and residents also had ready access to the alluring worlds of the theater and the silver screen. During the winter months, La Plaza offered stage shows featuring major performers such as Anna Pavlova, Tom Mix, and Sophie Tucker, while around the corner the Pheil Theatre presented films and more modest stage productions. This was impressive enough for a city of fewer than forty thousand people, but, in September 1926, St. Petersburg celebrated the opening of the sumptuous Florida Theatre. With twenty-three hundred seats, nine dressing rooms, a rooftop garden, and towering interior walls covered with suits of Spanish armor, tapestries, and other works of pseudo-Renaissance elegance, the Florida Theatre was a masterpiece of 1920s-style garishness. The Florida had everything, including a state-of-the-art air conditioning system which almost ruined the theatre's grand opening. Underestimating the power of their new cooling plant, "the proud management had the temperature down so low that ladies in evening dresses almost froze!"[25]

In addition to its theaters and dance halls, boomtime St. Petersburg boasted numerous attractions aimed at the post-Freudian libido. To the dismay of local traditionalists, an increasingly tolerant attitude towards sexual licentiousness was an important part of the city's racy new image. Prostitution was on the rise, or at least it was more in the open, and the city's beaches were filled with men and women cavorting in daring new bathing suits—an attraction brazenly advertised in John Lodwick's famous Purity League publicity stunt. The sexual theme was also underscored by a city-owned solarium where patrons could sunbathe in the nude and by an annual Festival of States parade that featured plenty of female pulchritude. Sun and fun, and sex and booze—it all seemed to fit with the speculative excess that dominated the local real estate scene. After all, if men and women could not enjoy themselves in a tropical resort city dedicated to the good life, where could they enjoy themselves? As the recalls of Mayor Mitchell and Mayor Pulver demonstrated, St. Petersburg retained a hardy strain of moralistic Victorianism. But this did not stop the flappers and the smart set from giving the city an extended taste of Jazz Age permissiveness.

Some St. Petersburg residents regarded the boom as one long glorious party. But, for a variety of reasons, many others had mixed feelings about what was happening to the city.

While nearly everyone welcomed the economic benefits of the boom, a number of people recoiled from at least some of its social by-products. Faced with a bewildering array of new conditions that required adaptation and compromise, some groups and individuals drew back in fear and anxiety. Moralists were troubled by questionable business ethics, an orgy of hedonism and conspicuous consumption, and a blatant disregard for temperance laws and religious admonitions. Nativists were concerned about the city's newfound ethnic and religious heterogeneity. And traditionalists of all persuasions were bothered by a seemingly uncontrollable pace of change. "It set out with malice aforethought to make itself a winter resort city par excellence," travel writer Ralph Henry Barbour wrote of St. Petersburg in 1926, "and so it has no one to blame for what has happened. Take it in January, and the sidewalks are so thronged with persons milling around, the streets so crowded with automobiles scraping bumpers and mudguards, and the parks and playgrounds so filled with children—from one to eighty—that a stranger from some quiet place like Chicago, Philadelphia, or New York feels confused and nervous."[26]

Not surprisingly, some of the city's more seasoned inhabitants looked to the past for order and solace. In July 1920, Mary Eaton, the co-owner of the city's most celebrated orange grove, and thirty-four others organized the St. Petersburg Memorial Historical Society. A mix of old families and newer upper-class residents, the group represented the local gentry and regarded themselves as trustees of the local historical record. At one level, the society's founding reflected the simple fact that the city was finally old enough to have a history. However, for many of the society's enthusiasts, the institutionalization of local history was also an act of social self-preservation. In a community dominated by interlopers and parvenus, someone had to remind the newcomers that the cash nexus was not the determinant of social status. The pioneer families of St. Petersburg had managed quite well before the coming of the boomers, and they were not about to relinquish their

Fire Station No. 2, at the corner of Ninth Street North and Burlington Avenue, circa 1921. The station building was constructed in 1913. Courtesy Pinellas County Historical Society

hard-earned elevation in the local hierarchy. Old money and pioneer status did not carry much weight in a relatively new city like St. Petersburg, but the museum that the society constructed on the waterfront in 1922 provided a comforting, if largely symbolic, expression of respect for the community's past.

The boom was also a bittersweet experience for St. Petersburg's black community. On the positive side, wages were up, and there was no shortage of work. Between 1921 and 1926, local building contractors dispatched labor agents to Alabama and Georgia to recruit black workers, and the resulting influx swelled the population of the black community. During the 1920s, the local black community tripled in size, from 2,444 to 7,416, as black population growth kept pace with white population growth. At the end of the decade, the black proportion of the city's population continued to hover around 18 percent. The expanded black community was serviced by a growing number of businesses, schools, and churches (twenty-six in 1930), as the institutional structure of the community took on an air of vitality and permanence. Improved medical care was facili-

tated by the expansion of Mercy Hospital, and the problem of maintaining public health in the black community was at least recognized in 1926 when Dr. James Ponder was asked to serve as the black community's "city physician." Ponder's appointment reflected the fact that the black community continued to exercise some political power. In many Southern cities, by the 1920s the black electorate had been all but eliminated. But in St. Petersburg, more than a third of the potential black electorate was still registered to vote in 1920. Black voters provided Noel Mitchell with solid support in the mayoral elections of 1921 and 1922, and they continued to vote in large numbers throughout the decade.

On the negative side, the 1920s brought a noticeable tightening of the Jim Crow system. Despite a large influx of non-Southern whites, local customs and laws imposed cradle-to-grave segregation. Indeed, the influx probably encouraged segregation, as image-conscious businessmen and city officials became increasingly concerned about the visibility of the black community. Hoping to render the growing black labor force as unobtrusive as possible, white leaders made every effort to encourage residential and social segregation. Unless they were domestics taking care of white children, black men and women were not allowed to use the city's parks or beaches, or even to sit on its famous green benches. Almost all of the city's new subdivisions had restrictive covenants or gentleman's agreements which excluded black residents. Since many deeds included clauses such as "No lot shall be sold, rented or conveyed to any colored person or person of African descent," even middle-class blacks had severely limited housing options.[27] As white settlement pushed outward from the downtown area, overcrowding became a serious problem in the black community. Despite boomtime wages, most blacks continued to live in substandard houses owned by white landlords. The black community had few paved roads and limited access to city gas and water mains, and many black residences had no electricity or indoor plumbing.

These deficiencies were obvious to anyone who ventured into the black section of town, but whites seldom did so. With very few exceptions, white business, religious, and fraternal organizations adopted an attitude of malign neglect toward blacks, and the local press limited its coverage of black affairs to crime reports. At election time, white politicians sometimes solicited black votes, usually surreptitiously, but the limited political clout of the black electorate fell far short of what was needed to bring about an equitable distribution of city services. Thus, despite their contributions to the city's growth, blacks were consigned to live on the underside of the boom.

To make matters worse, the surging popularity of the Ku Klux Klan during the early and mid-1920s made it extremely dangerous for blacks to speak out against racial discrimination. For blacks and other beleaguered minorities, this was a time to wait and hope for the best. This was certainly true for St. Petersburg's Jewish community, which found itself under attack from the Klan throughout the decade. During the winter of 1924-1925, a series of signs placed along Gandy Boulevard and Fourth Street North, the main route leading into the city, delivered a stark message: "Gentiles Only Wanted—No Jews Wanted Here."[28] The signs were the brainchild of Jim Coad, the outspoken secretary of the St. Petersburg Chamber of Commerce. A militant anti-Semite and nativist, Coad spoke for millions of fearful, white Anglo-Saxon Protestants when he called for a return to traditional, old-stock "Americanism." "The time has come to make this a hundred per cent American and Gentile city," he announced in 1925, "as free from foreigners as from slums."[29] The Ku Klux Klan was on the march, and Jim Coad, who helped to organize St. Petersburg's Olustee Klan No. 20, was right in step.

Coad's call for action was a direct response to recent Jewish migration into the city. Although a small number of Jews had lived in St. Petersburg since before the turn of the century, the 1920s brought the first large influx of Jewish residents and tourists. As late as 1920, the city's Jewish population was limited to nine families, several of whom had migrated from Key West prior to World War I. Only with the arrival of the Jacobs family in November 1920 did St. Petersburg Jews achieve a *Minyan*—the quorum of ten families required for official religious ceremonies. All of the original ten families were of Eastern European origin, all lived and worked in or near the downtown business district, and all were merchants. Tightly knit and interdependent, they socialized together and quietly worshipped in each other's homes. Relations with their Christian neighbors were generally cordial, and overt anti-Semitism was rare.

However, all of this changed in the 1920s. As Jim Coad and other image-conscious civic leaders nervously looked on, an identifiable Jewish community began to take shape. In 1923, the conservative congregation of B'Nai Israel was founded, and by mid-decade there were enough local Jewish children in need of religious education to justify periodic visits by a Tampa rabbi. By 1926, the city had its own rabbi, Maurice Lesseroux. Kosher food still had to be shipped in from Tampa, and Rabbi Lesseroux was forced to conduct services in a storefront, but a viable local Jewish community was clearly emerging.

The local establishment reacted to this

Patrons at the open-air post office, circa 1921. Courtesy Earl Jacobs Collection, Nelson Poynter Library, University of South Florida at St. Petersburg

changing situation with a mixture of fear and confusion. Although many of St. Petersburg's non-Jewish citizens rejected Jim Coad's virulent anti-Semitism—local leaders disavowed any responsibility for the controversial signs and reassured the city's Jewish merchants that their rights would be protected—many others sympathized with Coad's aims, if not his methods. In St. Petersburg, as in most of the nation, anti-Semitism was becoming increasingly respectable. At the very least, Coad's beliefs were respectable enough to allow his promotion to the executive vice-presidency of the Chamber of Commerce in 1926. It was no secret that several of the city's most prominent citizens belonged to the local chapter of the Klan. One of the strongest klaverns in the state, the Olustee Klan periodically held spectacular torch-lit initiation ceremonies on Pass-a-Grille Beach.

Although St. Petersburg Jews were fortunate enough to escape the worst excesses of the Klan, such as beatings and tar-and-featherings, less violent expressions of anti-Semitism became relatively common during the 1920s. A complex web of social restrictions, although legally less imposing than the Jim Crow system that separated blacks and whites, effectively excluded Jews from the mainstream of local life. All of the

city's private clubs and organizations had restrictive policies which barred Jews from membership. Restrictive covenants kept Jewish families out of the city's most fashionable neighborhoods. And many local hotels and restaurants openly displayed signs which read: "Restricted Clientele," "Gentiles Only," or "Christians Only." Restrictive policies were rigorously enforced at the city's most stylish hotels such as the Vinoy Park and the Soreno. Although some local hotels welcomed Jewish guests, the probability of rejection increased with each passing year. When the Don CeSar Hotel opened in 1928, Jews discovered that there was yet another place where they could not go. The ban applied to Jewish tourists as well as to local Jews, and even extended to the Jewish sportswriters who came to the city to cover spring training.

The ambiguous plight of Jews, blacks, and nostalgic pioneers underscored the complexity of the boom era. In retrospect, it seems clear that it was neither the best of times nor the worst of times—even for those who rode the boom to prosperity. As paper fortunes mounted and the idea of progress was corrupted by unrestrained acquisitiveness and greed, many people lost touch with reality—a reality that would ultimately and abruptly reassert itself. When several Northern newspapers—sensing

that the Florida real estate market was approaching its saturation point in 1925—began to forecast an impending crash, the high-rollers and binder boys responded with a flood of upbeat rhetoric. But even the giddiest of sand merchants—lost as they were in the ballyhoo of the Jazz Age—must have suspected that the days of easy money were numbered.

The development of the Coffee Pot Bayou area was just beginning when this aerial photograph was taken during the early 1920s. The area later known as Snell Isle can be seen in the background. Courtesy Earl Jacobs Collection, Nelson Poynter Library. University of South Florida at St. Petersburg

Looking south along First Street South, circa 1921. Bayboro Harbor, as yet undeveloped, can be seen in the background. Courtesy Earl Jacobs Collection, Nelson Poynter Library, University of South Florida at St. Petersburg

Still a cow town? This photograph was taken at the corner of Ninth Street and Twenty-first Avenue North circa 1922. The streetcar tracks and part of Eaton's citrus grove can be seen on the left. Courtesy St. Petersburg Historical Society

Members of the St. Petersburg Women's Club, 1919. The building in the background is the First Avenue Methodist Episcopal Church. Courtesy St. Petersburg Historical Society

The St. Petersburg Memorial Historical Society Museum, shown in 1923, was located at the western end of the Municipal Recreation Pier. The museum opened in 1922. Courtesy St. Petersburg Historical Society

During the early 1920s, the local chapter of the American Legion built this imposing structure on the waterfront near the foot of Central Avenue. This photograph was taken in 1924. Courtesy St. Petersburg Historical Society

Tin-can tourists enjoying the rustic life at St. Petersburg's Tent City, 1921. Courtesy Special Collections, University of South Florida Library, Tampa

"Where the Iceman, cuts no ice ~
Or the Gas, or the Coal, or the Rent-man, either."

This early 1920s postcard depicts a tin-can tourist campground near Lake Maggiore. Courtesy of Fritz Wilder

Looking like a twentieth-century frontiersman, this tin-can tourist pitched his tent in a wooded area near Lake Maggiore in 1925. Courtesy St. Petersburg Historical Society

Mayor Noel Mitchell, 1921. Courtesy Pinellas County Historical Society

John Lodwick served as the city's chief publicity agent from 1919 to 1942. Courtesy St. Petersburg Times

Construction of the Gandy Bridge commences, September 24, 1922. Photograph by Burgert Brothers, courtesy St. Petersburg Historical Society

Frank Fortune Pulver, 1920. Billed as the "millionaire bachelor mayor," Pulver was a strong-willed and flamboyant leader. He was mayor from 1922 to 1924. Courtesy St. Petersburg Historical Society

Sixty-seven people joined hands to measure the width of the Gandy Bridge causeway fill, 1922. Photograph by Burgert Brothers, courtesy St. Petersburg Historical Society

Road workers in 1922 grade Fourth Street North, which was to be the connecting link between Gandy Boulevard and downtown St. Petersburg. Photograph by Burgert Brothers, courtesy St. Petersburg Historical Society

Bridge builder George S. "Dad" Gandy, Sr., was the man of the hour in November 1924. Courtesy St. Petersburg Historical Society

The Gandy Bridge, 1925. Courtesy St. Petersburg Historical Society

For many years the Durant block on the northwest corner of Central Avenue and Fourth Street housed the real estate office of Noel Mitchell, but in 1914 Mitchell sold the block to Perry Snell and J. C. Hamlett's North Shore Company. This photograph was taken circa 1921. Courtesy Earl Jacobs Collection, Nelson Poynter Library, University of South Florida at St. Petersburg

Looking north along Fifth
Street, near First Avenue South
and Central Avenue, 1921. La
Plaza Theatre can be seen on the
left, and the St. Petersburg
Times *building and the real
estate office of Charles Roser can
be seen on the right. Photograph
by Burgert Brothers, courtesy
Florida State Archives*

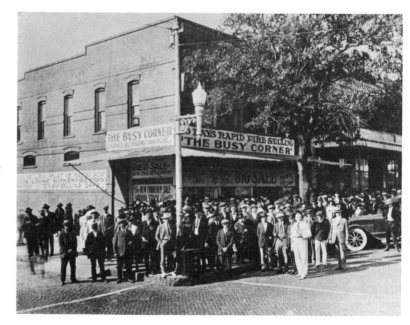

*Salesmanship was the name of
the game at "The Busy Corner,"
J. Bruce Smith's dry goods store
on the southwest corner of Central Avenue and Third Street
South, circa 1925. Courtesy*
St. Petersburg Times

A classic St. Petersburg scene—boardinghouse, green benches, and a "For Sale" sign, circa 1925. The St. Clair boardinghouse was located at 626 Central Avenue. Courtesy St. Petersburg Times

A street-paving crew laying bricks on Fortieth Street South, circa 1925. Courtesy St. Petersburg Times

A panoramic view of the Lake Vista subdivision, near Lake Maggiore, circa 1924. Courtesy St. Petersburg Historical Society

Perry Snell's Granada Terrace subdivision featured ornate "Spanish castles" and a central boulevard adorned with Stonehenge-like megaliths. Courtesy St. Petersburg Historical Society

*Bungalow-style houses like the
one pictured above were built by
the hundreds in St. Petersburg
during the 1920s. Courtesy
St. Petersburg Historical Society*

A prairie-style home in Roser Park, circa 1924. Photograph by Samuel H. Beck, courtesy St. Petersburg Historical Society

Cade Allen started his Allendale subdivision with the construction of this unusual stone, tile, and stucco home (3410 Ninth Street North) in 1922. Courtesy St. Petersburg City News Bureau

Built in 1919, this wooden bridge connected Snell Isle with Coffee Pot Boulevard until it was replaced by a more substantial masonry bridge in 1931. The Japanese-style buildings on the right served as the clubhouse of the Coffee Pot Gulf Club. Developed by Perry Snell, the Coffee Pot course opened in January 1920. This photograph was taken circa 1924. Courtesy St. Petersburg City News Bureau

Looking southwest along Snell Isle Boulevard, 1926. The Snell Isle subdivision was in an early stage of development when this photograph was taken. The building in the foreground is the clubhouse of the Snell Isle Golf Club. Courtesy St. Petersburg Historical Society

The courtyard of the Snell Isle Gardens apartment building, as it looked during the late 1920s. Opened in 1926, the Snell Isle Gardens complex was designed for clients who were awaiting the completion of their Snell Isle residences. Each apartment was filled with stylish furnishings, including a Steinway Piano. Photograph by Burgert Brothers, courtesy St. Petersburg Historical Society

Photo from the Historical Collection of Walter P. Fuller.

The year was 1926

St. Petersburg was still basking in the sunset of the "Golden Years". Almost everyone knew at least one land millionaire and, in spite of the harbingers of the gloomier days to come, the general expectation was that "things would pick up again soon".

Life was pleasant. There was fishing, boating in the Bay and golf! The sportier men of the golf set were garbed in knickers. The sportier cars featured wire wheels, fancy radiator ornaments and, for the really ardent devotee of the links, a fender mounted wicker basket for carrying clubs.

The smart set enjoying the good life in St. Petersburg, 1926. Courtesy St. Petersburg Historical Society

Former Mayor Noel Mitchell was billed as "The William Jennings Bryan of the Florida Rushes" in this mid-1920s advertisement. Courtesy St. Petersburg Times

Realtors on parade, circa 1925. The annual Festival of States celebration was prime selling time during the boom years. Courtesy Earl Jacobs Collection, Nelson Poynter Library, University of South Florida at St. Petersburg

Ohio's entry in the Festival of States parade, circa 1923. Courtesy Earl Jacobs Collection, Nelson Poynter Library, University of South Florida at St. Petersburg

The Ladies Auxiliary of the Grand Army of the Republic sponsored this float in the 1922 Festival of States parade. Courtesy St. Petersburg Historical Society

John C. Williams's cradle added a touch of nostalgia to the 1922 Festival of States parade. The float was sponsored by the St. Petersburg Memorial Historical Society, organized in 1920. Courtesy St. Petersburg Historical Society

A view of the waterfront in 1924. The eighty-five room Hotel Ponce de Leon (center) opened in 1922. The Spa, the St. Petersburg Yacht Club (with its 1922 addition), and the American Legion Hall can be seen on the right. Courtesy Earl Jacobs Collection, Nelson Poynter Library, University of South Florida at St. Petersburg

A view of the Central Yacht Basin and the Spa, 1925. Courtesy William L. Straub Collection, St. Petersburg Historical Society

The Soreno Hotel, circa 1926. Billed as the city's first million-dollar hotel, the Soreno opened in 1924. Courtesy Earl Jacobs Collection, Nelson Poynter Library, University of South Florida at St. Petersburg

Yacht Basin St. Petersburg, Florida.

*Swimming in the shallows at
Spa Beach, circa 1923. Courtesy
St. Petersburg Historical Society*

*The West Coast Inn, located near
the intersection of Third Avenue
South and First Street, as it
looked during the 1920s. This
distinctive brick building, with
its shingled tower and wrap-
around verandas, was demolished in 1967. Photograph by
Samuel H. Beck, courtesy St.
Petersburg Historical Society*

Young swimmers on the diving platform at Spa Beach, circa 1923. Courtesy St. Petersburg City News Bureau

The Hotel Alexander, on Central Avenue between Fifth and Sixth streets, circa 1926. Built in 1919, the Alexander's neo-Classical facade and symmetrical split plan made it one of the city's most striking buildings. It was designed by Atlanta architect Neel Reid. Courtesy Earl Jacobs Collection, Nelson Poynter Library, University of South Florida at St. Petersburg

The Princess Martha Hotel, 1926. Opened in 1924 as the Mason Hotel, this large neo-Classical brick hotel was renamed the Princess Martha following an early bankruptcy and change of ownership. It was designed by Boston architect F. Jonsberg. Courtesy Earl Jacobs Collection, Nelson Poynter Library, University of South Florida at St. Petersburg

The Jungle Country Club Hotel, shortly after its completion in 1925. This sprawling Mediter-ranean Revival structure was the centerpiece of Walter P. Fuller's Jungle subdivision. In 1945, the Jungle County Club Hotel build-ing was transformed into Ad-miral Farragut Academy. Cour-tesy Earl Jacobs Collection, Nelson Poynter Library, Univer-sity of South Florida at St. Petersburg

The clubhouse of the Jungle Club Golf Course, 1925. Real estate developer Walter P. Fuller purchased the St. Petersburg Country Club in January 1924 and turned it into the popular Jungle Club course. Courtesy Earl Jacobs Collection, Nelson Poynter Library, University of South Florida at St. Petersburg

I. M. "Handsome Jack" Taylor, the flamboyant promoter of Pasadena Estates, opened the posh Rolyat (Taylor spelled backwards) Hotel in January 1926. Courtesy Special Collections, University of South Florida Library, Tampa

Another view of the Rolyat Hotel.
Courtesy Special Collections,
University of South Florida
Library, Tampa

I. M. "Handsome Jack" Taylor.
Courtesy St. Petersburg Histori-
cal Society

The entrance to the Vinoy Park Hotel, circa 1926. Courtesy Special Collections, University of South Florida Library, Tampa

The elegant Mediterranean Revival-style Vinoy Park Hotel was still under construction when this photograph was taken in 1925. Designed by architect Henry Taylor and owned by Pennsylvania oilman Aymer Vinoy Laughner, the Vinoy Park opened in January 1926. Courtesy Earl Jacobs Collection, Nelson Poynter Library, University of South Florida at St. Petersburg

A stylish "knickerbocker boy" relaxing on a green bench near the Vinoy Park Hotel, circa 1926. Courtesy Earl Jacobs Collection, Nelson Poynter Library, University of South Florida at St. Petersburg

Looking north along Beach Drive, circa 1926. The small white building in the center is the St. Petersburg Art Club. Part of the Soreno Hotel can be seen on the left. Courtesy Earl Jacobs Collection, Nelson Poynter Library, University of South Florida at St. Petersburg

The waterfront, as seen from the top of the Vinoy Park Hotel, 1926. Courtesy Earl Jacobs Collection, Nelson Poynter Library, University of South Florida at St. Petersburg

The Pass-a-Grille Casino, circa 1926. Photograph by Burgert Brothers, courtesy Florida State Archives

Tourists enjoy the good life at Pass-a-Grille beach, circa 1926. Courtesy Earl Jacobs Collection, Nelson Poynter Library, University of South Florida at St. Petersburg

The Moorish-style Coliseum dance hall opened in November 1924. Located on Fourth Avenue North, the Coliseum quickly became a local landmark and a symbol of the city's Roaring Twenties culture. Courtesy Earl Jacobs Collection, Nelson Poynter Library, University of South Florida at St. Petersburg

The entrance to La Plaza Theatre, circa 1926. Courtesy Earl Jacobs Collection, Nelson Poynter Library, University of South Florida at St. Petersburg

The St. Petersburg Shuffle Board Club, north of Mirror Lake, circa 1925. Photograph by Burgert Brothers, courtesy St. Petersburg Historical Society

Bowling on the marl rink of the St. Petersburg Lawn Bowling Club, circa 1926. Founded in 1915, the club hosted several "world championships" during the 1920s. Courtesy St. Petersburg Historical Society

This waterfront ball park was the spring training home of the Boston Braves from 1922 to 1937. Courtesy St. Petersburg Historical Society

George Herman "Babe" Ruth, "the Sultan of Swat." Ruth and the New York Yankees began training in St. Petersburg in the spring of 1925. The Yankees' training facility was located at the southern end of Crescent Lake. Courtesy St. Petersburg Times

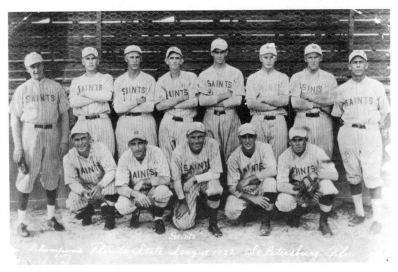

The 1922 St. Petersburg Saints, champions of the Florida State League. Courtesy St. Petersburg Historical Society

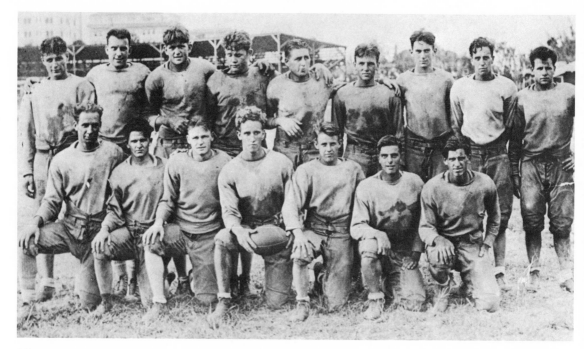

*The 1926-1927 St. Petersburg
High School football team. Courtesy* St. Petersburg Times

*A postcard view of St. Petersburg
High School, 1927. St. Petersburg High School moved to this
striking Mediterranean Revival-
style building in December 1926.
Located on Fifth Avenue North,
the one-million-dollar building
was designed by architect
William B. Ittner. Courtesy St.
Petersburg Historical Society*

The educational needs of black children, long ignored by city leaders, received some recognition when Davis Academy (later known as Davis Elementary School) opened in 1910. Located on Sixteenth Street South, near Fifth Avenue, the school was used until 1967. This photograph was taken during the 1920s. Photograph by Burgert Brothers, courtesy St. Petersburg Historical Society

Ruth Albury and her brother Joseph Albury, Jr., posing in front of the family car, circa 1923. Joseph Albury, Sr., was the first professional photographer to open a studio in St. Petersburg's black community. Photograph by Joseph Albury, Sr., courtesy of Joseph Albury, Jr.

The Mirror Lake section of downtown, 1925. The Suwannee Hotel (center) and the First Avenue Methodist Church (right) dominate the foreground, and the 1919 (center right) and 1911 (far right) high school buildings can be seen in the background. Courtesy Earl Jacobs Collection, Nelson Poynter Library, University of South Florida at St. Petersburg

The Atlantic Coast Line depot on First Avenue South, circa 1926. Courtesy Earl Jacobs Collection, Nelson Poynter Library, University of South Florida at St. Petersburg

Central Avenue storefronts, between Eighth and Ninth Streets, 1925. Courtesy St. Petersburg Historical Society

Black construction workers were a familiar sight in downtown St. Petersburg during the boom years. This photograph was taken in 1925. Courtesy St. Petersburg Times

The southeast corner of Central Avenue and Fourth Street, circa 1926. The distinctive neo-Classical facade of the American Bank and Trust Company can be seen on the far left. Courtesy Earl Jacobs Collection, Nelson Poynter Library, University of South Florida at St. Petersburg

The ten-story West Coast Title Building (also known as the Equitable Building), on the northeast corner of Central Avenue and Fourth Street, shortly after it opened in July 1926. Courtesy Earl Jacobs Collection, Nelson Poynter Library, University of South Florida at St. Petersburg

Relaxing on the green benches, on Fifth Street North, circa 1926. The Florida Power Building, La Plaza Theatre, and the Rutland Brothers department store can be seen in the background. Courtesy *St. Petersburg Times*

The Million Dollar Pier was nearing completion when this photograph was taken in 1926. Courtesy Earl Jacobs Collection, Nelson Poynter Library, University of South Florida at St. Petersburg

A view of the St. Petersburg Yacht Club and the Million Dollar Pier, 1926. Courtesy Earl Jacobs Collection, Nelson Poynter Library, University of South Florida at St. Petersburg

The St. Petersburg Yacht Club, circa 1926. Courtesy Special Collections, University of South Florida Library, Tampa

Feeding pelicans at the Million Dollar Pier, circa 1927. Courtesy St. Petersburg Historical Society

A prize catch being displayed at the Million Dollar Pier, circa 1927. Courtesy Earl Jacobs Collection, Nelson Poynter Library, University of South Florida at St. Petersburg

Chapter Seven

Hard Times

1927-1940

Members of a St. Petersburg carpenters' union protest the payment of low nonunion wages by local construction companies, 1938. Courtesy St. Petersburg Times

The collapse of the great Florida boom was inevitable, but in St. Petersburg the day of reckoning was hastened by a bit of bad luck. In early December 1925, the city hosted the annual convention of the Investment Bankers Association of America—an influential group of men who, it was hoped, would elevate the boom to new heights. John Lodwick and other local boosters envisioned a scenario in which, after spending a week in the warm sunshine, the bankers would return home to inform the investment world that the Sunshine City was bursting with opportunity. Unfortunately for the boosters, and for the local economy, the opening day of the convention Monday, December 7, turned out to be a day of steady rain. The rain did not let up on Tuesday, nor did it slacken on Wednesday. On Thursday and Friday, high winds and falling temperatures added to the conventioneers' misery. By the time the convention came to a close on Saturday, the departing bankers were in no mood to talk about the alleged charms of a city that had turned out to be a soggy, bone-chilling disappointment.

The relationship between the ill-fated bankers' convention and the subsequent collapse of the boom was undoubtedly more symbolic that causal, but many local observers would later look back on the convention as the beginning of the end. In January 1926, there was an encouraging flurry of real estate activity, but by early spring land sales were off markedly from previous years. Nearly everyone predicted that the market would rebound in the fall, but they were wrong. Although the city was full of tourists by October, the percentage looking for land was far too low to satisfy the inflated expectations of the army of sand merchants. Those who were interested in buying were no longer willing to pay inflated boom-era prices. Placed in a buyer's market where supply had obviously outstripped demand, all but the most naive buyers took advantage of the situation. In the words of Walter Fuller, who lost a multimillion dollar fortune during the bust, "the supply of suckers ha[d] run out."[1] As a result, the price of land plummeted, setting off a chain reaction of panic selling and foreclosures. By the spring of

1927, the whole inverted pyramid created by uncontrolled speculation had collapsed, but by that time Jack Taylor and most of the other high rollers had long since skipped town.

Although it lasted little more than half a decade, the big boom of the 1920s left indelible marks on the city of St. Petersburg. Even though the frenetic pace of the boom was gone, never to return, the spatial, architectural, and cultural legacies of the boom would influence the city's character for decades to come. Spatially, the proliferation of boom-era subdivisions gave the city a distinctive, spread-out, suburban quality. Architecturally, the Mediterranean Revival landmarks created during the 1920s added a touch of romantic frivolity that solidified the city's identification with leisure. At the same time, the boom experience reinforced and deepened the city's long-standing dependence on tourism. From the mid-1920s onward, few people doubted that the city's destiny lay more with consumption than production. For better or worse, St. Petersburg was a resort city, and there was no turning back from its reliance on advertising, public relations, and tourist-oriented institutions such as the Festival of States and the state societies. Finally, the massive influx of Northern settlers during the 1920s altered the demographic and cultural makeup of the city, creating a more heterogeneous community and ensuring that St. Petersburg would always be a quasi-Northern city in a Southern setting.

The cultural legacy of the boom became apparent in 1928, when the local electorate sent a Republican, Albert R. Welsh, to the state senate. Welsh's amazing showing—he was the first Republican to serve in the state legislature since Reconstruction—was based in part on the Hoovercrat phenomenon; in the 1928 presidential election, more than half of the city's Democrats temporarily abandoned their party to vote for Herbert Hoover, the Iowa Quaker who ran roughshod over Governor Al Smith, the Irish-American Catholic from New York. But the surprising strength of the local Republican Party in subsequent elections suggests that Welsh's victory represented more that the triumph of anti-Catholic prejudice. To the dismay of Florida Democrats, St. Petersburg had become one of the few cities in the South where local culture and demography fostered competitive two-party politics.

The bust also left its imprint on the city, although its legacy tended to be more psychological than socioeconomic. For many of those who experienced the roller-coaster ride of the 1920s, the image of the boom as a golden age would always be tempered by painful memories of the bust. Some, of course, repudiated the boom mentality altogether. "The 1925 boom was not an urge to retire in a pleasant cottage in Florida or to bask in luxurious villas or seaside hotels." Walter Fuller wrote in 1954, "It was, instead, a greedy delirium to acquire riches over night without benefit of effort, brains, or services rendered."[2] Perhaps so, but Fuller's insinuation that the boom-bust cycle of the 1920s was unrelated to the Florida Dream of free and easy living is open to serious question.

As important as it was, the bust was not the all encompassing historical watershed that it sometimes has been made out to be. At the very least, the short-term impact of the bust has frequently been exaggerated. Although shell-shocked realtors probably felt otherwise, the immediate post-boom era was not a time of social stasis or general economic despair. During the late 1920s, the city continued to grow, although at a much slower rate that during the boom. Between 1925 and 1930, St. Petersburg's year-round population rose from 26,847 to 40,425, an increase of 50.6 percent. At the same time, the institutional superstructure of the city continued to expand. In 1927 alone, city residents saw the opening of St. Petersburg Junior College, Jonathan C. Gibbs High School, the American Legion Hospital for Crippled Children, and the United States Coast Guard base at Bayboro Harbor. For people living in the shadow of the boom, much of this was obscured by a strong sense of relative deprivation. But the growth was real nonetheless.

The tendency to overestimate the impact of the bust has become a permanent part of local folklore, even finding its way into serious historical accounts. In *St. Petersburg and Its People*, for example, Walter Fuller gives the false impression that St. Petersburg's Great Depression began in 1926, not in 1929. The collapse of the boom wiped out a number of paper fortunes, including Fuller's. It also lowered expectations all around. But it did not plunge the city into a full-scale economic depression. Because of the big bull market on Wall Street, much of the nation was riding a wave of prosperity, and St. Petersburg, bust or no bust, was buoyed by the state of the national economy.

In South Florida, where the end of the boom was punctuated by the devastating Labor Day hurricane of 1926, the regional economy was dealt a knock-out blow. But on Florida's Gulf coast, which escaped the full fury of the storm, the economic downturn was much more gradual. Indeed, in the short run, Gulf coast resort cities like St. Petersburg probably benefited from the storm, as a large proportion of the Gold Coast's tourist trade was at least temporarily diverted to other parts of the state. For this and other reasons—one of which was a redoubled effort to advertise the city's charms—St. Petersburg enjoyed banner tourist seasons throughout the late 1920s. To the dismay of the local real estate industry, which continued to flounder, the tourists of the post-boom era tended to avoid anything that suggested land speculation. But, to the relief of storekeepers, hotel owners, and other merchants, they seemed to have plenty of money to spend on other things. Nothing could save the fortunes of the high-stake real estate speculators, but the healthy tourist trade went a long way toward shoring up the rest of the local economy.

One notable exception was the building industry. As the figures in Table 2 demonstrate, the pace of construction fell off dramatically after the bust of 1926.

Table 2

Bank Deposits and Building Permits, City of St. Petersburg, 1920-1940

Year	Total Value of Bank Deposits $	Total Value of Building Permits $
1920	5,928,171	2,901,120
1921	9,790,445	4,608,820
1922	10,076,812	4,107,655
1923	16,069,307	7,124,560
1924	24,177,642	9,557,500
1925	46,167,038	24,081,700
1926	27,410,713	15,580,200
1927	21,605,300	2,907,300
1928	25,258,149	1,849,900
1929	15,506,317	1,445,800
1930	6,344,068	797,525
1931	4,336,777	672,600
1932	4,616,512	278,100
1933	5,256,356	381,650
1934	7,632,513	1,271,500
1935	9,453,506	1,501,354
1936	12,909,731	2,000,960
1937	12,605,783	3,075,476
1938	15,554,625	3,017,250
1939	19,172,570	4,731,200
1940	21,793,398	5,830,539

Source: Walter P. Fuller, *St. Petersburg and Its People* (St. Petersburg: Great Outdoors Publishing, 1972), pp. 254, 258.

These figures understate the amount of construction going on during the late 1920s, since several major projects begun during the boom—including Snell Isle, the Snell Arcade, and the Don CeSar Hotel—carried over into post-boom era. But the actual decline was sharp enough to drive a majority of the city's carpenters and day laborers into other lines of work.

For a time, the economic malaise among building contractors and real estate agents threatened to cast a pall over the entire city. But, as the decade drew to a close, the city of sunshine and salesmanship seemed to regain its confidence, taking on an air of cautious optimism. For many local political and business leaders, the shock of the bust was finally beginning to wear off, and even the city council, which had been nearly paralyzed by the community's high level of bonded indebtedness, began to loosen its purse strings. Signs of renewed confidence were all around, but one of the most striking was the decision to construct a municipal airport on a stretch of landfill east of Bayboro Harbor. In October 1928, the city council authorized the construction of a field to be named in honor of Albert Whitted, a celebrated local flyer who had been killed in a plane crash near Pensacola in 1923. Opened during the summer of 1929, Whitted Airport was a modest facility with only one short runway. Indeed, it was a bit too modest for city publicity agent John Lodwick, who decided to add a little excitement to the city's latest public works project.

Shortly after the airport's opening, Lodwick convinced the Goodyear Tire and Rubber Company to station one of its blimps at the new field. The dirigible craze was then in full swing, and Lodwick was sure that the blimp would become a popular tourist attraction and a symbol of the city's economic recovery. At his urging, the city council appropriated an additional $33,062 for a municipal blimp hangar in September 1929. The hangar was completed by December, and a month later the blimp *Goodyear* flew into the city. By that time, however, Lodwick and the city council were already fending off complaints that they had saddled the city with yet another white elephant. Even Lodwick, the master of the well-timed publicity stunt, had not foreseen the stock market crash of October 1929. As the hangar went up, the value of stocks went down. And as the blimp glided among the clouds, the lofty dreams of the Sunshine City came crashing down to earth.

The national economic depression that followed hard on the heels of the stock market crash hit the city with devastating force. The local economy had barely survived the real estate bust of 1926, and now it faced a new and even graver set of challenges—a drying up of credit, a sharp decline in consumer spending, and a deflationary spiral of unprecedented proportions. During the late 1920s, a relatively healthy tourist trade had kept the local economy afloat, providing partial compensation for the depressed condition of the local real estate and construction industries. But as the nation sank into depression, the number of tourists visiting the city fell off markedly. Many people no longer had the funds for a winter vacation in Florida, and others were simply too nervous about the state of the nation to stray too far from home. Even the tourists who did show up were seldom in a spending mood. Refusing to panic, Chamber of Commerce officials and city publicists issued a steady barrage of hopeful projections. But no amount of upbeat rhetoric or wishful thinking could disguise the fact that there was big trouble in paradise. Empty hotel rooms, unsold inventories, and worried looks told the true story.

The decline in the tourist trade propelled the local economy into a five-year-long tailspin. Beginning in the spring of 1930, there were business failures and mortgage foreclosures by the hundreds. There was massive unemployment, particularly among unskilled laborers. Even those who managed to hold on to their jobs were often forced to accept sharply reduced wages. In some sectors of the economy, such as the construction industry, the collapse was almost total; as shown in Table 2, the value of building permits issued in the city during the early 1930s was only a small fraction of the comparable figures for the boom years of the mid-1920s.

Not everyone suffered equally—or even suffered at all. Indeed for the fortunate few who had money to spare, the deflation of the 1930s produced an unlimited number of bargains, particularly in real estate. According to Karl Grismer, "North Shore houses which cost $40,000 and more to build could be purchased for as little as $7,000," while "store buildings, large and small, were offered at from 10 to 15 percent of the construction costs."[3] But for the vast majority of the city's residents there was little thought of profiting from the Depression. They were too busy trying to survive. By 1932, the assessed valuation of real and personal property in the city was barely

half of what it had been in 1927. Even more alarmingly, the value of bank deposits in the city plummeted. In 1925, at the height of the boom, the value of bank deposits had been over $46 million and as late as 1929 the figure had still been $15 million. But by 1931-1932, deposits had fallen to less than $5 million.

The complete collapse of the city's financial institutions was perhaps the best index of the severity of the crisis. Between April 1930 and April 1931, every bank in the city was forced to close. Even venerable institutions such as the First National Bank of St. Petersburg were unable to meet the demands of panicking depositors who wished to make withdrawals. All together, more than $10 million in depositors' assets was frozen, and in the end most depositors were forced to settle for a fraction of their actual holdings. Some received as much as fifty-two cents on the dollar, but most received far less. Those who had entrusted their money to the American Bank and Trust Company, for example, recovered less than 1 percent of their money. It is little wonder that when two new banks opened in late 1930, many local residents completely avoided them.

The banking community was not the only local institution to suffer a decline in public confidence during the early 1930s. City hall also took increasing criticism. Despite a wealth of good intentions, local officials seemed powerless in the face of the city's mounting economic difficulties. No city government in America was fully prepared to deal with the economic and social problems of the Great Depression. But in St. Petersburg the situation was exacerbated by the community's profligate past. The expensive bond issues of the boom era, which amounted to millions of dollars of unreimbursed spending on streets and other public improvements, left the city in a precarious financial position. Indeed, the city's bonded indebtedness per capita—$802.06—was the second highest in the nation in 1930. In the context of a national depression, this level of debt became a formula for disaster, and in May 1930 the city had no choice but to default on its bond payments. The payments were not resumed until 1937.

Automobiles, streetcars, and strolling pedestrians on the busy Million Dollar Pier, circa 1928. Courtesy St. Petersburg Times

Looking west from the Million Dollar Pier's Casino building, circa 1928. Courtesy St. Petersburg Times

Not surprisingly, the default triggered a movement for governmental reorganization, and in July 1931 a new city charter was adopted. The new charter called for the hiring of a professional city manager and the election of a seven-member city council, with each councilman representing a specific geographical district. The council members were empowered to choose the mayor from their own ranks, which ostensibly lowered the mayor's profile, and an additional provision of the new charter allowed city officials to raise funds by selling tax-delinquent property at public auctions.

The first city manager to be hired under the new system, Wilbur Cotton, was a capable administrator who gave the city professional leadership. But governmental reorganization alone could not restore the city to economic health. Despite Cotton's best efforts, the economic situation continued to deteriorate, and in the worst days of 1931 and 1932, the city could not even meet its own payroll, much less solve the problems of the private sector. The biggest problem was an acute shortage of cash which made economic recovery all but impossible. The shortage became so severe that a group of local business leaders eventually formed the Citizens' Emergency Committee, which sanctioned the use of scrip certificates as a substitute for cash. Several of the city's largest employers, including the county school board, paid their employees with a combination of cash and scrip. The *St. Petersburg Times* even set up an arrangement which allowed advertisers to trade scrip for column space. "We bought all our groceries, clothing and almost anything, including automobiles," one local resident recalled many years later, "with scrip and part cash."[4]

Another sign of the times was the city council's reliance on a group known as the Home Patronage Committee. Throughout the Depression, St. Petersburg and other Florida cities attracted large numbers of unemployed migrants. They came from all over the eastern United States, a wandering army of bedraggled and forlorn refugees who left their homes in search of a better life. Some were drawn to the state by the Florida Dream, by a vague notion that the land of sunshine and sand merchants would somehow change their luck. And some simply rode the rails until they reached the end of the line. But, whatever their expectations, they invariably received a rude welcome once they arrived in the Sunshine State. This was certainly the case in St. Petersburg, where the Home Patronage Committee posted a series of signs displaying the warning: "DO NOT COME HERE SEEKING WORK—A CITY'S FIRST DUTY IS TO EMPLOY ITS OWN CITIZENS."[5] Considering the state of the local economy, the committee's attempt to rid the community of unemployed migrants was hardly surprising. But few people seemed to appreciate the irony of the situation—institutionalized inhospitality in a city that depended on visitors for its very existence.

The techniques used by the Home Patronage and Citizens' Emergency committees were stopgap measures, acts of desperation which were implemented to save the city from social chaos. But few people had any illusions that such measures would significantly advance the cause of economic recovery. By 1932, it had become clear that St. Petersburg's political and business leaders had failed to find an internal solution to the city's economic problems. Although the local elite hated to admit it, economic recovery would require help from either Tallahassee or Washington. And since Florida's state government was on the verge of bankruptcy throughout the early 1930s, the only real hope was the federal government in Washington.

Very few American cities received much economic help from the federal government during the Hoover years, but due to the efforts of two resourceful leaders, Florida Congressman J. Hardin Peterson and Herman Dann, a former president of the local chamber of commerce, St. Petersburg was one of the exceptions. After learning that the Veterans' Administration planned to build a major hospital and regional office somewhere in Florida, Peterson and Dann mounted a spirited campaign to bring the facility to St. Petersburg. Veterans' Administration officials drove a hard bargain, insisting that the city donate all of the land needed for the site. But unused land was one commodity that St. Petersburg had in abundance during the Great Depression. The deal was completed in 1931 when a large tract of newly acquired city land at Long Bayou, on Boca Ciega Bay, was turned over to the Veterans' Administration. Construction began in early 1932, providing the city with a glimmer of economic hope during the worst year of the Depression. The first stage of the project, which employed nearly a thousand construction workers, took a year to complete, with the regional office opening in January 1933, and the hospital in March. Over the next five years several additional buildings were constructed at Bay Pines, providing the local construction industry with a much-needed boost and creating a sprawling complex that employed a large staff of doctors and nurses.

During the 1932 presidential campaign, local Republicans pointed to the Bay Pines project as a symbol of President Hoover's successful economic recovery program. But after two years of the Depression, no amount of rhetoric—and certainly no single project—could fully restore public confidence in the tottering Hoover administration. On election day, the President received 49 percent of the vote in St. Petersburg, which was far more support than he received in the rest of the county (30 percent), or in the state as a whole (25 percent). Nevertheless, his showing represented a sharp decline from 1928, when he received 79.2 percent of the city's vote. Saddled with the Depression and unable to exploit the anti-Catholic prejudice that had worked so well against his 1928 opponent, Governor Al Smith of New York, Hoover was an easy mark for Franklin Roosevelt and the resurgent Democratic Party. Although St. Petersburg would remain something of a Republican stronghold (relative to other Southern cities) for decades to come, the Hoovercrat phenomenon, which had taken the city and much of the state by storm in 1928, was clearly over.

When Franklin Roosevelt replaced Herbert Hoover as President of the United States in March 1933, the confusion and inaction of the Hoover era gave way to the drive and dynamism of the New Deal. Beginning with the whirlwind period known as the First Hundred Days, Roosevelt presided over a massive expansion of the federal bureaucracy. Encouraged by a brain trust of advisors who advocated a wide-ranging and experimental approach to economic and social reform, Roosevelt and his congressional lieutenants created dozens of new agencies, including the Agricultural Adjustment Administration (AAA), the Federal Emergency Relief Administration (FERA), the Federal Deposit Insurance Corporation (FDIC), the Civil Works Administration (CWA) and the Public Works Administration (PWA). Through a combination of federal spending and national planning, the New Dealers hoped to revive the economy and restore public confidence in the nation's future. Grounded in the pragmatic traditions of the Progressive Movement and expressly designed to buttress the capitalist system, the New Deal stopped far short of socialism. Nevertheless, the unprecedented scope and

pace of the Roosevelt administration's reforms frightened diehard conservatives, who condemned the New Deal as a socialistic threat to free enterprise. Even so, most Americans—particularly those who were unemployed or otherwise down on their luck—applauded Roosevelt's efforts at reform, showering him with votes and affection.

This was certainly the case in St. Petersburg, where the New Deal's offer of federal aid was generally viewed as a godsend. Here, as elsewhere, the New Deal's activist response to the Great Depression radically altered the relationship between local government and the federal bureaucracy in Washington. Prior to the 1930s, city officials almost ignored national politics, which in their experience had little impact on local affairs other than determining the partisanship of the local postmaster. In a city like St. Petersburg, which was overwhelmingly Democratic prior to the mid-1920s, this feeling of detachment was reinforced by the states' rights ideology of the Solid South and by decades of Republican dominance in Washington (with the exception of the Woodrow Wilson interregnum of 1913-21, the Republican Party had controlled the White House since 1897). However, St. Petersburg's civic and business leaders did not take very long to adjust to the realities of New Deal economics. As the depression deepened and as state and local relief funds ran out, traditional attachments to local autonomy and self-reliance were quietly set aside.

Mayor Robert Blanc, City Manager Wilbur Cotton, and other city officials were extremely aggressive when it came to soliciting federal aid, which is not surprising considering the desperate state of the local economy. Pointing to the real estate bust of 1926, they pleaded for special consideration, arguing, with some justification, that the residents of St. Petersburg had already suffered through seven years of economic hardship—three years more than most Americans. Many other Florida communities made similar claims, and federal authorities never officially endorsed the idea that St. Petersburg deserved special treatment. But the city's ultimate success in the fierce competition for federal aid suggests that the

Swinging chairs at Spa Beach on the Million Dollar Pier, circa 1927. Courtesy St. Petersburg Times

argument may have carried some weight.

Between 1933 and 1941, the federal government pumped more than $10 million into St. Petersburg's economy—an unusually large figure for a small city. This infusion of federal money and influence took several forms—relief payments, public works projects, and military expenditures—and left few lives untouched. Although federal aid was no panacea for hard times, the local activities of the FERA, the CWA, the FDIC (St. Petersburg's First Federal Savings and Loan Association was granted a charter in August 1933) brought the first stirring of economic and psychological recovery. In addition to saving the city's economy from total collapse, federal aid reduced the toll of human misery and suffering by providing some of the city's least fortunate families with temporary sustenance and a measure of hope.

The first New Deal agency to have an impact on St. Petersburg was the Civil Works Administration. The brainchild of FERA administrator Harry Hopkins, the CWA was established during the summer of 1933 as a temporary alternative to the Public Works Administration. At that point, the PWA projects that eventually would provide employment for several hundred thousand workers were still in the planning stage. Thus, during the desperate winter of 1933-34, the

CWA—which specialized in short-term projects—became a critically important source of work relief. At the height of its influence, in January 1934, the CWA employed more than 4 million workers, most of whom were unskilled or semiskilled laborers. The average CWA employee earned fifteen dollars a week—a paltry sum by middle-class standards but more than twice the amount of the average FERA relief payment. In St. Petersburg, the CWA employed several hundred laborers who worked on everything from mosquito control to road repairs. Working closely with city officials, CWA administrators initiated dozens of local public works projects, including the expansion of Albert Whitted Airport and the transformation of a southside swamp into Bartlett Park.

The CWA was dismantled in the spring of 1934, but many of the local projects were extended under the auspices of the FERA, the PWA, and eventually the Works Progress Administration (WPA). Prior to the creation of the WPA in April 1935, the FERA carried the brunt of the load. Designed to supersede the Reconstruction Finance Corporation, which had loaned federal money to state governments, the FERA went far toward federalizing the nation's relief system. In St. Petersburg, the FERA was involved in a wide variety of relief projects, ranging from the distribution of surplus beef and cane syrup to the installation of glass reflectors on county highways. Among other projects, the agency put men to work on the roads, converted a factory on North Disston Avenue into a home for elderly male transients, distributed toys to poor children on Christmas, and poured several hundred thousand dollars into local schools, mostly for teachers' salaries. FERA funds did not always reach those who needed the help the most, particularly in the black community. But for many local families the FERA was the last best hope during the dark days of 1934 and 1935.

The PWA was a heavily funded agency—the initial appropriation was $3.3 billion—but it did not become active locally until late 1935, when two large projects were approved: a $90,000 addition at Mound Park City Hospital and a $294,545 appropriation for a beach water system. The hospital addition was completed in 1937, and a year later the PWA became involved in an even more ambitious project—the construction of a new city hall. The existing city hall, a two-story brick structure built in 1902 and originally designed as a manual training school annex, was totally inadequate for a community the size of St. Petersburg, and local boosters had been demanding a new building for years. Although government regulations during the new Deal made it extremely difficult to expend federal funds on city hall construction projects, local leaders and PWA officials eventually found a way to fund the building with public utilities appropriations. Construction began in late 1938 and continued for nearly a year. Formally opened in November 1939, St. Petersburg's stylish new $389,415 city hall became a symbol of the city's successful partnership with the New Deal.

The most influential and certainly the most visible federal agency in St. Petersburg was the WPA. Created by executive order following the Emergency Relief Appropriation of 1936, the WPA was the political cornerstone of the so-called Second New Deal. Conceived as a replacement for the FERA, the agency was directed by former FERA administrator Harry Hopkins, who hoped to restore the morale of the unemployed by providing socially purposeful work relief. Hopkins was deter-

mined to avoid unfulfilling make-work projects, and for the most part he was successful. In St. Petersburg, the WPA provided a livelihood for more than a thousand local families during the mid- and late-1930s, paying them wages from $25 to $55 a month. It also put people to work on projects that permanently benefited the community, projects such as the construction of a United States Coast Guard air station near Bayboro Harbor, the laying of the North Shore sewer system, and the continuing development of Bartlett Park, which was turned into one of the city's premier recreational facilities. WPA funds and workers were also instrumental in the creation of a National Guard armory, as well as a new campus for St. Petersburg Junior College. At the same time, the agency sponsored a wide range of cultural activities. The WPA operated sewing rooms, organized orchestras and art clubs and theater projects, conducted property surveys, compiled indexes of historical material, reorganized and catalogued public records, and even recorded the life histories of ex-slaves living in the city. No federal agency, before or since, has ever tried to do so much.

The activities of the WPA and other New Deal agencies helped to brighten the mood of the city during the mid- and late-1930s. But the major news in St. Petersburg during these years—the reality that overshadowed everything else—was the return of the tourists, a development that brought partial economic recovery to the city. Relative to the boom era, times were still hard. Many families continued to suffer, particularly in the black community. But the overall economic picture was not nearly as bleak as it had been earlier in the decade. For most of the city's residents, the worst of the Depression was over by 1935. Ironically, the same factor that had made the city so vulnerable during the early years of the Depression—dependence on the tourist trade—had proved to be the city's salvation.

A number of factors contributed to the revival of St. Petersburg's tourist economy: a slight improvement in the national economy, a run of good weather throughout the mid-1930s, a community-wide effort to treat tourists like visiting royalty, and perhaps most important, an ability to capitalize on the strikes and other signs of social upheaval that were becoming increasingly common in the industrial Northeast and Midwest. For those who could afford it, escape to a haven in the sun where there were no picket lines and no boarded-up factories was an increasingly attractive and viable option, and resort cities like St. Petersburg were more than willing to take full advantage of the situation.

As always, John Lodwick and his publicity staff did what they could to prime the pump. Travel agencies in Northern cities were outfitted with elaborate window displays advertising the charms of the city, and Sunshine City brochures and press releases were distributed by the thousands. Lodwick used everything from babies to bathing beauties to sell the city, which he touted as "America's convenient winter playground." In 1936, after the city had gone eighteen months without a sunshineless day, he assembled a group of eighteen-month-old toddlers, snapped an unforgettable photograph, and added the caption, "Sunshine Babies—never have known a cloudy day."[6] The Sunshine Babies press release was an unqualified success, but Lodwick's stock-in-trade was the "Florida fantasy" bathing beauty photograph. As one observer put it, he gave readers of Northern newspapers the distinct impression "that the city was populated solely by beautiful women and their grandparents."[7] At one point, he even enlisted the talents of the famous fan-dancer Sally Rand. As a semi-nude Miss Rand shivered in the shallows of Spa Beach, Lodwick created a St. Petersburg version of the popular painting *September Morn*. The resulting press release scandalized local religious leaders and other guardians of public decency. But the national press accepted it eagerly.

Lodwick argued that St. Petersburg was the perfect place to wait out the Depression. Judging by the steady flow of tourists who made annual pilgrimages to the city during the mid- and late-1930s, a large number of people agreed with him. The city was approaching the height of its beauty in the 1930s; trees planted earlier in the century had finally reached maturity, providing the downtown area with a beautiful array of foliage; the green benches,

the red brick streets, and the architectural monuments of the boom were still in good repair; and the efforts of hundreds of WPA workers kept the city's parks and other public spaces clean and attractive.

For some, the mere thought of sitting in the sunshine beneath a swaying palm attracted them to the city. But visitors who wanted more than an aesthetic respite on a green bench could choose from an impressive variety of recreational activities. In addition to the Gulf beaches and other natural attractions, there were dances and radio shows at the Million Dollar Pier, big-name entertainers at La Plaza Theatre, strutting showgirls at Spanish Bob's nightclub on the roof of the Snell Arcade, dog races at the St. Petersburg Kennel Club, band concerts at Williams Park, and countless picnics and outings organized by the city's state tourist societies. Retirees had the Kids and Kubs softball league, which was organized by the Three-Quarter Century Club in 1930 and which quickly became a symbol of the city's energetic approach to retirement living. For sailing enthusiasts of all ages, there was the annual St. Petersburg-to-Havana race, which began in 1930 with five boats but which quickly developed into a major yachting event.

And for baseball fans there was the blissful ritual known as spring training. With ex-Mayor Al Lang leading the way as the city's unofficial ambassador of baseball, St. Petersburg solidified its status as the hub of Florida's "grapefruit league" during the immense popularity of the New York Yankees, who each spring drew thousands of additional tourists to the city. Perennial pennant contenders, the Bronx Bombers won four consecutive world championships between 1936 and 1939. Although Babe Ruth left the team after the 1934 season, colorful stars such as Joe DiMaggio, Lefty Gomez, Lou Gehrig, and Bill Dickey perpetuated the Yankee mystique. In 1937, St. Petersburg's other adopted team, the Boston Braves, left the city after a sixteen-year stay, but by the following spring they had been replaced by the St. Louis Cardinals. Although less successful than the Yankees, the Cardinals were a team with a mystique of its own. In 1934, player-manager Frankie Frisch and his

celebrated "Gas House Gang" had captured not only the world championship but also the hearts of millions of fans. Thus, from 1938 on, St. Petersburg showcased two of the most popular teams in baseball.

The whirl of tourist activity began every November and continued for six hectic months, coming to a crescendo in early spring with the annual Festival of States. During the lean years of the early 1930s, the festival was scaled down to fit the city's austere circumstances. But from 1935 on, the city's annual rite of spring became increasingly elaborate and successful. The 1938 Festival, perhaps the most memorable in the city's history, featured a Golden Jubilee marking the fiftieth anniversary of the city's founding. The organizers of the Jubilee entertained the city's visitors with a lavishly costumed Gay Nineties pageant and even reenacted the opening of the Orange Belt Railroad using a replica of a late-nineteenth-century wood-burning locomotive.

Ironically, this same year of elaborate celebration witnessed the temporary return of the desperate economic conditions of the worst Depression years. In St. Petersburg these conditions were the backdrop of the strike-breaking defeat of a carpenters' union which was protesting wage cuts imposed by George Deeb, one of the city's largest contractors. These workers were not the only ones left out economically. The ambience in St. Petersburg during the mid- and late-1930s was a curious mixture of decadence and despair, dominated by the stark contrast between men and women who divided their time between the golf course and the veranda and the destitute who had nothing to divide.

Although everyone acknowledged that tourist dollars were essential to the city's survival, the widening gap between privileged visitors and the less fortunate majority of the city's population must have added to the sting of hard times. The local business community did everything it could to keep this resentment in check. Politicians, editors, businessmen—everyone cooperated in the effort to sustain the escapist fantasies of the city's guests. Everything was done to protect the tourists from the problems of the real world. Since St. Petersburg billed itself as an alternative to the real world, the city's business leaders enthusiastically participated in a conspiracy of silence, banishing the word "depression" from the local lexicon.

But there was one man who took another tack, who gloried in the struggle against economic adversity and who turned that struggle into his own form of picaresque escapism. James Earl "Doc" Webb, marketing wizard of the first order, was a self-made man who turned his life into a rags-to-riches success story worthy of Horatio Alger. Born in Nashville, Tennessee, in 1899, Webb was forced to drop out of school at the age of nine after his father was seriously injured in a truck accident. Left to his own devices, he tried everything from pin-setting at a bowling alley to peddling milk and vegetables on the streets before finding his calling in the "medicine man" game. By the age of twenty, he had become "Doc" Webb—the slick-talking purveyor of patent medicines, magical herbs, and good cheer. As the manager and part-owner of Economy Drugs in Knoxville, he dispensed "Doc's 608," "Wahoo Indian Bitters," "Sorbo-Rub," and other miraculous remedies for constipation, venereal disease, and catarrh. Webb eventually became one of Knoxville's best-known pharmacists, but in 1925 a partnership offer from Hayworth Johnson, an old friend who had recently opened a small drugstore on the northern fringe of St. Petersburg's black ghetto, attracted him to Florida.

Webb was eager to make his mark on the Florida boom, but within a year of his arrival the boom collapsed. Undaunted, Webb bought out his discouraged partner and changed the store's name to Webb's Cut Rate Drug Company. As the self-styled king of cut-rate prices, Webb developed a faithful clientele during the late 1920s, and when the deflationary spiral of the Great Depression hit the city in 1930, he was ready to take advantage of the situation. By catering to the lower end of the mass market and by promising to undersell his competition

by at least 10 percent on every item, he established himself as the "little man's friend." At a time when most businesses were undergoing retrenchment, he expanded his operation to include the sale of everything from groceries to men's clothing. Offering dress shirts for sixty-eight cents, packs of cigarettes for five cents, and breakfasts for two cents, he kept his cash registers ringing even during the worst moments of the Depression. To the relief of the down and out, he accepted all manner of scrip and IOUs, and he rarely turned anyone away. "I didn't care a damn about money," he recalled many years later "I wanted customers."[8]

Low prices and easy credit were the roots of Webb's success. But his customers also loved him for his showmanship. Adapting medicine-show techniques to the retail trade, he surrounded his price-cutting antics with a nonstop carnival of entertainment and attractions. Vaudeville and circus acts, dancing chickens, talking mermaids, scantily clad bathing beauties known as "Poster Girls," oversized floats in the Festival of States parade—no advertising gimmick was too bizarre or too outrageous for Doc Webb, the master showman of volume sales. Despite countless giveaways and untold hours devoted to seemingly mindless promotional stunts, all the showmanship worked to Webb's economic advantage in the end. By the mid-1930s, he had turned a tiny drugstore, seventeen by twenty-eight feet, into "the World's Most Unusual Drug Store"—a complex of stores which sprawled over several city blocks. A forerunner of the post-World War II shopping center, Webb's City had everything: a floral shop, a bakery, a grocery store, a meat market, a beauty salon, a travel agency, a hardware store, a gift shop, clothing emporiums, several coffee shops and soda fountains, a cafeteria, and even a drugstore. As early as 1936, Webb's annual sales topped $1 million, and by 1941 he was bringing in almost $4 million a year.

All of this activity made Webb a wealthy man, as well as a celebrity. Nevertheless, he kept his distance from the local business establishment and remained a maverick whose passionate commitment to unrestricted competition set him apart from the rest of the business community. An inveterate opponent of economic cooperation or anything that hinted at price-fixing, Webb insisted on going his own way. In this spirit he challenged the corporate giant Bristol-Myers in 1938, refusing to sell Ipana toothpaste at the price suggested by the corporation. Bristol-Myers took him to court. The ensuing legal battle gave Webb months of free publicity and added to his populistic mystique. In the end, the state supreme court ruled in his favor, issuing a verdict that drew applause from Webb's customers but not from his competitors. Many local businessmen regarded him as a demagogic troublemaker, a commercial version of Huey Long or Franklin Roosevelt. Indeed, the consternation over Webb's refusal to play by the rules was probably heightened by the volatile political backdrop of the mid-1930s. Many of the same businessmen who criticized Doc Webb's maverick ways were equally critical of Franklin Roosevelt's New Deal.

Although Roosevelt received 57.3 percent of the vote in St. Petersburg in the 1936 election—6.3 percent more than he had received in 1932—in relative terms St. Petersburg remained a conservative Republican stronghold. No other city in Florida gave the Republican Alf Landon such a large vote, and many of the city's most influential citizens were bitterly opposed to Roosevelt and the New Deal. As the crisis mentality of the early 1930s subsided, traditional attitudes toward local autonomy and governmental involvement in the economy reemerged. Not surprisingly, the backlash was generally limited to middle- and upper-class whites who felt increasingly confident that they could maintain their economic and social status without the help of federal bureaucrats. In effect, the New Deal tended to polarize local politics along class lines. Among the disadvantaged and the dispossessed, Roosevelt was a full-fledged hero. Among Republicans and conservative Democrats, Roosevelt often was a convenient symbol of everything that they disliked about modern American society. Dependence on federal aid bred resentment, and anti-Roosevelt sentiment was fueled as much by the New Deal's successes as by its failures. Business and civic leaders who were accustomed to having things their own way and who were determined to control their own destiny resented the intrusion of federal power into local life. Although the impact of the New Deal on local institutions was often exaggerated for political purposes, the general sense, that the power and prerogatives of the local elite were beginning to erode was correct.

The local establishment felt especially vulnerable in the area of race relations. Even though New Deal officials made a concerted effort to soothe the fears of white supremacists, the mere presence of federal power was enough to raise the level of white anxiety. The suspicion that the New Deal was the entering wedge of a second Reconstruction was common all across the South, but in St. Petersburg opposition to desegregation was accentuated by the city's dependence on the tourist trade. When city leaders attempted to revive the Depression-ravaged tourist economy, they redoubled their efforts to provide tourists with a sanitized social environment. In racial terms, this translated into a renewed commitment to Jim Crow institutions. Although the black community was regarded as an invaluable source of menial labor, the concept of black participation in the mainstream of city life was anathema to local boosters. The black residents of St. Petersburg had their place, but that place was not on the green benches, or on the Million Dollar Pier, or in the parks along the waterfront.

Despite the local economy's dependence on black labor, the city's image-conscious leaders were determined to downplay the importance and the size of the local black community. In 1930, the same year that the federal census revealed that blacks accounted for 18 percent of the city's population, the official city directory claimed that St. Petersburg was only 9 percent black. Clearly, in a city that had harbored a substantial black population for decades, the 1930 census figures told city leaders what they already knew but were unwilling to admit. The task of reconciling the city's self-styled image with demographic reality became even more difficult during the 1930s, when the local black population increased at a faster rate than the white population. Between 1930 and 1940, St. Petersburg's black population rose from 7,416 to 11,982, a 61.6 percent increase. During this same period, the local white population increased by only 48 percent.

As the black community grew in size and visibility, a number of anxious white leaders called for a stricter and more formalized system of residential segregation. In terms of residential patterns, St. Petersburg was already one of the most segregated cities in the United States. But, according to the new municipal charter adopted in 1931, one of St. Petersburg's primary civic goals was "to establish and set apart in said city separate residential limits or districts for white and negro residents." The enforcement of residential segregation would no longer be entrusted to restrictive covenants or racial custom; instead, the city charter empowered city officials "to prohibit any white person from taking up or establishing a place of residence or business within the territorial limits of said city so set apart and established for the residence of negroes, and to prohibit any negro from taking up or establishing a place of residence or business within the territorial limits of said city so set apart and established for the residence of white persons."[9]

For a variety of reasons—black resistance, preoccupation with economic problems, the fear that the new city charter could not survive a constitutional challenge, and the logistical difficulties inherent in mass relocation—strict enforcement of this segregationist mandate proved to be impractical. But the proponents of the "city within a city" concept did not given up easily. Beginning in the mid-1930s, the city council sponsored an Inter-Racial Relations Committee which sought to improve local race relations by sharply reducing interaction between blacks and whites. Led by its outspoken chairman, City Councilman Milledge D. Wever, the committee developed a series of proposals aimed at bringing the city into compliance with the segregationist provisions of the 1931 charter. In May 1936, at Wever's request, the city council unanimously approved a resolution that required all blacks to live in an area seventeen blocks long west of Seventeenth Street and south of Sixth Avenue South. Implementation of the Wever resolution was stymied by insurmountable logistical problems—enforcement would have required the relocation of more than a thousand black families, and the designated area was much too small to accommodate the city's entire black population. But the mere fact that the city council had endorsed such an extreme measure served notice that the spirit of Jim Crow was still a dominant force in St. Petersburg. The expansion of the black community had provoked a new vigilance among white supremacists, temporarily silencing the moderate white voices that had given the black minority a measure of hope in earlier times.

During the mid- and late-1930s, white anxiety about the visibility of the black community seemed to center around the problems of keeping blacks away from the downtown waterfront. The South Mole at the foot of First Avenue South was the only place on the waterfront where blacks were traditionally allowed to swim, but even this one exception became increasingly unacceptable to many white residents. After the city charter of 1931 sanctioned a heightened awareness of racial geography, employment in the white community became the only acceptable reason for a black man or woman to leave the black section of the city. Thus, whenever groups of blacks walked through the downtown area to get to the South Mole, some whites considered their passing through a serious breach of racial etiquette. Their resentment resulted in several ugly incidents, which prompted the city council to search for a black swimming area that was compatible with white supremacist sensibilities.

From 1936 to 1939, the city council's Inter-Racial Relations Committee spent much of its time on the black beach issue, but none of the committee's proposed solutions came to fruition. In May 1936, for example, after

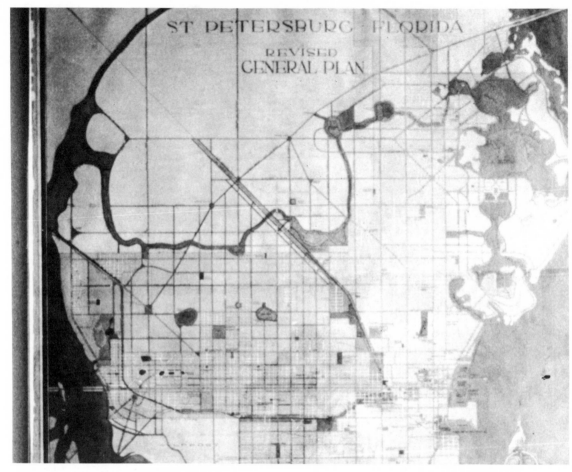

considering and rejecting several proposed areas—including the north end of Madeira Beach, the east end of Corey Causeway, the southwest corner of Lake Maggiore, and an isolated section on the northwest shore of Papy's Bayou—the city council purchased a small stretch of beach in Pasadena. However, the resulting uproar among the all-white residents of Pasadena and nearby Gulfport forced the council to cancel the plan. City officials later worked out a plan to turn part of Booker Creek into a black swimming hole, but black leaders rejected the idea, insisting that the black community needed access to a saltwater beach. The refusal to settle for a freshwater swimming hole angered and confused city officials. Such assertiveness would have been unimaginable in the 1910s or the 1920s, and

many whites attributed this unwelcome change to the intrusions of the New Deal.

Although, at this point, the black community was incapable of mounting a full-fledged civil rights struggle, the traditional patterns of black passivity and resignation were definitely declining. Led by the local chapter of the National Association for the Advancement of Colored People, the black community exhibited a new determination to defend itself against the worst excesses of racial discrimination. To some extent, the new militance was grounded in subtle changes at the grass-roots level. But it also reflected the emergence of the local black middle class. Despite its limitations, the black middle class had produced a sophisticated group of community leaders. Middle-class blacks did not always understand or empathize with the problems of their working-class neighbors. And some middle-class black power brokers clearly served their own interests at the expense of the black community. But the best of the city's black leaders were courageous reformers who worked for change while helping their constituents to make the best of a bad situation. On balance, the presence of middle-class black leaders made it much more difficult for whites to ignore the needs and aspirations of the black community. At the very least, white leaders could no longer pretend that the black community was an undifferentiated mass of illiterate domestics and day laborers.

Unfortunately, and somewhat ironically, the emergence of the black middle class was counterbalanced by a decline in black political power. During the 1930s, black political activity in St. Petersburg was circumscribed by a "white primary" clause in the new city charter. Although a significant number of black voters continued to participate in general elections, the specter of total disfranchisement haunted the black community throughout the decade. As a general rule, city officials were willing to tolerate a limited amount of black suffrage, although some white leaders periodically expressed concern that even a small black vote had the potential to become the balance of power in local politics. This concern surfaced in July 1937, when black participation in a civil service law referendum triggered a storm of protest in the white community.

The referendum and the accompanying controversy over black voting grew out of a bitter struggle between the local civil service board and chief of police Raymond Noel. To the dismay of the civil service board, the city charter of 1931 gave Chief Noel the authority to run the police department almost independently. According to the board, Noel was a power-hungry official who abused his authority. But such criticism only increased Noel's determination to remain independent from the board. For a time, Chief Noel and A.C. McEachern, the chairman of the civil service board, simply traded threats and insults. But after Noel demoted Detective John Siers, one of McEachern's staunchest allies, to dog catcher, the feud turned into a political donnybrook.

During the fall of 1936, the civil service board formed a special committee to investigate allegations that cronyism and corruption were widespread in the police department. Some of these allegations concerned minor personnel infractions, but the most serious charges alleged collusion with criminal elements in the black community. According to Chairman McEachern, Chief Noel had allowed "bolita rackets, bootleg joints, and disreputable houses" to operate in the black community with impunity; he had reclassified dangerous convicts as trustees, providing them with unreserved furlough privileges; and on one occasion he had even refused to arrest a black murderer, forcing the city council to turn to the county sheriff for help.[10] Although the case against Noel was hampered by a lack of solid evidence, the investigating committee's deliberations eventually led to a referendum which gave the electorate the opportunity to repeal the city's civil service law—a repeal that, in effect, would remove Noel from office.

Noel fought back, but the beleaguered chief found few supporters outside the police department. In the weeks leading up to the referendum, the entire political establishment lined up against him—a situation that ultimately forced him to turn in desperation to the black electorate. Since openly courting the black vote would have been tantamount to political suicide, Noel made every effort to camouflage his political alliance with the black community. But this discretion did not stop the opposition from mounting one of the most virulent race-baiting campaigns in the city's history. Noel's alleged violation of racial solidarity provoked a passionate response from white supremacists, and on the eve of the referendum more then two hundred robed and hooded Ku Klux Klansmen descended upon the black community. The Klan had not marched in St. Petersburg for more than ten years, but the July 1937 march attracted Klan delegations from as far away as Lakeland and Sarasota. During the hour-long, torch-lit procession, the Klansmen warned black onlookers to stay away from the polls. "Our organization is for Americanism," one Klan leader bellowed, "and using the negro vote for personal gain has no part in our conception of Americanism."[11] Although no blacks were harmed during the march, this unprecedented show of force carried a clear message of intimidation and potential violence.

An angry Chief Noel encouraged the black community to ignore the Klan's threats and promised police protection, but most observers predicted that the great majority of registered black voters would stay home on election day. They were wrong. The combination of police power and the black community's determination to exercise the right to vote resulted in a relatively high black turnout. The size of the black vote surprised almost everyone, including the *St. Petersburg Times* reporter who covered the election. "In open defiance of the Knights of the Ku Klux Klan," the reporter marveled, "St. Petersburg negro voters flocked to the polls today. . . . They went in taxicabs, afoot, and reportedly in police cruisers to pile up what will probably be the heaviest negro vote in the history of the city, thereby openly defying the 200 Klansmen who staged an eerie march through the black belt last night as a warning against negroes seeking political power."[12] Although Chief Noel and his black supporters ended up on the losing side—the civil service law was repealed by a vote of 4,016 to 1,312—the black electorate's willingness to stand up to the Klan would be a source of

community pride for years to come.

However, the black community paid a heavy price for its alliance with Chief Noel. In October 1937, the new city manager removed Noel from office, replacing him with E. D. "Doc" Vaughn. An experienced policeman who had already served a term as policy chief during the 1920s. Vaughn was known as an uncompromising advocate of white supremacy. Under his leadership, the police department's activities in the black community became increasingly brutal and repressive. On October 16, less than three weeks after Chief Vaughn assumed his new duties, a shootout between police and a young black laborer, J. C. "Honeybaby" Moses, left two policemen dead. Although Moses was later cornered and shot to death by police, a vengeance-seeking white mob threatened to turn the affair into a full-scale race riot. In the end, Chief Vaughn prevented the mob from mutilating Moses' body, but his willingness to put the body on public display angered many local blacks.

The Moses case was only the first in a series of incidents that poisoned the relationship between Chief Vaughn's police department and the black community. Working-class blacks bore the brunt of the police department's heavy-handed approach to law and order, as periodic "vagrancy sweeps" and "crackdowns" were carried out with ruthless efficiency. But on occasion even middle-class blacks felt the sting of white supremacist law enforcement. For example, in June 1938, a squad of club-swinging police broke up a black teachers' picnic in the Shore Acres section of northeastern St. Petersburg. Unaware that the city manager had given the teachers verbal permission to hold the picnic, the police upbraided the picnickers for invading a white neighborhood and ordered them to leave. During the ensuing melee, Noah W. Griffin, the principal of Gibbs High School and the president of the local chapter of the NAACP, was knocked to the ground, and several other black teachers were roughed up. Many blacks, and even some whites, were outraged by the police overreaction, and in the aftermath of the affair YMCA secretary W. G. Coxhead and several other members of the Inter-Racial Relations Committee urged City Manager Leland to see to it that the police protected the rights of black citizens. The teachers also received strong support from the city's all-white Ministerial Association. In addition to condemning the "roughness of police officials," the ministers filed "an urgent request that the city council take immediate steps to provide some beach or bathing pool facilities for 11,000 negro citizens for whose legitimate rights our city has too long neglected to provide."[13]

The reaction of white moderates to the Shore Acres incident was an encouraging development, but no one in the black community had any illusion that fundamental change was in the offing. For every white moderate who was open to change, there were probably a dozen or more white supremacists determined to keep the black man in his place. At this point, the black community itself exhibited limited capacity for civil rights agitation. Despite the presence of the NAACP and a few black militants, economic vulnerability and the legitimate fear of white retaliation continued to encourage black passivity and resignation. Whatever their true feelings, most black leaders remained extremely reluctant to speak our against racial injustice.

One of the few exceptions was the Reverend John Wesley Carter, the charismatic pastor of the Bethel Metropolitan Baptist Church. A light-skinned mulatto who had moved to the city from St. Augustine in the early 1930s, Carter never missed an opportunity to remind his parishioners of the moral bankruptcy of racial discrimination. On a few occasions he even managed to deliver this message to the white community. In November 1939, Carter went before the city council to ask for a "new deal" for black St. Petersburg. Although he avoided a direct challenge to the sanctity of Jim Crow, he implored the councilmen to treat their black constituents with respect and humane consideration. Under his proposed new deal, city leaders would provide the black community with such needs as decent housing, paved streets, the right to vote, expanded park and recreation facilities, additional rooms and beds at Mercy Hospital,

public restroom facilities, and efficient police protection. Carter also urged the council to hire black policemen, to allow law-abiding black citizens to use the Million Dollar Pier, and to enforce the city charter's exclusion of white residents and businessmen from black neighborhoods.[14] As the last request demonstrates, Carter's primary goal was equal treatment, not desegregation. But this should not obscure the militance of his stance. In the context of the pre-World War II South, he had gone about as far as a black leader could go.

To its credit, the city council gave Carter a polite hearing, and Mayor Ian Boyer even formed a subcommittee of councilmen to study the minister's proposal. But civility did not mean acquiescence. In the absence of significant black political and economic power, Carter's eloquence counted for very little. Despite a growing awareness of black dissatisfaction with the status quo, it would be many years before black St. Petersburg received anything approaching a "new deal."

The emergence of a small cadre of civil rights activists and the ability of black political leaders to fend off disfranchisement were hopeful signs which provided the black community with a psychological lift. But the activities of political and religious leaders did little to ameliorate the underclass status that characterized the lives of most St. Petersburg blacks. During the Great Depression, even more than in earlier decades, the dominant reality in the black community was grinding poverty. As the unemployment rate soared and as financial resources were stretched to the breaking point, squalid living conditions became the norm. Overcrowding and substandard housing were increasingly serious problems, and the physical contrast between black and white neighborhoods was more striking than ever. In a city known for stylish homes and beautiful subdivisions, the unpaved streets and unpainted shacks of Methodist Town and other black neighborhoods were inescapable reminders of racial separation and inequality.

Most black families rented their homes from absentee white landlords, many of whom treated both property and tenants with malign neglect. In the words of Karl Grismer, "a large percentage of the houses were nothing but tumble-down shacks, hardly fit for cattle to live in."[15] As late as 1940, 59.2 percent of the city's black households had no electricity (the comparable figure for white households was 2 percent), and 17.6 percent had no running water (the figure for white households was less than .5 percent). Only 18.5 percent of the city's black families owned their own homes. Most of the homes owned by blacks were modest dwellings located on small lots. In 1940, the average black-owned home was worth less than two thousand dollars and only 4 of the city's 591 black-owned homes were valued at more than ten thousand dollars. As a WPA investigator described the scene in 1939, there were "a few substantial brick and frame residences" scattered among "the clutter of dilapidated shacks."[16]

Local reformers, both black and white, complained about these slumlike conditions throughout the 1920s and 1930s. But the first serious effort to alleviate the black community's housing problems did not come until after the passage of the Wagner-Steagall Housing Act in August 1937. Spearheaded by Senator Robert F. Wagner, one of the nation's leading advocates of slum clearance and urban renewal, the act created the United States Housing Authority (USHA), which was empowered to spend $500 million on the construction of public housing projects. Between 1938 and 1941, approximately 350 such projects were completed, including the highly successful Jordan Park project in St. Petersburg.

Soon after the passage of the Wagner-Steagall Housing Act, local urban renewal advocates began agitating for a USHA appropriation, prompting Mayor Vernon Agee to create a five-member St. Petersburg Housing Authority. Led by local attorney Walter Ramseur, the new city housing authority convinced federal officials that the local black community was in dire need of urban renewal, and in early December 1937 St. Petersburg became one of the first cities in the nation to be offered public housing funds. At first, several members of the city council, including Mayor Agee, were reluctant to accept the USHA's

offer, ostensibly because USHA regulations required the city to contribute 10 percent of the money needed to finance the project. But widespread support for public housing among local business and civic leaders—including the president of the Chamber of Commerce and the head of the downtown Merchants' Association—soon forced the city council to approve the project. Despite vocal opposition from white slumlords and Negrophobic conservatives, the city council and the USHA eventually agreed upon a plan that would eliminate one unit of slum property for each new unit of public housing. Thus, in August 1938, the USHA transferred nearly a million dollars in funds to the city's housing authority, which purchased a site of twenty-six acres on the outskirts of the black community. Construction of the Jordan Park project began in April 1939, and took nearly a year to complete. In April 1940 the first tenants moved in, and despite some initial confusion over eligibility requirements, all 242 units were soon occupied.

Pleased with its success, the St. Petersburg Housing Authority approached the city council in the summer of 1940 with a plan to add a second phase to the Jordan Park development. But the housing authority's negotiations with the city council immediately became entangled in a bitter controversy over utility rates. By July the squabble had evolved into a full-scale crisis, with the city council issuing a series of rulings that made it all but impossible to proceed with the proposed second phase. Local slumlords and other opponents of public housing were jubilant, but the city council's apparent obstructionism ultimately triggered a citywide protest led by the League of Women Voters. Drawing support from a wide variety of civic organizations—including the Chamber of Commerce, the Merchants' Association, the Board of Realtors, and the Urban League—the League of Women Voters mounted a petition campaign calling for a referendum on the public housing question. After being presented with more than four thousand signatures, an embarrassed city council agreed to submit the question to the electorate in a September 24 referendum. During the month preceding the refer-

The intersection of Fifth Street and Second Avenue South as it looked in 1927. The Florida Power building (left), completed in 1926, and the YMCA building (lower right), completed in 1927, were recent additions to the area. Courtesy St. Petersburg Times

The height of Mediterranean Revival splendor—the Snell Isle residence (375 Brightwaters Boulevard) of real estate developer Perry Snell, circa 1931. The third floor housed Snell's private art collection. Courtesy St. Petersburg Historical Society

The eastern facade of the Don CeSar Hotel, circa 1929. Courtesy Special Collections, University of South Florida Library, Tampa

endum, supporters and opponents of public housing traded arguments and insults at a series of public meetings. Although proponents of public housing had the solid backing of the local press, the opposition countered with a spirited grass-roots campaign that attacked public housing as a socialistic challenge to free enterprise and a threat to white supremacy. This attempt to manipulate antiradical and Negrophobic sentiment was not without success, but on election day the supporters of Jordan Park expansion carried the referendum by a surprisingly comfortable margin, 2,731 to 2,081. The housing authority was then able to continue with its plans, and the construction of Jordan Park's 204-unit second phase was completed in the fall of 1941.

The opening of Jordan Park was an important event in the history of St. Petersburg. But for blacks and whites who aspired to live in a racially equalitarian community, it was, at best, a bittersweet victory. The construction of an all-black public housing project posed no challenge to segregation; indeed, it probably enhanced the notion that "separate but equal" was an achievable and acceptable goal. And yet, within the confines of a fundamentally

inhumane caste system, decent housing did bring an added measure of human dignity and material improvement to men and women who had been systematically deprived of both. Revealing both the potential and the limitations of the city, the resolution of the Jordan Park controversy was symbolic of St. Petersburg's overall experience during the 1930s. In depression-era St. Petersburg, progress was difficult—but not impossible—to achieve, and the balance sheet at the end of the decade showed mixed results. Despite the efforts of the New Deal and the revival of the tourist trade, economic inequality and racial injustice continued to cast a dark shadow over the Sunshine City. On the other hand, the city and its people had weathered the worst social and economic crisis in American history. Almost incredibly, according to the 1940 federal census, the city's population had risen to 60,812—a 50 percent increase since 1930. Growth did not necessarily mean improvement, but the city had clearly entered a new stage of maturity. Like a ship that had sailed through a major storm, St. Petersburg had arrived at mid-passage with a hard-earned sense of its strengths and weaknesses.

A postcard view of the Snell Arcade Building, 1929. Built on the site of the old Durant Block, this architectural monument was designed by Richard Kiehnel of Miami. The pride and joy of developer Perry Snell, the opulent Snell Arcade featured European mosaics and statuary and a roof garden nightclub. Courtesy St. Petersburg Historical Society

The Snell Arcade's ground floor featured a lavishly appointed hallway leading to the open-air post office. Courtesy St. Petersburg Historical Society

Dancers perform at Spanish Bob's nightclub, on the roof of the Snell Arcade building, circa 1930. Courtesy St. Petersburg Historical Society

Resembling an Egyptian temple, the entrance to the Municipal Solarium stood on the Million Dollar Pier from 1930 to 1961. Radio personality Lowell Thomas served as master of ceremonies when the solarium was dedicated in 1930. Courtesy St. Petersburg City News Bureau

The interior of the solarium at the municipal spa on the Million Dollar Pier, 1933. Courtesy St. Petersburg Historical Society

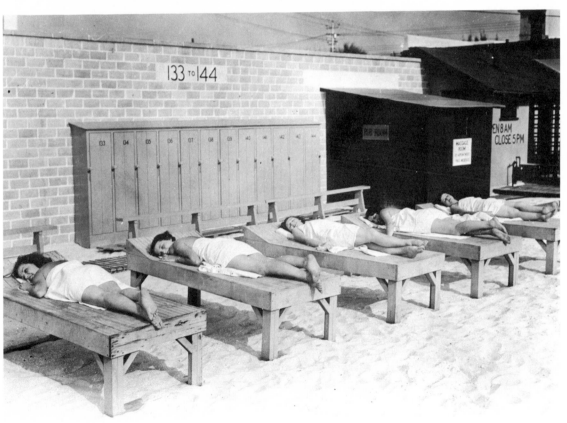

In 1930, the St. Petersburg Solaria, near the corner of Beach Drive and Fourth Avenue North, provided "sun and air baths with perfect privacy." The individual tanning units revolved on a circular track, and the openings on the top and sides were adjustable. Patrons were charged one dollar an hour. Photograph by Ray Robie, courtesy Florida State Archives

The interior of a solarium unit, 1930. Photograph by Ray Robie, courtesy Florida State Archives

Shades of Isadora Duncan—a classic Florida seaside publicity shot, circa 1930. Photograph by Ray Kendall Williams, courtesy St. Petersburg Times

Playing cards in Williams Park, circa 1931. Courtesy St. Petersburg Historical Society

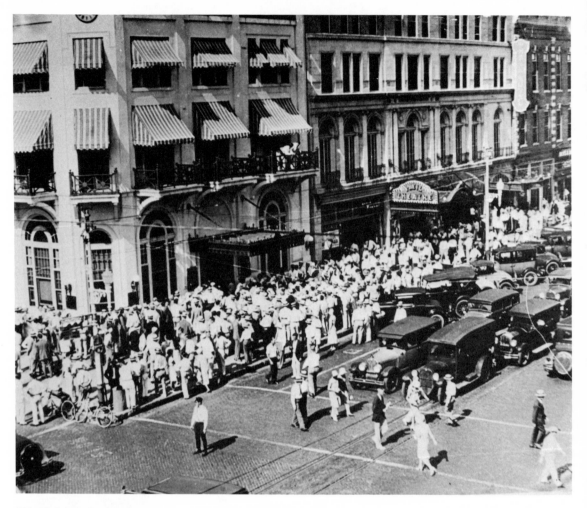

*Worried depositors make a run
on the financially troubled
Central National Bank in 1931.
After two such runs, the bank
went under on April 12, 1931.
Courtesy* St. Petersburg Times

WARNING
DO NOT
COME HERE
SEEKING
WORK

"A City's First Duty is to
Employ its own Citizens."
OFFICIAL NOTICE
HOME PATRONAGE COMMITTEE
ST. PETERSBURG, FLA.

During the Great Depression of the 1930s, St. Petersburg and other Florida cities attracted large numbers of unemployed men and women searching for work. More often than not, they received a rude welcome; signs like the one above could be seen throughout the city in 1932. Courtesy St. Petersburg Times

An aerial view of Bay Pines Veterans' Administration Center and Hospital, 1933. Construction of the Bay Pines complex began in 1932. Courtesy St. Petersburg Historical Society

Coast Guard vessels moored alongside the Million Dollar Pier, circa 1933. The Coast Guard base at Bayboro Harbor opened in 1927. Courtesy St. Petersburg Historical Society

Albert Whitted Airport, 1933. The building at the upper right is the Goodyear blimp hangar, built in 1929. Bayboro Harbor can be seen in the background. In October 1934, Whitted Airport became the headquarters for G. T. "Ted" Baker's National Airlines. Courtesy St. Petersburg City News Bureau

A Goodyear blimp easing into the blimp hangar at Albert Whitted Airport, circa 1930. Goodyear blimps were stationed at the airport from 1930 to 1939. Courtesy St. Petersburg City News Bureau

The St. Petersburg Police Department, 1933. Chief Raymond Noel, who later became embroiled in a bitter power struggle with the city's civil service board, is the fourth man from the left in the front row. Photograph by Samuel H. Beck, courtesy St. Petersburg Historical Society

Geriatric pugilism under the sun—the Health City image was alive and well during the 1930s. Courtesy St. Petersburg Historical Society

Founded in 1924, St. Petersburg's Three-Quarter Century Club developed into one of the city's most celebrated institutions. The photograph above was taken in March 1936, as the club embarked on a boat trip to Bradenton. The men dressed in white are members of the Kids and Kubs, a softball league organized by the Three-Quarter Century Club in 1930. Photograph by Clyde Fairfield, courtesy St. Petersburg Historical Society

Spring training, 1934. Local baseball booster Dick Mayes of Brooksville is flanked by Yankee greats Lou Gehrig (left) and Babe Ruth (right). 1934 was Ruth's last season with the Yankees, although he returned to St. Petersburg in the spring of 1935 as a member of the Boston Braves. Courtesy St. Petersburg Historical Society

"Specs" Lohr (far left) was one of St. Petersburg's best-known fishing guides during the 1930s. Courtesy St. Petersburg Historical Society

Spectators on the Million Dollar Pier view the start of the annual sailing race from St. Petersburg to Havana, circa 1934. The St. Petersburg-to-Havana race was first held in 1930. Courtesy St. Petersburg Historical Society

The massive 2,300-seat Florida Theatre, located at the corner of Central Avenue and Fifth Street South, opened in 1926. This photograph was taken in 1936. The theater was demolished in the late 1960s. Courtesy St. Petersburg Historical Society

Williams Park, 1936. Courtesy St. Petersburg Times

A "tropical paradise" publicity shot taken at Spa Beach, circa 1936. Photograph by Ray Kendall Williams, courtesy St. Petersburg Times

During the mid-1930s, even schoolchildren were enlisted in the effort to boost the winter tourist trade. This photograph was taken during a Festival of States parade. Courtesy St. Petersburg Historical Society

During the late 1930s and early 1940s, advertising displays similar to the one shown here appeared in travel agency windows all over the eastern half of the United States. This photograph was taken in Atlanta, circa 1938. Courtesy St. Petersburg Historical Society

George Deeb, owner of the Deeb Construction Company, passing out checks to nonunion carpenters in defiance of the local carpenters' union, 1938. Courtesy St. Petersburg Times

Railway workers and onlookers pose in front of a late nine-teenth-century wood-burning locomotive in March 1938. The city of St. Petersburg celebrated its fiftieth anniversary in 1938 by reenacting the June 1888 arrival of the first Orange Belt train. Courtesy St. Petersburg Times

The Reverend John Wesley Carter, circa 1935. Courtesy of Valkyrie Press

Transportation, old and new. When the Seaboard Air Line's Silver Meteor rolled into St. Petersburg for the first time in 1939, railroad officials asked Elijah Moore, a local peddler who sold produce from an oxcart, to pose next to the train. Born in South Carolina in 1880, Moore— who earned the nickname "I got 'em"—was also a well-known lay minister. He lived in St. Peters-burg from 1912 to 1972. Courtesy St. Petersburg Times

The United States Coast Guard
Station at Bayboro Harbor,
1938. Courtesy St. Petersburg
Historical Society

The new St. Petersburg City
Hall, on the southeast corner of
Fifth Street and Second Avenue
North, shortly after its comple-
tion in late 1939. This long-
awaited building was constructed
with federal funds. Courtesy
St. Petersburg Times

Mayor R. J. McCutcheon and eleven former mayors posed for this picture at the Suwannee Hotel in December 1941. Back row (left to right): Robert Blanc, John N. Brown, Arthur Thompson, Henry Adams, C. M. Blanc, J. D. Pearce, Ian Boyer. Front row (left to right): Isham Byrom, John S. Smith, R. J. McCutcheon, Al Lang, and Vernon Agee. Courtesy St. Petersburg Times

An aerial view of the Jordan Park public housing project while it was under construction in early 1940. Designed to replace slum dwellings that were prevalent in the black community, the project was financed by the United States Housing Authority. Construction of Phase One (242 units) was completed in April 1940. In 1941, 204 additional units were built. *Courtesy* St. Petersburg Times

The St. Petersburg Evening Independent *and* St. Petersburg Times *buildings at Fourth Street and First Avenue South, circa 1940. Courtesy* St. Petersburg Times

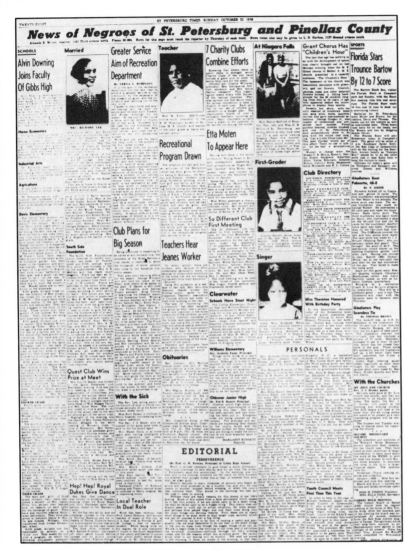

After the death of William L. Straub in 1939, St. Petersburg Times *editor and publisher Nelson Poynter became the city's most influential journalist. This photograph of Poynter was taken during the 1940s. Courtesy Nelson Poynter Collection, Nelson Poynter Library, University of South Florida at St. Petersburg*

The first issue of the St. Petersburg Times *"Negro News Page" appeared on October 22, 1939. The page carried articles about black church and school activities, sporting and social events, births, deaths, weddings, and other personal news. It was written exclusively by black reporters working out of their homes, and was only inserted in papers distributed in black neighborhoods. The "Negro News Page" went from a weekly to a daily in October 1948. It was discontinued in 1967. Courtesy* St. Petersburg Times

Members of the Modernistics, circa 1938. The Modernistics belonged to the City Federation of Colored Women's Clubs. Courtesy of Shirlye Whiting

*La Plaza Theatre, circa 1940.
Courtesy* St. Petersburg Times

*The Million Dollar Pier, circa
1940. Courtesy St. Petersburg
Historical Society*

*The McCray Foundational
School, circa 1936. The school
was located at Twelfth Street
South between Fifth and Dixie
Avenues and was operated by
Rev. Grant H. McCray, Sr., and
his wife Arline. Opened in 1927,
the school provided day care for
children of working black parents.
During the Great Depression, a
community kitchen at the Foundational School provided food for
struggling black families. Courtesy of Arline McCray*

Chapter Eight

War and Peace

1941-1950

A silhouette view of the Million Dollar Pier and the Central Yacht Basin at sunrise, 1945. Courtesy St. Petersburg Times

In the opinion of many observers, including a Federal Writers' Project investigator who visited the city in 1939, one of St. Petersburg's greatest strengths was its cosmopolitanism. St. Petersburg's cultural outlets," the investigator concluded, "offer a cosmopolitan blend found only in a city of diverse population."[1] As a regional melting pot and as the winter home of numerous writers, artists, and other intellectuals, St. Petersburg was one Southern city that knew something about the wider world. Perhaps so, but the citizens of the Sunshine City would learn a great deal more about the world in the years to come. The Second World War opened the city to new possibilities and new experiences, both pleasant and unpleasant. In varying degrees this was true of almost all American cities, but few cities felt the winds of war as early as St. Petersburg, and even fewer underwent such a thoroughgoing militarization during the war.

In the fall of 1939, more than two years before the United States declared war on the Axis powers, the United States Coast Guard Air Station at Bayboro Harbor—a facility built by the WPA in 1935 as an extension of Albert Whitted Airport—was conducting anti-submarine air patrols over the Gulf of Mexico. The Coast Guard's nightly patrols were prompted by an October 1939 Presidential proclamation prohibiting the submarines of belligerent nations from entering American ports or cruising in offshore areas, and by the growing number of German U-boats preying upon British merchant ships in the Gulf. In 1940, the Bayboro anti-submarine squadron included only five planes, but the number eventually grew to nineteen.

The Coast Guard also reopened its Bayboro Harbor naval base in late 1939. Originally commissioned as an anti-bootlegging operation, the Bayboro base had been abandoned since 1933. Recommissioned as a training facility when the Coast Guard was given the responsibility of training merchant seamen, the base by early 1940 was home to 250 recruits and two training ships, the *Joseph Conrad* and the *American Seaman*. During the next two years a steady flow of trainees passed through the base, and sailors became a familiar

sight on the city's streets, particularly after the passage of the Lend-Lease Act in March 1941. As the demand for merchant seamen increased, the Coast Guard expanded the base, using dredging and landfill to reshape the shores of Bayboro Harbor.

The Coast Guard's growing presence at Bayboro Harbor brought the war in Europe closer to home. But neither the war nor the presence of the Coast Guard had much effect on the overall mood of the city in 1940 and 1941. Even after the military draft of October 1940, which saw the registration of nearly ten thousand local men, the public seemed more concerned with the ups and downs of the tourist trade than with military preparedness or the Battle of Britain. In May of 1941, local officials tried to organize a Home Defense Unit, modeled after the Home Guard of Great Britain, but the number of volunteers was much smaller than expected. Most people, it seemed, were too busy or too apathetic to commit themselves to civil defense work, though some observers charitably attributed the poor response to the local citizenry's temporary preoccupation with local politics. In early July, after several weeks of public debate, the voters approved a new city charter which, among other things, restored the electorate's right to choose the city's mayor; under the 1931 charter the mayor had been chosen by the City Council. The summer of 1941 also witnessed a bitter controversy over a proposed "blue law" liquor ordinance. The voters endorsed the ordinance in a July referendum, but local liquor dealers later challenged the new law in court. On December 12, the circuit court ruled in favor of the city council, but by that time public attention had shifted to more serious concerns. Earlier in the week the Japanese attack on Pearl Harbor had shattered the illusion that the United States could keep its distance from a world at war. The events of December 7 catapulted the city and the nation into a new era, and nothing would ever be quite the same again.

The winter of 1941-42 was a difficult time in the United States. The aftershocks of Pearl Harbor, the subsequent fall of Manila, the expectation of the a full-scale Japanese invasion of the American mainland (in the immediate aftermath of Pearl Harbor, St. Petersburg's only two Japanese-owned businesses, the Nikko Inn and the Sone Gift Shop were closed down by federal authorities; the owners were later arrested by the FBI and placed in an internment camp for the duration of the war), and continuing German advances in Europe and North Africa produced fear and apprehension in a nation militarily unprepared for war. But fortunately for the Allied cause, this acute sense of crisis also produced a common resolve to fight back. By the beginning of 1942, military mobilization had become an all-encompassing national crusade, temporarily suspending the domestic debate over the proper scope and authority of the New Deal. In one way or another, nearly everyone was called upon to make personal sacrifices and adjustments to wartime conditions. Soldiers and sailors risked their lives on the battlefield, while on the homefront civilians put up with rationing, travel restrictions, blackouts, loneliness, and generally disrupted lives.

Most Americans shouldered the burdens of war with grace and good humor, an attitude borne not only of patriotism and concern for friends and relatives serving in the military, but also of economic optimism. For many Americans the war meant economic recovery. In less than a year, World War II accomplished what eight years of the New Deal had failed to accomplish—a sharp decline in unemployment and an end to the economic depression that had crippled the nation since 1929. This was certainly the case in St. Petersburg. At the beginning of the war the chances for such a recovery looked slim; indeed, for a time it appeared that the war would spell economic disaster for resort communities like St. Petersburg. During the early months of 1942, the city's economic prospects looked grimmer than ever, as tire and gas rationing, wartime travel restrictions, and the general social dislocation of military activity crippled the tourist trade. In a few short weeks, the economic gains of the late 1930s had been wiped out, or so it seemed. While other American cities were mobilizing for wartime production, nonindustrial St. Petersburg was languishing in the sunshine.

By February 1942, many of the city's hotels and boarding houses were almost empty. But ironically these empty hotel rooms would soon prove to be the city's salvation. St. Petersburg had no factories that could be adapted to the production of war materials, but it did have an abundance of buildings, both large and small, that could be converted to barracks. To solve its economic problems, the city needed only "to convince the government that its housing accommodations were an asset worth considering; that if servicemen were brought to the city for training, St. Petersburg could and would provide places for them to stay."[2] This proved to be no easy task, but after several weeks of aggressive lobbying by local officials the War Department selected St. Petersburg as a major technical services training center for the Army Air Corps.

Air Corps trainees began arriving in St. Petersburg in June 1942, and by mid-summer there were more than ten thousand soldiers in the city. Using the Vinoy Park Hotel as its local headquarters (the headquarters was later moved to a downtown office building), the Air Corps leased every major hotel in the city, except the Suwannee, and dozens of smaller hotels as well. Even so, the city's hotels could not always accommodate the massive influx of trainees (most trainees spent four to six weeks in the city), and at several points soldiers were forced to pitch their tents in the city parks or on hotel grounds. Indeed, at the height of the influx, in late 1942 and early 1943, approximately ten thousand soldiers were camped at the Piper-Fuller Airport and the adjoining Jungle Club golf course. Everywhere one looked there were khaki-clad recruits and Army jeeps. Training classes were held all across the city, often in the open air, and downtown streets were frequently jammed with marching platoons and armored convoys. By the time the training center was discontinued in July 1943, more the one hundred thousand trainees and instructors had passed through the city.

Fortunately for the local economy, the departure of the Army Air Corps trainees was counterbalanced by the continuing growth of the maritime training facility at Bayboro

Harbor. During the summer of 1942, the responsibility for training merchant seamen was transferred from the Coast Guard to the United States Maritime Service, which promptly expanded the Bayboro base. After the completion of new barracks and classroom buildings in January 1943, the number of trainees at the base increased dramatically. Eventually, the number became so large that the Maritime Service was forced to lease four of the large downtown hotels previously occupied by the Army Air Corps. By the end of the war, the instructors at Bayboro had trained more than twenty-five thousand merchant seamen. From August 1943 on, the Bayboro base also housed the Army Transport Corps Marine Officers Cadet School, a training center for junior deck and engineering officers.

The local military presence also included a United States Navy anti-submarine base on the south side of Bayboro Harbor, commissioned in October 1942; a coastal artillery battery at Pass-a-Grille; ;and from October 1943 on a convalescent hospital in the Don CeSar Hotel. Most importantly, throughout the war years the Tampa Bay region was one of the busiest pilot training areas in the eastern United States. With its warm climate and flat landscape, west central Florida presented an almost ideal location for flight training, and the Army Air Corps sent wave after wave of young pilots to train in the area. On the Pinellas side of the bay, there was a small training facility at Albert Whitted Airport and a much larger facility at the Pinellas Army Air Base, a converted county airport located on the western shore of Old Tampa Bay, nine miles north of St. Petersburg. Begun as a WPA project in

An aerial view of downtown St. Petersburg, 1941. Courtesy St. Petersburg Times

April 1941, the county airport was still under construction in 1942 when the Army Air Corps decided to use it as a training center for fighter pilots. The Air Corps lengthened the runways, installed a large control tower, and eventually constructed living quarters for fifteen hundred trainees. The first group of pilots arrived in August 1942, and for the remainder of the war the skies over Pinellas County were dotted with training planes.

The pilots at the Pinellas Army Air Base shared the local skies with hundreds of bombers and reconnaissance pilots stationed at training centers in Hillsborough County. In addition to the large bomber base at Tampa's MacDill Field, there were small bomber and reconnaissance training centers at Drew (the present site of Tampa International Airport) and Henderson Fields. Since Mullet Key, at the southern tip of Pinellas County, was the Air Corps's main gunnery and bombing practice area, the drone of B-17 and B-26 bombers (or the smaller UC-78 trainers, commonly known as "bamboo bombers") could be heard in St. Petersburg throughout the war.[3]

Fortunately for local merchants, the large military presence in Hillsborough County provided St. Petersburg with more than the sound of bombers. Drawn by the natural attractions of the lower Pinellas area—especially Spa Beach and St. Petersburg Beach—thousands of soldiers and sailors stationed on the Hillsborough side of the bay visited the city on weekends passes and furloughs. The roads and bridges between Hillsborough and Pinellas were jammed with vehicles, particularly after the tolls on the Gandy Bridge and the Davis Causeway (later renamed the Courtney Campbell Causeway) were eliminated (thanks to Senator Claude Pepper's influence) in the spring of 1944.

The net result was a sea of "khaki and olive drab," though not everyone who came to St. Petersburg during the war was in uniform.[4] The city also welcomed a large number of military wives. Most came to be near husbands who were assigned to training units in the area, but many remained in the city even after their husbands were shipped overseas. The presence of these women, plus that of the hundreds of other newcomers who decided to wait out the war in the sunshine, helped to swell the city's population to unprecedented levels, creating a severe housing shortage by the end of the war. During the last three years of the war, the total number of people in the city at any given time probably exceeded one hundred thousand. Thus, in terms of sheer numbers, the overall military presence in the city more than compensated for the sharp decline in the tourist trade.

The city's permanent residents did their best to take all of this in stride; as a seasonal tourist center, St. Petersburg was accustomed to large influxes of people. And yet somehow the wartime "invasion" was different, not only because of its military character but also because the psychological and social impact of the influx was magnified by the absence of many of the city's most familiar faces. More than eight thousand local residents served in the armed forces during the war, very few of whom were stationed in the Tampa Bay area. Sooner or later, most ended up overseas, where they experienced adventures and challenges that would have been unimaginable prior to the war.

Without a doubt, these military experiences were the focal point of the war for most families. But, in its own way, the drama of the homefront—where the vast majority of the city's population spent the war—was every bit

Army recruits camp on the grounds of the Vinoy Park Hotel in 1942. Most of St. Petersburg's large hotels were turned into barracks during World War II, but they could not always accommodate the massive influx of military personnel. Courtesy St. Petersburg Historical Society

as intense as the drama of the battlefield. For the largely unsung heroes of the homefront, the wartime experience was dominated by green ration books, blackout regulations, shortages, war bond drives, teary perusals of casualty lists, anxious trips to the post office, and the vicarious excitement of following the news from the front. It was a trying, exhausting time, and nearly everyone experienced moods that ran the gamut of human emotions, from anguish to joy, from stark fear to patriotic rage.

Even though many of the city's traditional activities were suspended during the war—from 1943 to 1945, there were no Festival of States parades, no St. Petersburg-to-Havana yacht races, and no spring training games (though some local baseball fans did catch an occasional glimpse of Joe DiMaggio, who was stationed at the Don CeSar in 1945)—wartime St. Petersburg rarely lacked for activity. Indeed, the thousands of servicemen and fellow travelers who crowded into St. Petersburg during the war gave the city an air of excitement that it had not experienced since the height of the 1920s boom. During the 1930s, the dominant image of the city had been that of a quiet haven for the elderly, the infirm, and the

wealthy. But with the coming of the military, "flaming youth" returned to the city in force. Everywhere there was nonstop action, from the bar stools to the beaches, with more than enough carousing to occupy the Army MPs and Navy Shore Patrol who patrolled the city. Downtown streets were crowded day and night, and restaurants, bars and dance halls were often filled to overflowing. Thus, despite rationing and the absence of the normal tourist trade, many local merchants did record-breaking business during the war.

Although it would be difficult to exaggerate the economic and social impact of the wartime military influx, some of the most important developments on the homefront had little or nothing to do with the presence of military personnel. Most obviously, wartime conditions prompted major adjustments in age and gender roles. With so many young men in uniform, retirees, women, teenagers, and even children were called upon to keep city services and private businesses going. At one time or another, nearly everyone shared these burdens, but much of the responsibility for maintaining the homefront fell upon the shoulders of young and middle-aged women. In addition to working as nurses, Red Cross volunteers, teachers, and clerical workers, women frequently found themselves working in previously all-male occupations. As early as March 1942, the city hired eleven women to work as bus and trolley operators, and by the end of the war women were filling difficult and important positions all over the city. For a time in 1943, local railroads were even hiring women as common laborers. Thus, even though St. Petersburg had no major defense plants, the city was not without its equivalents of "Rosie the Riveter." Here, as elsewhere, World War II expanded opportunities for women.

The situation was somewhat less favorable for the city's black minority. But the war years did witness subtle changes in local race relations, as well as some improvement in the economic and social conditions of the black community. The pace of change was still maddeningly slow, and there was no guarantee that change would continue to move in a progressive direction. But the overall trend was encouraging. The decline in racial bigotry was most apparent in the North, but even in Southern cities like St. Petersburg there was a noticeable shift in the racial attitudes of some whites. Although racial prejudice was still rife, Hitler's promotion of the Aryan as a racial superman tended to discredit racial extremism. Moreover, as the war progressed and as knowledge of the Holocaust spread, the American government's relentless anti-Nazi propaganda campaign weakened the moral and political position of militant white supremacists. Perhaps most importantly, when set against the backdrop of a war against a racist enemy, the willingness of black soldiers to fight and die for their country led many whites to acknowledge (often grudgingly) the legitimacy of black demands for civic equality.

In St. Petersburg the proportion of men and women in uniform was actually higher in the black community than in the white community. Nearly two thousand local blacks served in the armed forces during the war, though many whites were unaware of this fact. All of St. Petersburg's black servicemen were trained at special Jim Crow facilities and later assigned to segregated units. And with the exception of a few Navy stewards, no black servicemen were stationed anywhere in the Tampa Bay area. Even so, the black contribution to the war effort was a great source of pride in the black community. It was also a badly needed source of employment for many impoverished black families.

The economic impact of the war on the black St. Petersburg was mixed. On the negative side, the wartime decline in the building trades and the military occupation of the city's hotels put some black laborers and domestics out of work. Fortunately, these problems were offset by military employment, rationing, and the general improvement of the local economy. On balance, the average black family was probably slightly better off during wartime than during the late 1930s. In any event, most black families probably regarded these slight economic gains as less important than the general social and political progress that marked the late 1930s and early 1940s.

One of the most important developments of this era, as far as the black community was concerned, was the liberalization of the city's most powerful newspaper, the *St. Petersburg Times*. As early as 1937, the *Times* had spoken out against the white primary and the Ku Klux Klan, but the paper did not make a clear break with its racially conservative past until after the death of William L. Straub in April 1939. With Straub's death, editorial control of the *Times* passed to Nelson Poynter, the thirty-five year old son of Paul Poynter, the paper's longtime publisher. A graduate of Indiana University and Yale University, where he earned a master's degree in economics, Nelson Poynter was a liberal-minded supporter of the New Deal and an avowed racial moderate. Traditionally, the *Times'* coverage of the black community had been limited to crime reports and condescending human interest stories. But under Poynter's leadership the *Times* gradually expanded and improved its treatment of black news.

Beginning in October 1939, the *Times* published a weekly "Negro News Page," a collection of articles about black church and school activities, sporting and social events, births, deaths, weddings, and other personal news. Written exclusively by black reporters

Soldiers stand in formation near the North Mole and the Vinoy Park Hotel in 1942. Courtesy St. Petersburg Historical Society

A wartime scene near the Million Dollar Pier in 1942. The "Little St. Mary's" public restroom, designed by noted architect Henry Taylor, can be seen in the background. The restroom bears a striking resemblance to St. Mary's Catholic Church (Fourth Street and Fifth Avenue South), which was also designed by Taylor. Courtesy St. Petersburg Times working out of their homes, the Negro News Page generally avoided controversial political and racial issues. But it did break a longstanding taboo against using courtesy titles such as "Mr." or "Mrs." or "Dr." when referring to black men and women. This breach of racial etiquette went almost unnoticed in the white community, largely because few whites knew of the Negro News Page's existence; the page was only inserted in papers distributed in black neighborhoods. Progress was slower in the regular pages of the *Times*, but the absence of racial epithets and slurs, plus the occasional appearance of feature stories on black celebrities such as Dr. George Washington Carver, signified that the paper was no longer a mirror of racist orthodoxy.

For many local blacks, an even more important development of the late 1930s and early 1940s was the dramatic reversal of the political decline that had threatened the black community in the early years of the Great Depression. St. Petersburg's black voter registration figures began to edge upward in 1937, the year the Florida legislature repealed the state poll tax. And by the early 1940s, many black leaders were beginning to believe that real political power was in the offing. The greatest impediment to black political power—the white primary system—was still in force and would remain so until after the end of the war. But by 1945 it was clear that the days of the white primary were numbered. In a series of landmark decisions, beginning with the *Classic* case of 1941 and culminating in *Smith v. Allwright* in 1944, the United States Supreme Court declared white-only primaries to be unconstitutional. This did not stop local Democratic leaders from announcing, in February 1945, that they had no plans to open their registration rolls to blacks. But this tacit defiance of the Court's mandate came to an end a year later, when Dr. Gilbert Leggett and several other black leaders successfully petitioned the circuit court to strike down the local white primary system. Hailed as a major victory for local Civil Rights advocates, the 1946 decision led to a sharp increase in black political activity. By the end of the decade, black participation in local Democrat pri-

maries had become commonplace, and the rate of black voter registration in St. Petersburg had risen to 30 percent, one of the highest rates in the South.

There was less progress in the legal justice system, and the repressive nature of the local police remained one of the most threatening aspects of black life. Yet even here there were encouraging signs. In December 1941, blacks were allowed to serve on a Pinellas County grand jury for the first time in the county's history, and soon thereafter J. P. Moses became St. Petersburg's first black bondsman. Although token in nature, these developments indicated that there were cracks in the mold, that a closed system was beginning to open, albeit ever so slowly. Unfortunately, real change would not come until 1949, when the police department hired four black patrolmen—the first black policemen in the city's history. Progressive community leaders, both black and white, had urged the hiring of black policemen for years. But their efforts had been stymied by the reluctance of city officials to challenge the power and authority of Police Chief E. D. "Doc" Vaughn. A militant white supremacist whose uncompromisingly harsh attitude toward the black community was a throwback to an earlier, more brutal era, Chief Vaughn was a folksy, self-styled "Florida cracker" who sometimes seemed out of place in a genteel resort city. He nonetheless received strong support from racial conservatives, both inside and outside of city hall.

During the war, the police department became increasingly repressive in its dealings with the city's black minority. Beginning in November 1942, when city officials issued a "Work or Jail" edict, the police conducted periodic raids on black bars and pool halls, in an effort to root out "loafers" and "idlers."[5] Black men who could not prove gainful employment were threatened with imprisonment if they did not cooperate with the police. These raids were stepped up later in the war, especially when there was a shortage of labor. Backed by the city council, which claimed that it would not tolerate loafing during wartime, the police were empowered to act as labor agents for city agencies and other local

Army Air Corps trainees stand in a chow line at the Tramor Cafeteria in 1942. Built in 1930, the Tramor was one of the many local restaurants taken over by the military during World War II. Courtesy St. Petersburg Times

employers short of labor. City officials generally defended the system in nonracial terms as a necessity of wartime, but the fact that such vagrancy sweeps were limited to black neighborhoods did not go unnoticed in the black community. During the course of the war, local blacks were also angered by several flagrant incidents of police brutality, including the killing of a black male suspect in August 1942, and the savage beating of a black female prisoner in October 1944. The latter case brought a formal reprimand from the city manager, Carleton Sharpe. Sharpe had tangled with Vaughn during an earlier tenure at city hall and had removed him from office in 1934. So it came as no surprise when Sharpe fired Vaughn again in 1945.

Sharpe was not the only local official to recognize the need to reform the city government's relationship with its black constituents. In 1943, the city planning commission issued a surprisingly candid appraisal of the economic and social blight that continued to plague much of the black community. In preparing a new master plan for the city, the commission concluded that the physical condition of the black community constituted a serious impediment to civic progress. Although the planners

cited the Jordan Park public housing project as an important step forward, they decried the prevalence of substandard housing in most of the city's black neighborhoods and acknowledged the stark contrast between black and white schools. Without exception, the city's black schools were overcrowded and underfunded, and some lacked even the most basic facilities. The critical shortage of space and facilities at Gibbs High School, where 781 students attended a school designed for 350 children, was especially glaring. The report also pointed out the need for additional park and recreation facilities in the black community.

To alleviate these deplorable conditions, the city planners called for a massive infusion of government funds and private capital in the black sections of the city. While black leaders welcomed this unprecedented show of social consciousness, few harbored any illusions that the proposed commitment of funds was compatible with the political realities of a white supremacist society. Despite their good intentions, the planners had failed to identify the primary source of the black community's problems; nowhere in the report was there even a hint that racial prejudice had contributed to the black population's plight, or that many of its problems could be partially ameliorated by an abandonment of Jim Crow restrictions.

The National Urban League offered a more probing analysis of black St. Petersburg in 1945. After spending several weeks in the city, a team of Urban League investigators issued a lengthy report that assessed the strengths and weaknesses of the black community and the character of local race relations. The investigators applauded the success of the Jordan Park housing project and noted the emergence of the city's black middle class, but on the whole they were discouraged by what they saw. Poverty, severe overcrowding, and dilapidated housing were the norm in almost all of the city's black neighborhoods, and, despite the recommendations issued by the city planning commission in 1943, little or nothing was being done to eradicate these conditions. The city's black schools—and the white public officials who were responsible for their condition—also came in for sharp criticism. The black school system had no kindergarten classes, no facilities for technical education, and no access to St. Petersburg Junior College, an institution that had become a major source of social mobility in the white community. Black teachers earned far less than their white counterparts (this particular problem would be partially alleviated by a 1946 federal court order), and everything from black-boards to school buses was in short supply.

The Urban League investigators were equally troubled by the poor condition, or in some cases, the absence of other black institutions. In a black population of nearly fifteen thousand, there were only two doctors and not a single lawyer. Mercy Hospital was overcrowded and understaffed. And after six decades the black community still had no public beach, no swimming pool, no library (a black branch of the public library opened in 1946), no blood bank, and no newspaper of its own (though an "underground" paper called *The Informer* had existed for a brief period during the 1930s). In the area of race relations, the investigators found that residential and social segregation were rigidly enforced, and that blacks and whites had very few opportuni-

ties to engage in interracial dialogue or cooperation, the major exception being an informal ministerial network set up by the St. Petersburg Council of Churches in 1940. The report provided numerous examples of the black community's exclusion and alienation from the mainstream of city life. But the most poignant example was the tradition of fear that kept blacks away from the city's famous green benches. Although city police no longer prevented blacks from sitting on downtown benches, the investigators discovered that very few black citizens felt secure enough to exercise this new freedom. The wounds of a lifetime would take a long time to heal.

Mending the wounds of war would also take time. Fortunately, the numerous sacrifices made on the battlefield—more than a hundred soldiers and sailors from St. Petersburg lost their lives during the war—were made more bearable by the unconditional surrender of the Axis powers in 1945. When V-J Day finally arrived in mid-August, exhaustion and sorrow turned to jubilation. In St. Petersburg, even an intense summer heat wave could not stop the joyous crowds from pouring into the streets. The city celebrated for days. Despite recent cutbacks in the number of military trainees, the city was still jammed with people at the end of the war. The 1945 state census placed the city population at 85,174, a 40 percent increase since 1940.

Despite all that happened between 1941 and 1945, the city was rapidly demilitarized after the war. Although the Coast Guard maintained a small peacetime facility at Bayboro Harbor and the Bayboro maritime base continued to train a small number of merchant seamen, men in uniform soon became a rarity in St. Petersburg. In October 1945, the decommissioned Pinellas Army Air Base became a civilian airport. And, with the exception of the Jungle Country Club Hotel, which became the home of Admiral Farragut Academy in January 1945, and the Rolyat, which had served as the home of Florida Military Institute since 1932, all of the city's hotels returned to civilian use. Even the military hospital in the Don CeSar Hotel was closed at the end of the war, though it would soon be converted into a Veterans' Administration office building. The patients at the Bay Pines Veterans' Hospital were a solemn reminder of the recent past, but for the most part the military drama of the war was over.

St. Petersburg would never again be a military town. However, the city would feel the impact of the Second World War for decades to come. Like the coming of the Orange Belt Railroad in 1888 and the boom and bust cycle of the 1920s, World War II proved to be a major watershed in the city's history. Many people had the profound sense that nearly everything was different after the war, and they were right. In countless ways the war accelerated technological and social change, propelling the city and the nation into a new age. Though all ages are ages of transition, it is little wonder that the generation that experienced the roller-coaster ride of depression and war felt especially cut off from previous generations.

Viewing the war as a psychological and historical turning point was a global phenomenon. But in St. Petersburg this sense of change was accentuated by a postwar demographic explosion that had its origins in the city's wartime militarization. During the immediate postwar era, St. Petersburg attracted thousands of veterans, many of whom had trained in the city during the war. Some returned only as tourists, but many others came back to stay. By the spring of 1946, the city was full of newcomers, men and women who had come from as far away as Oregon to make a fresh start in the Florida sunshine. A restless, optimistic lot, they had come to grab their share of the Florida Dream.

This mass in-migration of veterans and other transplants sparked a major postwar building boom. During the war, governmental restrictions had brought private building to a near standstill, but all this changed in the winter of 1945-46. After nearly twenty years of hard times, the local construction and real estate industries entered a period of unprecedented growth and prosperity. Between 1943 and 1946, the number of homes and apartments under construction rose from 11 to 1,533. Each year brought further expansion,

and by 1950 the number of units under construction had increased to 3,434. For the first time in the city's history, the value of residential building permits topped twenty million dollars.

Despite the absence of large commercial building projects—the new Maas Brothers department store completed in 1948 was the only major exception—the postwar building boom was even larger than the fabled boom of the 1920s. It was also fundamentally different. During the 1920s, the fortunes of the local real estate industry had been driven by land speculation and the sale of empty lots, not by housing needs. This was not true during the late 1940s (though the speculative impulse would reassert itself in later decades), when most land buyers actually intended to live in homes built on their property. Since the city was full of half-developed subdivisions that had been languishing since the bust of 1926, it was a buyer's market. The supply of available lots included hundreds of tax delinquent properties that had been seized by the city, and local officials were more than willing to do what they could to fuel the postwar real estate boom. During the late 1940s, the city held a series of public land auctions where prospective homebuyers and real estate speculators were able to purchase lots at bargain prices. At one point, the city even sponsored a special "lottery" auction for veterans, distributing some of the choicest empty lots in the city to those who selected the winning numbers.

The postwar residential building boom had a major impact on St. Petersburg. In addition to boosting the local economy, it changed the look and feel of much of the city. There were many elements in this transformation, but a big part of the change can be attributed to architectural style. The predominant styles of the 1920s and 1930s—from sprawling up-scale Mediterranean Revival and Southern Revival creations to California-style bungalows and tin-roofed "cracker" houses up on blocks—had been replaced by the mass-produced one-story tract house. The emphasis was on cost-efficiency and functionalism, and the only surviving connection with the city's fanciful past was the continuing popularity of the red-tile roof. Many of these new homes were modest structures placed on small lots. Designed for small households, they were well-suited to the needs of families with small or modest incomes, especially retirees living on pensions or social security benefits. They also proved to be readily adaptable to the residential air-conditioning revolution of the 1950s. After the Carrier Corporation introduced the low-cost window unit in 1951, the whir of compressors could be heard from one end of the city to the other.

By the early 1950s, small windows and compact floor plans were the order of the day, as virtually all of the city's building contractors had adapted to the requirements of air conditioning and mass production. During the late 1940s, James Rosati became the first local builder to use concrete block construction and terrazo floors on a large scale, but nearly all of his competitors soon followed suit. Rosati also built the city's first shopping center (excluding the unique and ever-expanding Webb's City). The opening of the Tyrone Gardens Shopping Center was a milestone in the city's history, though few observers realized it at the time. It was only after the opening of the city's second shopping center, a much larger complex known as Central Plaza, in 1952 that the negative impact on the downtown business community become clear.

By that time, the suburbanization of the city was in full swing. Most of St. Petersburg's postwar transplants bought homes in the central and western sections of the city, and many other gravitated to the city's suburban rim, to what historian Kenneth Jackson has aptly called the "crabgrass frontier."[6] Suburbs such as Gulfport, Pinellas Park, and Kenneth City, which was incorporated in 1947, expanded rapidly during the immediate postwar era, though their busiest days were yet to come. This decentralization was encouraged by a burgeoning system of county roads, and by the increasing popularity of trailer parks. At the same time, the postwar revival of the tourist trade—aided by the invention of the "motel"—drew thousands of newcomers to St. Petersburg Beach and other barrier island communities. Although it would be several years before a publicist invented the "Sun-coast," the metropolitanization of St. Petersburg and Pinellas County was well on its way by 1950.

The emergence of the suburban rim caught some people by surprise, probably because immediately after the war the downtown area was the focus of attention for most local political and business leaders. They were determined to refurbish the central business district, and for the first time in fifteen years they had the money to do it. A city government that had been close to bankruptcy during the Great Depression found itself blessed with a large revenue surplus at the close of the war, largely because municipally-owned utilities had reaped huge wartime profits. This surplus began to pile up as early as 1943, but federal regulations prevented the city from spending the money during the war. Consequently, city officials created a special "postwar fund." By the end of the war, the fund had accumulated more than a million dollars, allowing the city to launch an ambitious program of public improvements. The largest amount went for street improvements, but city officials also used the money to spruce up the Million Dollar Pier and the downtown waterfront, develop a large city park near Lake Maggiore, and construct a long-awaited replacement for the aging St. Petersburg Athletic Park.

Opened in March 1947, the new ballpark was named in honor of former mayor Al Lang, the man who had brought major league baseball to the city three decades earlier. As the spring training home of the New York Yankees and the St. Louis Cardinals, both of which returned to the city in 1946 after a four year absence, Al Lang Field quickly became an important landmark for the thousands of baseball fans who visited the city each spring. It also symbolized the city's postwar prosperity, though by 1947 signs of St. Petersburg's recent progress could be found all across the city. In the brief span of three years, between 1945 and 1948, the city constructed a number of new public buildings, including a police station, two fire stations, and a new city jail which replaced the infamous "city stockade."

Soldiers and friends pose in front of St. Mary's Catholic Church in 1942. Courtesy St. Petersburg Historical Society

This period also saw the expansion of Mound Park and Mercy Hospitals, the construction of a new city water tower, and the renovation of the city gas plant.

Ironically, one of the municipal utilities that had underwritten this postwar bonanza—the city trolley system—soon fell victim to St. Petersburg's newfound commitment to progress. For nearly half a century, streetcars had been a fixture of local life. Operated as a municipally-owned utility since 1919, the trolley system had played an important role in the expansion of the city, linking the downtown with outlying areas such as Gulfport and the Jungle. By the 1930s, nearly thirty miles of track crisscrossed the city, and thousands of local residents and tourists rode the streetcars every day. The system was especially popular during World War II, when gas and tire rationing limited automobile and bus travel. However, in the immediate postwar era local officials decreed that trolleys did not fit into

the city's plans for the future. The city's financial analysts concluded that a transit system using buses only would be cheaper and more practical than the existing system, which used both trolleys and buses. Most of St. Petersburg's streetcars dated from the 1920s, giving the system a charming, historic look. But not everyone appreciated this quaintness; many local citizens complained that the city's antiquated trolley cars were noisy and inefficient, and that they slowed down the flow of automobile traffic. Others were deeply attached to the system and fought hard to save it. But in the end the forces of "progress" won out.

In October, 1947, with Mayor Bruce Blackburn dissenting, the City Council voted to phase out all of the city's trolleys as soon as possible. A group of die-hard trolley enthusiasts challenged the city's right to purchase a new fleet of buses, but in January 1948 most of the city's streetcars were taken out of service and scrapped. The Gulfport and Jungle lines

Nearly two thousand local blacks served in the armed forces during World War II. All were assigned to segregated units. Courtesy of Shirlye Whiting

remained open until May 7, 1949, when Car 100 made St. Petersburg's final trolley run. With Mayor Blackburn, ex-Mayor Al Lang (who had presided over the purchase of the line in 1919), Bill "Alligator Man" Carpenter, and several other old timers on board, the car coasted to the end of the line in Gulfport with its windows draped in black crepe. A sign on the front of the car read "Not Dead Just Retired."[7]

The controversy surrounding the removal of the trolley system was symptomatic of the city's restless mood during the late 1940s. Rising expectations and the inevitable difficulties of postwar adjustment often led to group conflict and divisiveness, particularly in the area of labor-management relations. In St. Petersburg, as in many American cities, the immediate postwar era was marked by a series of strikes and walkouts. City sanitation workers staged a walkout in 1950, city transit workers followed suit a year later, and on three different occasions between 1945 and 1952 the *St. Petersburg Times* was hit by major strikes. The first newspaper strike began in November 1945, when the local printers' union demanded shorter hours and higher wages—a situation which put liberal editor Nelson Poynter in a peculiar position. A longtime supporter of organized labor, Poynter had fought for the pro-labor Wagner Act of 1935. And as recently as 1944, Poynter and the *Times* had crusaded against right-to-work laws. However, this did not stop him from crushing the local printers' union after negotiations between the paper and the union went sour. After the strike collapsed in January 1946, none of the strikers were rehired. Poynter went on to become the principal owner of the *Times* in 1947, and he and his staff continued to write pro-labor editorials. But when the paper's pressmen went out on strike in 1949 and 1952, management maintained its hard line, breaking both strikes in short order.

The local political scene also had its share of turmoil during the postwar years. After several years of battling with an uncooperative city council, City Manager Carleton Sharpe resigned in 1948. Sharpe's successor, Ross Windom, would remain in office for eleven years, the longest tenure in the city's history, but he too would have his frustrations. Despite his accomplishments, which included the reform of the police department and the completion of the Sunshine Skyway bridge in 1954, Windom's lack of success in negotiating with disgruntled city employees and civil rights advocates—especially his defiance of a United States Supreme Court order mandating the desegregation of the Municipal Spa Pool—ultimately tarnished his reputation, prompting his resignation in 1958.

Partisan and elective politics also took a dramatic turn after the war. In 1948, St. Petersburg elected its first Republican mayor, Stanley Minshall, and on the county level the local Republican party offered its first serious challenge to the ruling Democrats, winning four minor county offices. Two years later, for the first time in its history, the Republican party ran a full slate of candidates for city and country offices. To nearly everyone's surprise, the 1950 Republican effort swept dozens of Democratic incumbents out of office, ending the traditional local Democratic hegemony. (The 1950 election also launched the political career of Daisy K. Edwards, the first woman to win a seat on the St. Petersburg City Council in more than a quarter of a century.) Although no local Republican had served in the Florida legislature since 1931, the upstart Republicans garnered all three of Pinellas County's seats in the state house of representatives. One of the three new Republican legislators was William Cramer, a local war hero and Harvard Law School graduate who would later (1954-1970) serve eight terms in Congress.

A number of personal and political factors, including the complacency of the local Democratic machine, contributed to this abrupt political realignment. But, as longterm political trends would eventually demonstrate, the Republican revolution of 1950 was rooted in a fundamental demographic and social transformation. The 1950 federal census confirmed what everyone in St. Petersburg already knew—that the city was continuing to grow at a rapid pace; during the preceding decade the local population had increased from 60,812 to 96,838. But the census also revealed that the city's demographic profile was becoming progressively whiter, older, and less distinctively Southern. The black proportion of the city's population had fallen to 14.4 percent, the lowest figure since the early 1890s. In absolute terms, the number of blacks in the city was still increasing—from 11,982 in 1940 to 13,977 in 1950—but such gains were dwarfed by the accelerating pace of white in-migration.

St. Petersburg had always had more than its share of regional transplants, but the onrush of postwar migrants was beginning to rival the great migration of the boom era. In 1950, for the first time in the city's history, the percentage of local residents born in Florida dipped below 20 percent. At the same time, the proportion of elderly residents—those sixty-five years old or older—rose to 22.2 percent, double the figure of 1930. The senior citizen migration would not reach its peak until the early 1970s, when the proportion sixty-five years old or older passed 35 percent. But the process that would eventually make St. Petersburg synonymous with old age (leading quipsters to dub the city "God's Waiting Room") was well underway by midcentury.[8] Not all of the city's newcomers voted Republican, but the growing predominance of Northern-born voters—voters who in most cases had received their political socialization in two-party states—rapidly dispelled the mystique of Solid South politics.

The 1950 census captured a community on the threshold of a new era. Although the city had already undergone significant growth and change, St. Petersburg at midcentury was closer to its past than to its future. During the next thirty years, the city's population would triple in size, and the entire Tampa Bay region

*Merchant Marine trainees race
skiffs near the Million Dollar
Pier during World War II.
Courtesy St. Petersburg Historical Society*

would be transformed into a sprawling
metropolis. This spiralling growth would
present local residents with a series of difficult
challenges. Maintaining an expansive economy
without destroying the natural environment,
avoiding the placelessness of a landscape
overrun by chain stores and strip malls, and
generally reconciling progress and tradition—
these and other challenges, including the
necessity of overcoming the legacy of racial
discrimination, would stretch the city's moral
and intellectual resources to the limit. At the
same time, St. Petersburg would find it
increasingly difficult to sustain a positive
public image, a strange predicament for a city
that had pioneered the art of municipal public
relations. Once the city became closely identified with elderly retirees, it became an easy
mark for gerontophobic pundits. As the cult of
youth became a national obsession in the
1960s, St. Petersburg grew vulnerable to feelings of marginality and insecurity, so much so
that image-conscious city officials eventually
ordered the removal of the city's famous green
benches. Ironically, in the age of the Sunbelt
relaxing in the sunshine had become an
unacceptable symbol for a progressive city.

St. Petersburg today bears only a partial
resemblance to the small Southern city of 1950.
Indeed, it no longer considers itself a part of the
South. For better or worse, it now belongs to the
Sunbelt, a region where lack of tradition has
become a tradition, and where communal
feeling often has more to do with a shared
experience of migration and transience than
with local history. And yet, far more than most
Sunbelt cities, St. Petersburg maintains vital
links with the past. With all its imperfections
and self-doubt, the city remains a vivid
expression of the Florida Dream. The green
benches are gone, but the goal of striking a
humane balance between leisure and enterprise still dominates St. Petersburg's public life.
A century after its founding, the city stands
apart from the mainstream of urban and
industrial America, a continuing testament to
the charms of life on the subtropical rim.

The United States Army purchased the Don CeSar Hotel in 1942, and turned it into a military hospital. This photograph, with hospital patients and employees in the foreground, was taken in February 1944. Courtesy Florida State Archives

An aerial view of the Merchant Marine Training Base at Bayboro Harbor on May 22, 1945. Courtesy St. Petersburg Historical Society

Merchant Marine recruits at a beachside firing range, circa 1943. Courtesy St. Petersburg Historical Society

Graduation day at Bayboro Harbor's Merchant Marine training base in 1945. The three-masted sailing ship in the back-ground is the U.S.S. Joseph Conrad. *Courtesy St. Petersburg Historical Society*

Webb's City, the home of cut-rate prices, in 1943. Beginning with a small store in 1925, James Earl "Doc" Webb eventually presided over Webb's City, a 77-store complex covering seven city blocks. Despite its status as a local landmark, Webb's City closed its doors for good in August 1979. Courtesy St. Petersburg Historical Society

Motorists wait for a jammed Gandy drawbridge to be lowered on August 31, 1944. The delay lasted three hours, but at least there was no toll, thanks to an April 1944 executive order issued by President Franklin Roosevelt. Courtesy St. Petersburg Times

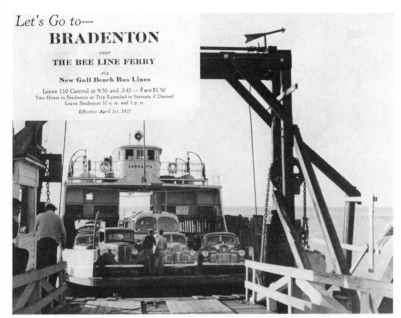

Prior to the opening of the Sunshine Skyway in 1954, the Bee Line Ferry was the main connection between St. Petersburg and the Sarasota-Bradenton area to the south. The Bee Line opened in 1926. This photograph was taken at the Bee Line's Piney Point terminal (south of Ruskin) sometime during the 1940s. Courtesy St. Petersburg Historical Society

A night scene on crowded Central Avenue in late November 1943. Courtesy St. Petersburg Times

An open-air Coast Guard Reserve recruiting station, circa 1944. Courtesy St. Petersburg Times

Children collecting scrap metal for the war effort in 1943. Courtesy St. Petersburg Times

American Legion volunteers collecting phonograph records "for our fighting men," circa 1943. Courtesy St. Petersburg Historical Society

This World War II window display at Rutland Brothers department store urged Americans to buy war bonds and "to send your personally autographed bomb to Hitler or Tojo!" Courtesy St. Petersburg Historical Society

KIDS -- THREE QUARTER CENTURY SOFTBALL CLUB, INC. ST. PETERSBURG, FLA. -- KUBS
- 1944 -

LINCOLN - ME. = ROBERTS - OHIO = VEITCH - N.D. = WEGT - N.Y. = BORAN - N.J. = WILKEN - MICH = YESBERGER - OHIO = HOOD - MICH = JOHNSON - ILL = WALKER =
75   81   78   77   81   87   86   77   79 -   77
                                                        REC. SEC.   PRESIDENT   CA. TINDER.

EATON = SCHELER - ILL = EISENHUTH - WIS. = DOUBLEDAY - MICH = PECKINPAUGH - OHIO = LAWCOCK - MICH = COLEMAN - N.Y. HARRINGTON - N.Y. = WHITE - MICH = SWARTLEY - PA. = BOWES - N.Y. = MORWICK
UMPIRE - 81 -   80 -   75   84   75   77   75 -   76   83   76 - UMPIRE

MINTO = McCULLOUGH - MINN = ROSS - N.Y. = WARNER - IND = HAWK - MANAGER = WALDEN - W.VA. = BOWEN - IOWA = SCOFIELD - N.Y. = MERRILL - MASS. HEIDEN =
AST. UME   77 -   81 -   77   82   75   79   79   - TRAINER

Founded in 1930, the Kids and Kubs softball club limits its membership to players seventy-five years old and older. This photograph was taken in 1944. Courtesy St. Petersburg Historical Society

Prisoners and guards stand in front of the infamous City Stockade in 1945. Courtesy St. Petersburg Times

La Plaza Theatre in the rain, circa 1945. Courtesy St. Petersburg Times

Celebrating V-J Day on Central Avenue, August 15, 1945. Courtesy St. Petersburg Times

Peace at last, August 1945. Courtesy St. Petersburg Times

Dancing at the Casino on the Million Dollar Pier, circa 1940. Courtesy St. Petersburg Times

An aerial view of the downtown waterfront, looking north from Albert Whitted Airport, 1947. Courtesy St. Petersburg Historical Society

Spring training on the water-front—Al Lang Field in 1947. Named for Mayor Al Lang, the transplanted Pennsylvanian who was instrumental in bringing major league baseball to the city in 1914, Al Lang Field was built in 1947 as a replacement for St. Petersburg Athletic Park (one block north of the Al Lang site). Courtesy St. Petersburg Historical Society

The St. Petersburg Kennel Club (later known as Derby Lane) dog track opened in January 1925. This photograph was taken circa 1947. Courtesy St. Petersburg Historical Society

The Municipal Spa, as it looked during the late 1940s. The Spa building was demolished in 1962. Courtesy St. Petersburg Historical Society

During the early and mid-1940s, St. Petersburg boasted approximately 30 tourist camps. One of the city's most popular tourist havens, the Treasure Village Tourist Camp (5151 Fourth Street North) offered cottages and mobile home lots at "reasonable rates" in 1945. Courtesy St. Petersburg Times

The building of Maas Brothers department store in the heart of downtown was one of the city's most important postwar construction projects. This photograph was taken on July 3, 1947. Courtesy St. Petersburg Times

A lively conversation on a downtown green bench, circa 1948. Courtesy St. Petersburg Times

An aerial view of the John's Pass Bridge, between Madeira Beach and Treasure Island, circa 1948. The development of the peninsula's barrier islands and the emergence of the "Pinellas Suncoast" concept would transform the local economy and much of the local landscape during the post-1950 era. Courtesy St. Petersburg Historical Society

Silas Dent, the "hermit of Cabbage Key," at home, circa 1950. One of the Pinellas region's best-known characters, Dent lived on Cabbage Key (part of Tierra Verde) from the turn of the century until his death at the age of seventy-six in 1952. Courtesy St. Petersburg Historical Society

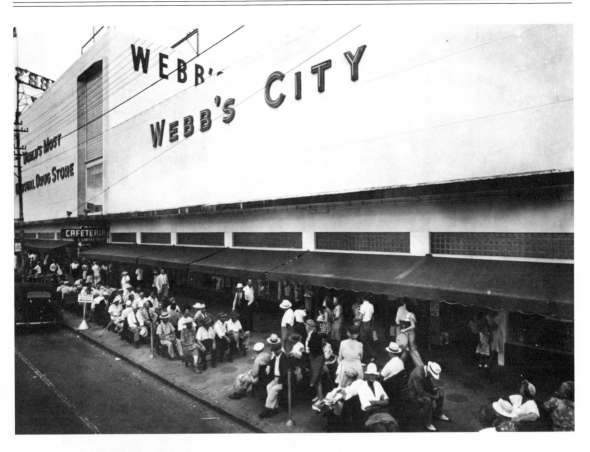

Webb's City, the "World's Most Unusual Drug Store," 1948. Photograph by Burgert Brothers, courtesy Florida State Archives

Shades of P. T. Barnum—Doc Webb, right, and Tennessee Slim, a frequent "visitor" at Webb's City in the postwar years. This photograph was taken during a Festival of States parade. Courtesy St. Petersburg Times

The ultimate "Florida Dream" publicity shot—the Webb's City Poster Girls on the beach in 1948. Beginning in 1939, Webb selected an annual bevy of poster girls to represent Webb's City. Courtesy St. Petersburg Times

The St. Petersburg Police Department hired its first black policemen in 1949. The local black community regarded the hiring of black policemen as a definite sign of progress, although it would be many years before black officers would be allowed to work in predominantly white neighborhoods. From left to right, Lt. Robinson, who supervised the black recruits; Sam Jones, who later became the department's first black sergeant; Titus Robinson; Willie Seay; and Louis Burrows. Courtesy St. Petersburg Times

Segregation at Al Lang Field, 1950. Courtesy St. Petersburg Times

Workers tend the coke furnace at the city gas plant, circa 1950. Courtesy St. Petersburg Times

The last run of the Big Bayou trolley, January 11, 1948. The man on the left, L. D. Childs, had been riding the Big Bayou trolley since 1914. The motorman on the right is E. F. Crawley. Courtesy St. Petersburg Times

The Municipal Negro Swimming Pool at Wildwood Park, shortly after it opened in 1954. Courtesy St. Petersburg Historical Society

Hope springs eternal at the
Fountain of Youth, circa 1950.
During the postwar era, St.
Petersburg welcomed a steady
stream of retirees, and sooner or
later most of them paid a visit to
the Fountain of Youth, the
famous sulfuric artesian well
created by Edwin Tomlinson at
the turn of the century. Courtesy
St. Petersburg Times

An Atlantic Coast Line
passenger train blocks traffic on
Ninth Street South in 1950.
During the post-World War II
era, many local residents considered train traffic in the
downtown business district to be
a nuisance. Despite periodic
complaints, the Atlantic Coast
Line terminal remained in the
downtown area until June 1963.
Courtesy St. Petersburg Times

The Orange Blossom Trailer
Park, 1950. Mobile-home living
became an increasingly popular
option for retirees and seasonal
visitors during the post-World
War II era. Courtesy St. Petersburg Historical Society

Culture in a quonset hut, 1951.
The Operetta, located on Ninth
Avenue North, was later turned
into a roller skating rink. Cour-
tesy St. Petersburg Historical
Society

The Soreno Hotel and the St. Petersburg Yacht Club, 1951. Courtesy St. Petersburg Times

*The Million Dollar Pier, circa
1950. Courtesy St. Petersburg
Historical Society*

*Water skiing near the Million
Dollar Pier, 1953. Courtesy* St.
Petersburg Times

*The demolition of La Plaza
Theatre, 1957. Courtesy* St.
Petersburg Times

The end of an era—the demoli-
tion of the Million Dollar Pier's
Casino building, 1967. Courtesy
St. Petersburg Times

An aerial view of the Municipal Pier, circa 1975. The pier head building with the inverted pyramid design opened in 1971. The large building in the background is the Bayfront Tower condominium. Courtesy St. Petersburg Historical Society.

Notes for Quotations

Chapter 1

1. Alfred W. Crosby, Jr., *The Columbian Exchange: Biological and Cultural Consequences of 1492* (Westport, Connecticut: Greenwood Press, 1972).

2. Samuel Eliot Morison, *The European Discovery of America: The Southern Voyages, 1492-1616* (New York: Oxford University Press, 1974), 518, 520.

3. Ibid., 527.

4. Walter P. Fuller, *St. Petersburg and Its People* (St. Petersburg: Great Outdoors Publishing Company, 1972), 1, 96.

5. Gloria Jahoda, *River of the Golden Ibis* (New York: Holt, Rinehart and Winston, 1972), 82.

6. J. Leitch Wright, Jr., *Creeks and Seminoles: Destruction and Regeneration of the Muscogulge People* (Lincoln: University of Nebraska Press, 1986), 4.

7. Fuller, *St. Petersburg and Its People*, 48.

Chapter 2

1. Hampton Dunn, *Yesterday's St. Petersburg* (Miami: E. A. Seeman, 1973), 16.

2. John A. Bethell, *Pinellas, A Brief History of the Lower Point* (St. Petersburg: Independent Press, 1914), 20.

3. Raymond Arsenault and Gary Mormino, "From Dixie to Dreamland: Demographic and Cultural Change in Florida, 1880-1980," In Randall M. Miller and George E. Pozzetta, eds., *Shades of the Sunbelt: Essays on Ethnicity, Race, and the Urban South* (Westport, Connecticut: Greenwood Press, 1988), 163; Nelson M. Blake, *Land Into Water—Water Into Land: A History of Water Management in Florida* (Tallahassee: University Presses of Florida, 1980), 25.

4. *The Sea Breeze* (Disston City, Florida), May 1, 1886.

5. Kirk Monroe, quoted in Gary R. Mormino and Anthony P. Pizzo, *Tampa: The Treasure City* (Tulsa: Continental Heritage Press, 1983), 79.

Chapter 3

1. W. C. Van Bibber, "Peninsular and Sub-Peninsular Air and Climates," *Journal of the American Medical Association* 4 (1885): 542.

2. Karl H. Grismer, *The Story of St. Petersburg* (St. Petersburg: P. K. Smith and Company, 1948), 72.

3. Hampton Dunn, *Yesterday's St. Petersburg* (Miami: E. A. Seeman, 1973), 18. See also Walter P. Fuller, *St. Petersburg and Its People* (St. Petersburg: Great Outdoors Publishing Company, 1972), 70-73.

4. Dunn, *Yesterday's St. Petersburg*, 21.

5. Grismer, *The Story of St. Petersburg*, 69.

6. *The Weekly South Florida Home* (St. Petersburg), March 4, 1892, quoted in ibid., 88.

7. Grismer, *The Story of St. Petersburg*, 91.

Chapter 4

1. John A. Bethell, *Pinellas, A History of the Lower Point* (St. Petersburg: Independent Press, 1914), 56-57.

2. *St. Petersburg Times*, Exposition Edition, September 1897; St. Petersburg and Sanford Railroad brochure (c. 1896), located in the St. Petersburg Map Collection, St. Petersburg Historical Society.

3. W. C. Van Bibber, "Peninsular and Sub-Peninsular Air and Climates," *Journal of the American Medical Association* 4 (1885): 536 ff.

4. Gary R. Mormino and Anthony P. Pizzo, *Tampa: The Treasure City* (Tulsa: Continental Heritage Press, 1983), 121, 128.

5. *St. Petersburg Times*, Exposition Edition, September 1897.

6. Karl H. Grismer, *The Story of St. Petersburg* (St. Petersburg: P. K. Smith and Company, 1948), 94.

7. Ibid; *St. Petersburg Times*, Exposition Edition, September 1897.

8. Robert Hooker, ed., *The Times and its times, A History* (St. Petersburg: Times Publishing Company, 1984), 14.

9. *St. Petersburg Times*, May 10, 1902.

10. Walter P. Fuller, *St. Petersburg and Its*

People (St. Petersburg: Great Outdoors Publishing Company, 1972), 123.

11. *St. Petersburg Times*, April 12, 1902; Grismer, *The Story of St. Petersburg*, 230.

12. See Leo Marx, *The Machine in the Garden: Technology and the Pastoral Ideal in America* (New York: Oxford University Press, 1964).

Chapter 5

1. C. Vann Woodward, *The Strange Career of Jim Crow* (New York: Oxford University Press, 1973). See also Joel Williamson, *The Crucible of Race: Black-White Relations in the American South Since Emancipation* (New York: Oxford University Press, 1984).

2. Walter P. Fuller, *St. Petersburg and Its People* (St. Petersburg: Great Outdoors Publishing Company, 1972), 328.

3. Samuel Davis, "The Black Community of St. Petersburg, 1920," (Seminar Paper, University of South Florida, 1983), 1.

4. See Eugene D. Genovese, *Roll, Jordan, Roll: The World the Slaves Made* (New York: Pantheon, 1974).

5. *St. Petersburg Times*, January 21, 1920.

6. *St. Petersburg Evening Independent*, June 23, 1913; Jon L. Wilson, "Days of Fear: A Lynching in St. Petersburg," *Tampa Bay History* 5 (Fall/Winter 1983): 11.

7. *St. Petersburg Evening Independent*, June 24, 1913; Wilson, "Days of Fear: A Lynching in St. Petersburg," 11.

8. Fuller, *St. Petersburg and Its People*, 281.

9. Ibid.

10. Wilson, "Days of Fear: A Lynching in St. Petersburg," 4-5; *St. Petersburg Times*, November 12, 1914.

11. Luther Atkins, quoted in Wilson, "Days of Fear: A Lynching in St. Petersburg," 17.

12. Wilson, "Days of Fear: A Lynching in St. Petersburg," 7.

13. Ibid., 22.

14. Robert Hooker, ed., *The Times and Its times, A History* (St. Petersburg: Times

Publishing Company, 1984), 18.

15. *St. Petersburg Evening Independent*, November 14, 1914; Wilson, "Days of Fear: A Lynching in St. Petersburg." 19.

16. *St. Petersburg Times,* November 17, 1914; Wilson, "Days of Fear: A Lynching in St. Petersburg," 19.

17. *St. Petersburg City Directory 1912* (St. Petersburg: Times Publishing Company, 1912), 14.

18. Paul Barco quoted in Wilson, "Days of Fear: A Lynching in St. Petersburg," 11.

19. Karl H. Grismer, *The Story of St. Petersburg* (St. Petersburg: P. K. Smith and Company, 1948), 202.

20. See Maria Vesperi, *City of Green Benches: Growing Old in a New Downtown* (Ithaca: Cornell University Press, 1985); Grismer, *The Story of St. Petersburg*, 201-203.

21. Hap Hatton, *Tropical Splendor: An Architectural History of Florida* (New York: Alfred A. Knopf, 1987), 75.

22. Gloria Jahoda, *River of the Golden Ibis* (New York: Holt, Rinehart, and Winston, 1973), 281.

23. Grismer, *The Story of St. Petersburg*, 122.

24. *St. Petersburg Evening Independent*, September 1, 1910.

25. *St. Petersburg Times*, July 2, 1906; Milton Polk, "The Man, His Hammer, and His House: W. L. Straub, the *St. Petersburg Times*, and the Creation of Pinellas County," (Seminar Paper, University of South Florida, 1987), 23.

26. *Tampa Morning Tribune*, February 27, 1907; Polk, "The Man, His Hammer, and His House," 13.

27. T. F. McCall, quoted in *St. Petersburg Times*, April 21, 1911; Polk, "The Man, His Hammer, and His House," 48.

28. Grismer, *The Story of St. Petersburg*, 300.

29. Ibid., 203, 314; Karl H. Grismer, *History of St. Petersburg, Historical and Biographical* (St. Petersburg: Tourist News,

1924), 87, 277.

30. Dick Bothwell, *Sunrise 200* (St. Petersburg: Times Publishing Company, 1975), 22-23; June Hurley Young, *Florida's Pinellas Peninsula* (St. Petersburg: Byron Kennedy and Co., 1984), 56.

31. Grismer, *History of St. Petersburg*, 195.

32. Ibid., 196.

33. Bothwell, *Sunrise 200,* 51.

Chapter 6

1. Walter P. Fuller, *St. Petersburg and Its People* (St. Petersburg: Great Outdoors Publishing Company, 1972), 165.

2. Ibid., 157.

3. Ibid., 141.

4. See Roderick Nash, *The Nervous Generation: American Thought, 1917-1930* (Chicago: Rand McNally, 1970).

5. See Gary R. Mormino, "Roadsides and Broadsides: A History of Florida Tourism," in *Essays in Florida History* (Tampa: Florida Endowment for the Humanities, 1986), 17.

6. Noel A. Mitchell, "Outlines Plan for City Work," *Tourist News* 1 (December 4, 1920): 15.

7. J. Fred Kurtz, "In Defense of St. Petersburg," (letter to "The Open Forum") *Tourist News* 1 (December 4, 1920): 21; Del Marth, *St. Petersburg: Once Upon a Time* (St. Petersburg: City of St. Petersburg, 1976), 21.

8. Jack Edwards Dadswell, "In the City of Tourist's Tents," *Tourist News* 1 (December 4, 1920): 3.

9. Mitchell, "Outlines Plan for City Work," 15.

10. *St. Petersburg Times,* July 6, 1921.

11. *St. Petersburg Times,* June 1, 1921; David Shedden, "Boosting the Boom: St. Petersburg and Its *Times,* 1921-1926," (Seminar Paper, University of South Florida, 1984), 1.

12. *St. Petersburg Times*, March 21, 1926.

13. *Tourist News* 1 (December 4, 1920): 3.

14. "Millions Spent in Buildings Here," *Tourist News* 1 (December 4, 1920): 18.

15. Robert Hooker, ed., *The Times and its times, A History* (St. Petersburg: Times Publishing Company, 1984), 33.

16. Fuller, *St. Petersburg and Its People,* 157.

17. Karl H. Grismer, *The Story of St. Petersburg* (St. Petersburg: P. K. Smith and Company, 1948), 320.

18. Ibid., 153-154.

19. David Nolan *Fifty Feet in Paradise: The Booming of Florida* (San Diego: Harcourt Brace Jovanovich, 1984), 200.

20. *St. Petersburg Times*, November 24, 1924; Dick Bothwell, *Sunrise 200* (St. Petersburg: Times Publishing Company, 1975), 68.

21. Bothwell, *Sunrise 200*, 69.

22. Ibid., 79.

23. Karl H. Grismer, *History of St. Petersburg, Historical and Biographical* (St. Petersburg: Tourist News, 1924), 284.

24. Bothwell, *Sunrise 200*, 70.

25. *St. Petersburg Times,* July 15, 1966; Raymond Arsenault, "The End of the Long Hot Summer: The Air Conditioner and Southern Culture," *Journal of Southern History* 50 (November 1984): 604.

26. Ralph Henry Barbour, *Let's Go to Florida!* (New York: Dodd, Mead, and Company, 1926), 205.

27. See Samuel Davis, "The Same Deal: Blacks in St. Petersburg in the 1930s" (Seminar Paper, University of South Florida, 1986), 5.

28. *St. Petersburg Times,* July 23, 1978; Interview with Leonard Cooperman, St. Petersburg, Florida, November 2, 1981; Interviews with Goldie Jacobs Schuster, St. Petersburg Beach, Florida, November 13, 1981, November 16, 1982; George E. Mowry and Blaine Brownell, *The Urban Nation 1920-1980* (Revised Edition) (New York: Hill and Wang, 1981), 30: Raymond Arsenault and Jacob Vonk, "Gentiles Only Wanted: Anti-Semitism in St. Petersburg, Florida, 1920-1980," Paper presented at the Annual Meeting of the Southern Jewish Historical Society, New Orleans, Louisiana, November 21, 1982, 1.

29. Mowry and Brownell, *The Urban Nation 1920-1980*, 30.

Chapter 7

1. Walter P. Fuller, *St. Petersburg and Its People* (St. Petersburg: Great Outdoors Publishing Company, 1972), 176.

2. Walter P. Fuller, *This Was Florida's Boom* (St. Petersburg: Times Publishing Company, 1954), 22.

3. Karl H. Grismer, *The Story of St. Petersburg* (St. Petersburg: P. K. Smith and Company, 1948), 170.

4. Ralph Reed, quoted in Robert Hooker, ed., *The Times and its times, A History* (St. Petersburg: Times Publishing Company, 1984), 36.

5. Ibid., 35.

6. Dick Bothwell, *Sunrise 200* (St. Petersburg: Times Publishing Company, 1975), 31.

7. Ibid.

8. Ibid., 45.

9. *Charter of the City of St. Petersburg, Florida* (Tallahassee: Florida State Legislature, 1931), 9.

10. *St. Petersburg Times*, September 11, 1936; William E. Watts, "St. Petersburg: The Sunshine City 1936-1940" (Seminar Paper, University of South Florida, 1987), 4.

11. *St. Petersburg Times*, July 20, 1937.

12. Ibid.

13. Ibid., June 21, 1938.

14. Ibid., November 8, 1939.

15. Grismer, *The Story of St. Petersburg*, 189.

16. Federal Writers' Project, *Florida: A Guide to the Southernmost State* (New York: Oxford University Press, 1939), 260.

Chapter 8

1. Federal Writers' Project, *Florida: A Guide to the Southernmost State* (New York: Oxford University Press, 1939), 261.

2. Karl H. Grismer, *The Story of St. Petersburg* (St. Petersburg: P. K. Smith and Company, 1948), 192.

3. *St. Petersburg Times*, February 21, 1988.

4. Robert Hooker, ed., *The Times and its times, A History* (St. Petersburg: Times Publishing Company, 1984), 42.

5. *St. Petersburg Times*, November 24, 1942.

6. Kenneth T. Jackson, *The Crabgrass Frontier: The Suburbanization of America* (New York: Oxford University Press, 1985).

7. James Buckley, *Street Railways of St.*

Petersburg, Florida (Forty Fort, Pa.: Harold E. Cox, 1983), 32.

8. Dick Bothwell, *Sunrise 200* (St. Petersburg: Times Publishing Company, 1975), 77; *St. Petersburg Times*, May 27, 1988, 1A, 20A, and May 29, 1988, 1D, 3D; Raymond Arsenault and Gary R. Mormino, "From Dixie to Dreamland: Demographic and Cultural Change in Florida, 1880-1980," in Randall K. Miller and George E. Pozzetta, eds., *Shades of the Sunbelt: Essays on Ethnicity, Race, and the Urban South* (Westport, Connecticut: Greenwood Press, 1988), 165, 182.

Selected Bibliography

The following bibliography represents only a partial listing of the sources used for this study. It does not include primary materials such as federal and state census data, city and county records, and oral history interviews.

MANUSCRIPT AND DOCUMENT COLLECTIONS:

Largo, Florida. Heritage Park Museum, Pinellas County Historical Society.
   Harvey L. Wells Collection
   Pinellas County Map Collection

St. Petersburg, Florida. St. Petersburg Historical Society.
   Benoist Collection.
   Department of Leisure Services Scrapbook.
   Mary W. Eaton Papers.
   Gandy Collection.
   A. L. Johnson Papers.
   Alfred E. Newman Collection.
   Orange Belt Railroad Collection.
   St. Petersburg Advertising and Promotional Materials File.
   St. Petersburg and Pinellas County Map Collection.
   St. Petersburg Schools File.
   Jay D. Smith Papers.
   William L. Straub Papers.
   Webb's City Collection.
   Woman's Town Improvement Association Papers.

St. Petersburg, Florida. St. Petersburg League of Women Voters.
   Historical Files.

St. Petersburg, Florida. St. Petersburg Public Library.
   Luther Atkins Scrapbooks.
   Pinellas County Newspaper Index (compiled by the Works Progress Administration, 1938-39), 16 volumes.

David A. Watt Diary.
St. Petersburg City Scrapbooks, 1918-1944 (21 volumes).

St. Petersburg, Florida. Nelson Poynter Library, University of South Florida at St. Petersburg,
   Nelson Poynter Papers.

Tampa, Florida. University of South Florida Library, Special Collections.
   Florida Historical Society Map Collection.
   Walter P. Fuller Papers.

NEWSPAPERS AND PERIODICALS:

The Florida Peninsular (Tampa), 1855-1862.
The Herald (Point Pinellas), 1887.
St. Petersburg Evening Independent, 1908-1950.
St. Petersburg Times, 1901-1950
The Sea Breeze (Disston City, Florida), 1886-1887.
South Florida Home (St. Petersburg), 1893.
The Sunshine City Weekly Bulletin (St. Petersburg), 1927.
Tampa Journal, 1889.
Tampa Tribune, 1895-1912
The Tourist News (St. Petersburg), 1920-1929.

BOOKS AND PAMPHLETS:

Barbour, Ralph Henry. *Let's Go to Florida!*. New York: Dodd, Mead, and Company, 1926.
Bethell, John A. *Pinellas, A Brief History of the Lower Point*. St. Petersburg: Independent Press, 1914. Reprinted as *Bethell's History of Point Pinellas*. St. Petersburg: Great Outdoors Publishing Company, 1962.
Blake, Nelson M. *Land Into Water—Water Into Land: A History of Water Management in Florida*. Tallahassee: University Presses of Florida, 1980.
Bothwell, Dick. *Sunrise 200*. St. Petersburg: Times Publishing Company, 1975.
Brandon, William. *Indians*. New York: American Heritage Press, 1985.
Brown, Rosemary; Nuccio, Margaret; and Loeb, Karen, *St. Petersburg's Historic Suite:*

Watercolor Paintings by Milton Howarth. St. Petersburg: St. Petersburg Arts Commission, 1980.

Buckley, James. *Street Railways of St. Petersburg, Florida*. Forty Fort, Pa: Harold E. Cox, 1983.

Cabeza de Vaca, A. N. *Adventures in the Unknown Interior of America*. New York: Collier Books, 1961.

Cash, W. T. *History of the Democratic Party in Florida*. Live Oak, Florida: Democratic Historical Foundation, 1936.

Celi, Francisco Maria. *From Havana to the Port of Tampa: Year of 1757: A Journal of Surveys, Atlantic Ocean-Northern Part*. Transcribed and translated with notes by John D. Ware, Tampa: n.p., 1966.

Chalmers, David. *Hooded Americanism: The History of the Ku Klux Klan*. New York: Doubleday, 1965.

Cherbonneaux, Mattie Lou. *Mamaw's Memoirs*. St. Petersburg: Privately Printed, 1979.

City of St. Petersburg Community Development Department Planning Division. *St. Petersburg's Architectural and Historic Resources*. St. Petersburg: City of St. Petersburg Community Development Department Planning Division, 1981.

Crane, Verner W. *The Southern Frontier 1670-1732*. New York: W. W. Norton, 1981.

Coker, William S. and Watson, Thomas D. *Indian Traders of the Southeastern Spanish Borderlands: Panton, Leslie and Company and John Forbes and Company, 1783-1847*. Gainesville: University Presses of Florida, 1986.

Costrini, Patricia Perez, ed. *A Tradition of Excellence: Pinellas County Schools, 1912-1987*. Clearwater: Pinellas County School Board, 1988.

Covington, James W. *The Billy Bowlegs War, 1855-1858*. Chuluota, Fl.: Mickler House Publishing, 1982.

Covington, James W. *The Story of Southwestern Florida*. New York: Lewis Publishing Company, 1957.

Crosby, Alfred W., Jr. *The Columbian Exchange: Biological and Cultural Consequences of 1492*. Westport,

Connecticut: Greenwood Press, 1972.

Crosby, Alfred W., Jr. *Ecological Imperialism: The Biological Expansion of Europe, 900-1900*. Cambridge: Cambridge University Press, 1986.

Davis, Enoch Douglas. *On the Bethel Trail*. St. Petersburg: Valkyrie Press, 1979.

Davis, William Watson. *The Civil War and Reconstruction in Florida*. New York: Columbia University Press, 1913.

Dobyns, Henry F. *Their Number Become Thinned: Native American Population Dynamics in Eastern North America*. Knoxville: University of Tennessee Press, 1983.

Douglas, Marjory Stoneman. *The Everglades: River of Grass*. New York: Holt, Rinehart and Winston, 1947.

Douglas, Marjory Stoneman. *Florida: The Long Frontier*. New York: Harper and Row, 1967.

Dunlop, Beth. *Florida's Vanishing Architecture*. Englewood, Florida: Pineapple Press, 1987.

Dunn, Hampton. *Yesterday's St. Petersburg*. Miami: E. A. Seeman, 1973.

Eberson, Frederick. *Early Medical History of Pinellas County: A Quadricentennial Epoch*. St. Petersburg: Valkyrie Press, 1978.

Elliott, J. H. *Imperial Spain 1469-1716*. Harmondworth, England: Penguin Books, 1970.

Federal Writers' Project. *The WPA Guide to Florida*. New York: Pantheon, 1984. Originally published as *Florida: A Guide to the Southernmost State*. New York: Oxford University Press, 1939.

Fernald, Edward A., ed. *Atlas of Florida*. Tallahassee: Florida State University Foundation, 1981.

Fuller, Walter P. *This Was Florida's Boom*. St. Petersburg: Times Publishing Company, 1954.

Fuller, Walter P. *St. Petersburg and Its People*. St. Petersburg: Great Outdoors Publishing Company, 1972.

Fuller, Walter P. *This Was Florida's Boom*. St. Petersburg: Times Publishing Company, 1954.

Garcilaso de la Vega. Translated and Edited by John Grier Varner and Jeanette J. Varner. *The Florida of the Inca*. Austin: University of

Texas Press, 1951.

Gill, Joan E. and Read, Beth R., eds. *Born of the Sun*. Hollywood, Florida: Worth International Communications Corporation, 1975.

Gould, Rita Slaght. *Pioneer St. Petersburg: Life In and Around 1888*. St. Petersburg: Page Creations, 1987.

Grismer, Karl H. *History of St. Petersburg, Historical and Biographical*. St. Petersburg: Tourist News Publishing Company, 1924.

Grismer, Karl H. *The Story of St. Petersburg*. St. Petersburg: P. K. Smith and Company, 1948.

Gulfport Historical Society. *Our Story of Gulfport, Florida*. Gulfport: Gulfport Historical Society, 1985.

Hann, John H. *Apalachee: The Land between the Rivers*. Gainesville: University Presses of Florida, 1988.

Hatton, Hap. *Tropical Splendor: An Architectural History of Florida*. New York: Alfred A. Knopf, 1987.

Hoffmeister, John Edward. *Land from the Sea: The Geologic Story of South Florida*. Coral Gables: University of Miami Press, 1974.

Hooker, Robert, ed. *The Times and its times, A History* (July 25, 1884 to July 25, 1984). St. Petersburg: Times Publishing Company, 1984.

Hurley, Frank J., Jr. *Surf, Sand, and Post Card Sunsets: A History of Pass-a-Grille and the Gulf Beaches*. St. Petersburg: Great Outdoors Publishing Company, 1977.

Hurley, June. *The Don Ce-Sar Story*. St. Petersburg Beach: Partnership Press, 1974.

Jackson, Kenneth T. *The Crabgrass Frontier: The Suburbanization of America*. New York: Oxford University Press, 1985.

Jakle, John A. *The Tourist: Travel in Twentieth-Century North America*. Lincoln: University of Nebraska Press, 1985.

Jackson, Page, *An Informal History of St. Petersburg*. St. Petersburg: Great Outdoors Publishing Company, 1962.

Jahoda, Gloria. *Florida, A Bicentennial History*. New York: W. W. Norton, 1976.

Jahoda, Gloria. *River of the Golden Ibis*. New York: Holt, Rinehart, and Winston, 1973.

Johns, John E. *Florida During the Civil War*. Gainesville: University of Florida Press, 1963.

Kennedy, Margery and Waltz, Doris, eds. *Pass-a-Grille: A Patchwork Collection of Memories*. Franklin, N.C.: Macon Graphics, 1981.

Kennedy, Stetson. *Palmetto Country*. New York: Duell, Sloan and Pearce, 1942.

Klingman, Peter D. *Neither Dies Nor Surrenders: A History of the Republican Party in Florida, 1867-1970*. Gainesville: University Presses of Florida, 1984.

Lanier, Sidney. *Florida: Its Scenery, Climate and History*. Philadelphia: J. B. Lippincott and Company, 1876.

Larson, Lewis H. *Aboriginal Subsistence Technology on the Southeastern Coastal Plain during the Late Prehistoric Period*. Gainesville: University Presses of Florida, 1980.

Lazarus, William C. *Wings in the Sun: the Annals of Aviation in Florida*. Orlando: Tyn Cobb's Florida Press, 1951.

Lorant, Stefan, ed. *The New World: The First Pictures of America, Made by John White and Jacques Le Moyne and Engraved by Theodore de Bry*. . . . New Revised Edition. New York: Duell, Sloan and Pearce, 1965.

Lyon, Eugene. *The Enterprise of Florida: Pedro Menéndez de Avilés and the Spanish Conquest of 1565-1568*. Gainesville: University of Florida Press, 1976.

Leuchtenberg, William E. *Franklin D. Roosevelt and the New Deal, 1932-1940*. New York: Harper and Row, 1963.

Leuchtenberg, William E. *The Perils of Prosperity, 1914-32*. Chicago: University of Chicago Press, 1958.

Mahon, John K. *History of the Second Seminole War*. Gainesville: University of Florida Press, 1967.

Marx, Leo. *The Machine in the Garden: Technology and the Pastoral Ideal in America*. New York: Oxford University Press, 1964.

Mathews, Janet Snyder. *Edge of Wilderness: A Settlement History of Manatee River and Sarasota Bay*. Sarasota: Coastal Press, 1983.

Matson, George and Sanford, Samuel. *Geology and Ground Waters of Florida*. Washington, D.C.: Government Printing Office, 1913.

Marth, Del. *St. Petersburg: Once Upon a Time*. St. Petersburg: City of St. Petersburg, 1976.

McElvaine, Robert S. *The Great Depression: America, 1929-1941*. New York: Times Books, 1984.

McKay, D. B., ed. *Pioneer Florida*. 3 vols. Tampa: Southern Publishing Company, 1959.

McReynolds, Edwin C. *The Seminoles*. Norman: University of Oklahoma Press, 1957.

Mergen, Bernard. *Recreational Vehicles and Travel: A Resource Guide*. Westport, Connecticut: Greenwood Press, 1985.

Milanich, Jerald and Fairbanks, Charles H. *Florida Archaeology*. New York: Academic Press, 1980.

Milanich, Jerald and Proctor, Samuel, eds. *Tacachale: Essays on the Indians of Florida and Southeastern Georgia during the Historic Period*. Gainesville: University Presses of Florida, 1978.

Miller, Randall M. and Pozzetta, George E., eds. *Shades of the Sunbelt: Essays on Ethnicity, Race, and the Urban South*. Westport, Connecticut: Greenwood Press, 1988.

Mohl, Raymond A. *The New City: Urban American in the Industrial Age, 1860-1920*. Arlington Heights, Illinois: Harlan Davidson, 1985.

Morison, Samuel Eliot. *The European Discovery of America: The Southern Voyages, 1492-1616*. New York: Oxford University Press, 1974.

Mormino, Gary R. and Pizzo, Anthony P. *Tampa: The Treasure City*. Tulsa: Continental Heritage Press, 1983.

Mormino, Gary R. and Pozzetta, George E. *The Immigrant World of Ybor City: Italians and Their Latin Neighbors in Tampa, 1885-1985*. Urbana: University of Illinois Press, 1987.

Mowatt, Charles L. *East Florida as a British Province, 1763-1784*. Berkeley: University of California Press, 1943.

Mowry, George E. and Brownell, Blaine. *The Urban Nation 1920-1980*. Revised Edition. New York: Hill and Wang, 1981.

Nash, Roderick. *The Nervous Generation: American Thought, 1917-1930*. Chicago: Rand McNally, 1970.

National Urban League. *Report of the Social and Economic Conditions of the Negro Population of St. Petersburg, 1945-1946*. New York: National Urban League, 1945.

Nolan, David. *Fifty Feet in Paradise: The Booming of Florida*. San Diego: Harcourt Brace Jovanovich, 1984.

Parry, Albert. *Full Steam Ahead! The Story of Peter Demens*. St. Petersburg: Great Outdoors Publishing Company, 1987.

Pearce, Donn. *Dying in the Sun*. New York: Charterhouse, 1974.

Pinellas County Planning Council. *Pinellas County Historical Background*. Clearwater: Pinellas County Planning Council, 1986.

Richardson, Joseph M. *The Negro in the Reconstruction of Florida*. Tallahassee: Florida State University Press, 1965.

Robertson, James A. Translator and Editor. *Narrative of a Gentleman of Elvas*. DeLand, Florida: Florida State Historical Society, 1933.

Robinson, Ernest Lauren. *History of Hillsborough County, Florida: Narrative and Biographical*. St. Augustine: The Record Company, 1928.

Romans, Bernard. *A Concise and Natural History of East and West Florida, 1775*. Edited by Rembert W. Patrick. Floridiana Facsimile and Reprint Series. Gainesville: University of Florida Press, 1962.

Rothchild, John. *Up for Grabs: A Trip Through Time and Space in the Sunshine State*. New York: Viking Press, 1985.

Rowe, Anne E. *The Idea of Florida in the American Literary Imagination*. Baton Rouge: Louisiana State University Press, 1986.

St. Petersburg City Directory (1908 and 1912). St. Petersburg: Times Publishing Company, 1908, 1912.

St. Petersburg City Directory (1914-1950). Jacksonville, Florida: R. L. Polk, 1914-1950. (Published in Richmond, Virginia from 1944 on).

St. Petersburg, Florida—The Sunshine City. n.p.: n.p., c. 1934.

St. Petersburg Historical Society, *Historic Downtown Walking Tour, St. Petersburg, Florida*. St. Petersburg: St. Petersburg Historical Society, 1987.

St. Petersburg in 1908, Illustrated and Descriptive. Spartanburg, S.C.: Band and White, 1908.

Shofner, Jerrell H. *Nor Is It Over Yet: Florida in the Era of Reconstruction, 1863-1877*. Gainesville: University of Florida Press, 1974.

Sider, Don, ed. *Mark 75: St. Petersburg Times Seventy-fifth Anniversary*. St. Petersburg: Times Publishing Company, 1959.

Silverberg, Robert. *The Mound Builders*. Athens, Ohio: Ohio University Press, 1986.

Slacum, Marcia; Harwood, John; DeLoache, Frank; and White, Theresa. *Blacks in St. Petersburg 1980*. St. Petersburg: Times Publishing Company, 1980.

Smith, Buckingham. *Narratives of de Soto in the Conquest of Florida*. Gainesville: University of Florida Press, 1968. Originally published in 1866.

Smith, Julia Floyd. *Slavery and Plantation Growth in Ante-Bellum Florida, 1821-1860*. Gainesville: University of Florida Press, 1973.

Smyth, G. Hutchinson. *The Life of Henry Bradley Plant*. New York: G. P. Putnam's Sons, 1898.

Starkey, Jay. *Things I Remember, 1899-1979*. Brooksville: Southwest Florida Water Management District, 1980.

Starr, J. Barton. *Tories, Dons, and Rebels: The American Revolution in West Florida*. Gainesville: University of Florida Press, 1976.

Straub, William L. *History of Pinellas County, Florida*. St. Augustine: The Record Company, 1929.

Tannehill, Ivan Ray. *Hurricanes: Their Nature and History*. Princeton: Princeton University Press, 1938.

Tebeau, Charlton. *A History of Florida*. Coral Gables: University of Miami Press, 1980. Revised Edition.

Todorov, Tzvetan. Translated by Richard Howard. *The Conquest of America*. New York: Harper and Row, 1984.

Vesperi, Maria. *City of Green Benches: Growing Old in a New Downtown*. Ithaca: Cornell University Press, 1985.

White, Dorothy K. *Florida Painters: Past and Present*. St. Petersburg: St. Petersburg Historical Society, 1985.

White, Gay Blair. Edited by Warren J. Brown. *The World's First Airline: The St. Petersburg-Tampa Airboat Line*. Largo: Aero-Medical Consultants, Inc., 1984. Second Edition.

Willey, Gordon Randolph. *Archeology of the Florida Gulf Coast*. Washington, D.C.: Smithsonian Institution, 1949.

Williamson, Edward C. *Florida Politics in the Gilded Age, 1877-1893*. Gainesville: University of Florida Press, 1976.

Williamson, Joel. *The Crucible of Race: Black-White Relations in the American South Since Emancipation*. New York: Oxford University Press, 1984.

Woodward, C. Vann. *The Strange Career of Jim Crow*. Third Revised Edition. New York: Oxford University Press, 1973.

Wright, J. Leitch, Jr. *Creeks and Seminoles: Destruction and Regeneration of the Muscogulge People*. Lincoln: University of Nebraska Press, 1986.

Wright, J. Leitch, Jr. *The Only Land They Knew: The Tragic Story of the American Indians in the Old South*. New York: The Free Press, 1981.

Young, June Hurley. *Florida's Pinellas Peninsula*. St. Petersburg: Byron Kennedy and Co., 1984.

Zaiser, Marion. *The Beneficent Blaze: The Story of Major Lew B. Brown*. New York: Pageant Press, 1960.

ARTICLES:

Allen, Robert V. "Peter Demens: The Redoubtable Hustler." *The Quarterly Journal of the Library of Congress* 34 (July 1977): 208-26.

Arnade, Charles W. "Celi's Expedition to Tampa Bay: A Historical Analysis." *Florida Historical Quarterly* 47 (July 1968): 1-7.

Arnade, Charles W. "The Juan Baptista Franco Document of Tampa Bay, 1756." *Tequesta* 28 (1968): 99-101.

Arnade, Charles W. "The Tampa Bay Area from the Aborigines to the Spanish." *Tampa Bay History* 1 (Spring/Summer 1979): 5-16.

Arsenault, Raymond. "The End of the Long Hot Summer: The Air Conditioner and

Southern Culture." *The Journal of Southern History* 50 (November 1984): 598-627.

Arsenault, Raymond and Mormino, Gary. "From Dixie to Dreamland: Demographic and Cultural Change in Florida, 1880-1980." in Miller, Randall M. and Pozzetta, George E., eds. *Shades of the Sunbelt: Essays on Ethnicity, Race, and the Urban South.* Westport, Connecticut: Greenwood Press, 1988), 161-191.

Babb, Ellen and St. Julien, Milly. "Public and Private Lives: Women in St. Petersburg at the Turn of the Century." *Tampa Bay History* 8 (Spring/Summer 1986): 4-27.

Barker, Eirlys. "A Sneaky, Cowardly Enemy": Tampa's Yellow Fever Epidemic of 1887-88." *Tampa Bay History* 8 (Fall/Winter 1986): 4-22.

Bash, Evelyn C. "Profiles of Early Settlers on the Pinellas Peninsula." *Tampa Bay History* 5 (Spring/Summer 1983): 82-93.

Bullen, Ripley P. "Archaeology in the Tampa Bay Area." *Florida Historical Quarterly* 34 (July 1955): 51-63.

Bushnell, David I., Jr. "Investigations of Shell and Sand Mounds on Pinellas Peninsula, Florida." *Smithsonian Miscellaneous Collections* 78 (1926): 125-132.

Bushnell, Frank F. "The Maximo Point Site-1962." *Florida Anthropologist* 15 (1962): 89-101.

Camp, Paul Eugen, ed. "St. Petersburg's First Public School." *Tampa Bay History* 7 (Spring/Summer 1985): 76-82.

Chamberlin, Donald L. "Fort Brooke: Frontier Outpost, 1824-42." *Tampa Bay History* 7 (Spring/Summer 1985): 5-29.

Cook, Wythe. "Fossil Man and Pleistocene Vertebrates in Florida." *American Journal of Science.* 5th Series. 12 (1926): 441-452.

Covington, James W. "The Armed Occupation Act of 1842." *Florida Historical Quarterly* 40 (July 1961): 41-52.

Covington, James W. "Life at Fort Brooke, 1824-1836." *Florida Historical Quarterly* 36 (April 1958): 319-330.

Covington, James W. "Trade Relations Between Southwestern Florida and Cuba, 1600-1840." *Florida Historical Quarterly* 38 (October 1960): 114-128.

Davis, Jack E. "The Spirits of St. Petersburg: The Struggle for Local Prohibition, 1892-1919." *Tampa Bay History* 10 (Spring/Summer 1988): 19-33.

DeFoot, J. Allison, II. "Odet Philippe in South Florida." *Tampa Bay History* 8 (Spring/Summer 1986): 28-37.

"The Depression Decade: A Photo Essay." *Tampa Bay History* 3 (Spring/Summer 1981): 32-47.

Dillon, Rodney E. Jr. "South Florida in 1860." *Florida Historical Quarterly* 60 (April 1982): 440-454.

Dobkin, J.B. "Trails to Tampa Bay: A Photo Essay." *Tampa Bay History* 1 (Spring/Summer 1979): 24-30.

Dodd, Dorothy. "Captain Bunce's Tampa Bay Fisheries, 1835-1840." *Florida Historical Quarterly* 25 (January 1947): 246-256.

Edwards, R. L. and Merrill, A. S. "A Reconstruction of the Continental Shelf Areas of Eestern North America for the Times 9,500 B.P. and 12,500 B.P." *Archaeology of Eastern North America* 5 (1977): 1-43.

Farnell, Cheryl. "Dawn of the Automobile Age: A Photo Essay." *Tampa Bay History* 7 (Spring/Summer 1985): 42-60.

Fewkes, J. Walter. "Preliminary Archaeological Explorations at Weeden Island, Florida." *Smithsonian Miscellaneous Collections* 76, No. 13 (1924): 1-26.

Goodyear, Albert C. "Pinellas Point: A Possible Site of Continuous Indian Habitation." *Florida Anthropologist* 21 (1968): 74-82.

Goodyear, Albert C., et al. "Paleo-Indian Manifestations in the Tampa Bay Region." *Florida Anthropologist* 36 (1983): 40-66.

Holmes, Jack D. L. "Spanish Interest in Tampa Bay during the 18th Century." *Tampa Bay History* 5 (Spring/Summer 1983): 5-23.

Holmes, Jack D. L. "Two Spanish Expeditions to Southwest Florida, 1783-1793." *Tequesta* 25 (1965): 97-107.

Holmes, Jack D. L. and Ware, John D. "Juan Baptista Franco and Tampa Bay, 1756." *Tequesta* 28 (1968): 91-97.

Lardner, Ring, "The Golden Honeymoon," in *The Best Short Stories of Ring Lardner*. New York: Charles Scribner's Sons, 1957, pp.

189-203.

Long, Durward. "The Making of Modern Tampa: A City of the New South, 1885-1911." *Florida Historical Quarterly* 49 (April 1971): 333-345.

Luer, George M. and Almy, Marion. "A Definition of the Manasota Culture." *Florida Anthropologist* 35 (March 1982): 34-53.

Luer, George M. and Almy, Marion. "The Development of Some Aboriginal Pottery of the Central Peninsular Gulf Coast of Florida." *Florida Anthropologist* 33 (December 1980): 207-225.

Luer, George M. and Almy, Marion. "Temple Mounds of the Tampa Bay Area." *Florida Anthropologist* 34 (September 1981): 127-155.

Milanich, Jerald T. "Tracing the Route of Hernando de Soto Through Florida." in *Essays in Florida History*. Tampa: Florida Endowment for the Humanities, 1986, 8-13.

Milanich, Jerald T. "Corn and Calusa: De Soto and Demography" in Gaines, Sylvia W., ed. *Coasts, Plains and Deserts: Essays in Honor of Reynold J. Ruppe*. Tempe: Arizona State University Anthropological Research Papers No. 38, 1987, 173-184.

Mormino, Gary R. "Roadsides and Broadsides: A History of Florida Tourism." in *Essays in Florida History*. Tampa: Florida Endowment for the Humanities, 1986, 14-19.

Paulson, Darryl. "Stay Out, the Water's Fine: Desegregating Municipal Swimming Facilities in St. Petersburg, Florida." *Tampa Bay History* 4 (Fall/Winter 1982): 6-19.

Paulson, Darryl and St. Julien, Milly. "Desegregating Public Schools in Manatee and Pinellas Counties, 1954-71." *Tampa Bay History* 7 (Spring/Summer 1985): 30-41.

"Preserving for the Future: An Interview with Three Generations of the Starkey Family." *Tampa Bay History* 3 (Fall/Winter 1981): 58-75.

Ricci, James M. "The Bungalow: A History of the Most Predominant Style of Tampa Bay." *Tampa Bay History* 1 (Fall/Winter 1979): 6-13.

Ricci, James M. "Boasters, Boosters and Boom: Popular Images of Florida in the 1920s." *Tampa Bay History* 6 (Fall/Winter 1984): 31-57.

"The Roaring Twenties: A Photo Essay." *Tampa Bay History* 2 (Fall/Winter 1980): 30-40.

Rogers, Ben F. "Florida in World War II: Tourists and Citrus." *Florida Historical Quarterly* 39 (July 1960): 34-41.

Sanders, Michael L. "The Great Freeze of 1894-95 in Pinellas County." *Tampa Bay History* 2 (Spring/Summer 1980): 5-14.

Simonds, Willard B. "*The Sea Breeze*: The First Newspaper of the Lower Pinellas Peninsula." *Tampa Bay History* 5 (Fall/Winter 1983): 75-80.

"Sitting in the Sunshine." *Saturday Evening Post* 211 (April 1, 1939): 18-19+.

Smith, E. A. "Frog." "When Steamboats Left Tampa Bay." *Tampa Bay History* 2 (Spring/Summer 1980): 30-33.

Stafford, John W. "Egmont Key: Sentinel of Tampa Bay." *Tampa Bay History* 2 (Spring/Summer 1980): 15-29.

Stirling, Mathew W. "Prehistoric Mounds in the Vicinity of Tampa Bay, Florida." *Explorations and Field Work of the Smithsonian Institution for 1929*. Washington, D. C.: The Smithsonian Institution, 1930).

Tapley, Kay. "Camping and Cruising along the Suncoast in 1899." *Tampa Bay History* 2 (Fall/Winter 1980): 61-72.

Taylor, Robert A. "The Great War: A Photo Essay." *Tampa Bay History* 8 (Spring/Summer 1986): 47-64.

Tindall, George Brown. "The Bubble in the Sun." *American Heritage* 16 (August 1965): 76-83, 109-111.

Van Bibber, W. C. "Peninsular and Sub-Peninsular Air and Climates." *Journal of the American Medical Association* 4 (1885): 536ff.

Vanderblue, Homer B. "The Florida Land Boom." *Journal of Land and Public Utility Economics* 3 (May 1927): 113-131.

Ware, John D. "Tampa Bay in 1757: Francisco Maria Celi's Journal and Logbook, Part I." *Florida Historical Quarterly* 50 (October 1971): 158-179.

Watts, W. A. "Post Glacial and Interglacial Vegetation History of Southern Georgia and Central Florida." *Ecology* 52 (1971): 676-690.

Willey, Gordon R. "The Weeden Island

Culture: A Preliminary Definition."
American Antiquity 10 (1945): 225-254.
Wilson, Jon L. "Days of Fear: A Lynching in St.
Petersburg." *Tampa Bay History* 5
(Fall/Winter 1983): 4-26.

UNPUBLISHED THESES AND PAPERS:

Applefield, Helen. "A Little Bit of Social
History: The Banking Industry and the City
of St. Petersburg." Seminar Paper,
University of South Florida, 1984.

Arsenault, Raymond and Vonk, Jacob.
"Gentiles Only Wanted: Anti-Semitism in
St. Petersburg, Florida, 1920-1980." Paper
presented at the Annual Meeting of the
Southern Jewish Historical Society, New
Orleans, Louisiana, November 2, 1982.

Bell, Brad. "Blacks in St. Petersburg."
Seminar Paper, University of South Florida,
1986.

Carlson, Randy. "St. Petersburg, 1910-1915."
Seminar Paper, University of South Florida,
1987.

Cole, Bradley A. "The History of St.
Petersburg, Florida—The Nifty Fifties, 1951-
1955." Seminar Paper, University of South
Florida, 1987.

Dahlvik, Suzanne R. "Dr. James S. Hackney:
Fact and Folklore." Seminar Paper,
University of South Florida, 1988.

Davis, Samuel. "The Black Community of St.
Petersburg, 1920." Seminar Paper,
University of South Florida, 1983.

Davis, Samuel. "Interstate-275 and the Black
Community of St. Petersburg." Seminar
Paper, University of South Florida, 1984.

Davis, Samuel. "The Same Deal: Blacks in St.
Petersburg in the 1930s." Seminar Paper,
University of South Florida, 1986.

Davis, Samuel. "Segregation and the Black
Community of St. Petersburg." Seminar
Paper, University of South Florida, 1985.

De la Torre, Lynn. "St. Petersburg, 1955-
1959." Seminar Paper, University of South
Florida, 1987.

Fleming, Douglas L. "Toward Integration: The
Course of Race Relations in St. Petersburg,
1868-1963." M. A. Thesis, University of
South Florida, 1973.

Grigg, Irma B. "Persistence Patterns in St.
Petersburg Neighborhoods, 1915-1935."
Seminar Paper, University of South Florida,
1984.

Kuppler, Curtis. "St. Petersburg during the
War Years, 1941-1945." Seminar Paper,
University of South Florida, 1987.

Lesperance, Thomas. "The Development of
Medical Facilities from 1920 through 1980."
Seminar Paper, University of South Florida,
1984.

Maas, Steve. "The Tampa Bay Area:
Environment, Archaeological Research,
Prehistory, and History." Report prepared
for the Tampa Bay Regional Planning
Council, June 1988.

Merskin, Debra. "The City That Publicity
Built: St. Petersburg, Florida." Seminar
Paper, University of South Florida, 1986.

Nitz, Robin H. "St. Petersburg: A Passage in
Time, 1916-1920." Seminar Paper,
University of South Florida, 1987.

Polk, Milton. "The Man, His Hammer, and His
House: W. L. Straub, the *St. Petersburg
Times*, and the Creation of Pinellas County."
Seminar Paper, University of South Florida,
1987.

Roy, Beckey. "A Research of Marriage
Announcements in the *St. Petersburg Times*
for the Month of June during the Years 1920,
1940, 1960, and 1980." Seminar Paper,
University of South Florida, 1984.

Shedden, David. "Boosting the Boom: St.
Petersburg and its *Times*, 1921-1926."
Seminar Paper, University of South Florida,
1984.

Wagner, Steven M. "St. Petersburg History,
1906-1910." Seminar Paper, University of
South Florida, 1987.

Watts, William E. "St. Petersburg—the
Sunshine City, 1936-1940." Seminar Paper,
University of South Florida, 1987.

Whittier, James A. "St. Petersburg: Town to
City in 1923." Seminar Paper, University of
South Florida, 1981.

Williams, Ruth E. "The Black Community."
Seminar Paper, St. Petersburg Junior
College, 1983.

Williams, Ruth E. "St. Petersburg of
Yesteryear, Post-World War II, 1946-1950."

Seminar Paper, University of South Florida, 1987.

Wilson, Jon L. "St. Petersburg in 1888." Typescript, St. Petersburg Historical Society, 1985.

Index

Bethel Baptist Church, 127
Bethel Metropolitan Baptist Church, 269
Bethell, John, 37, 40, 42, 44-46, 78, 155
Bethell, Mary, 37
Bethell, Sarah, 36-37
Bethell, William, 40
Big Bayou, 27, 36-37, 40, 42-45, 47, 59, 87, 115-116, 137, 155, 199, 330
Bindaman, Edward, 194
Birth of a Nation, 126
Black Legend, 22
Black Point, 49
Blackburn, Bruce, 310-311
Blacks, 27, 29-31, 40-41, 48, 57, 85, 100, 120-121, 123-132, 134, 142,
    148, 162-163, 172-173, 187, 192-193, 206-208, 216, 243, 245, 263-270,
    272, 289, 292-295, 303, 305-307, 311-313, 320, 325, 328-330
Blanc, C. M., 291
Blanc, Robert, 258, 291
Blanche, 88, 169
Block, J. Kennedy, 197-198
Blocker, Albert T., 95, 103, 134-135, 141
Blocker, Hattie Dean, 103
Blocker, Marguerite, 151-152
Blocker House and Lodge, A. T., 95
B'Nai Israel, 207
Boatbuilding, 60, 80, 102
Boca Ciega Bay, 19, 29-30, 32, 35, 39, 42, 46, 136, 187, 202, 257
Bohrer family, 65
Bolshevik Revolution, 60, 187
Booker Creek, 27, 44, 60-61, 63, 87, 137, 148, 181, 266
Bonhomie, Hotel, 117
Booms, 38, 142, 147, 188, 190-209, 252-255, 261
Boston, Ma., 201-202, 232
Boston Braves, 143, 240, 283
Boulevard and Bay Land Devlopment Company, 198
Bowling Green, Ky., 137
Boy Scouts of America, 123
Boyer, Ian, 269, 291
Braddock, Captain David Cutler, 25
Bradenton, Fl., 19, 128, 135, 199, 282, 317
Bradshaw, James G., 91, 128, 155
Bradshaw, May, 155
Branch, John L., 42
Brantley, D. F. S., 80
Brantly Pier, 80, 88
Bridges, 53, 142, 148, 187-188, 196-197, 199, 214-217, 301,
    312, 316-317, 326
Bristol-Myers Corporation, 264
British, 11, 24-29, 31, 42, 45, 47, 52-53, 72, 81-82, 118-119,
    124, 132, 298
Brooke, Colonel George Mercer, 30
Brooksville, Fl., 284
Brown, John N., 201, 291
Brown, Lew B., 122, 128, 132, 138-139, 142-143, 145, 190, 192, 199
Bryan, William Jennings, 79, 84, 225
Bryant, Ira, 127
Bunce, William, 31, 38, 40
Burgert Brothers, 214-216, 218, 224, 237, 239, 243, 327
Burnside, Virginia, 188
Burrows, Louis, 328
Bussey Park, 172
Bussy, H. P., 81
Byrom, Isham, 291

C
Cabbage Key, 31, 38, 326
Cabeza de Vaca, A. Nunez, 20-21
Cable, Jerome, 122
California, 60, 201, 308
Caloosahatchie River, 18-19

Calusa Indians, 15, 18, 23-25, 29
Camden, N.J., 129, 132
Camden (N.J.) *Courier*, 132
Canadian Society, 118-119, 133
Canadians, 45, 47, 118-119, 133, 146
Cancer de Barbastro, Fray Luis, 22-23
Caribbean Sea, 19, 88
Carlos, Chief, 24
Carnegie Corporation, 142, 169
Carpenter, William, 145, 175-176, 311
Carpetbaggers, 41
Carrier Corporation, 309
Carter, John Wesley, 269, 289
Carver, Dr. George Washington, 305
Cascade Mountains, 28
Cascavela, 28
Castillo, M., and Sons, 81
Catholicism, Roman, 23, 135, 162, 179, 252, 258, 304, 309-310
Cattle industry, 38-39, 44, 63, 136, 210
Cedar Keys, Fl., 38, 43-44, 47, 65
Celi, Don Francisco Maria, 25-27
Central America, 22
Central Hotel, 72
Central National Bank, 278
Central Plaza, 308
Central Yacht Basin, 163, 228-229, 296-297
Chamber of Commerce (Board of Trade), 83, 87-88, 122-123,
    136, 138-139, 143, 145-146, 153, 186, 189, 195, 207-208,
    255, 257, 270
Charles V, of Spain, 19, 21
Charleston, S.C., 31
Charlotte Harbor, 14-15, 23, 29-30
Chase, John H., 86, 88
Chicago, Il., 52, 205
Childs, L. D., 330
Choctaw Indians, 28
Christianity, 17, 22, 24, 207-208
Churches, 65, 68-69, 85, 93, 97, 121, 125, 127, 135, 151, 155, 179,
    205-206, 211, 244, 261, 269, 289, 304, 307, 309
Churchill, John, 60
Cimarrónes, 27
Cincinnati Reds, 143
Citizens' Emergency Committee, 257
Citrus, 39, 42-44, 49, 57, 62, 66, 73, 85, 120, 154, 173, 210
City charters (St. Petersburg), 142, 194, 256, 265, 267, 298
City Federation of Colored Women's Clubs, 294
City hall, 74, 85, 260, 290
Civil War, 38-41, 133, 191
Civil Works Administration, 258-259
Clam Bayou, 39-40, 47
Clarenden Hotel, 64, 90-91
Classic case, 305
Clearwater, Fl., 42, 57, 65, 81, 130, 139-142
Clearwater Sun, 132
Cleveland, Horace, 87
Cleveland, Ohio, 186
Cleveland Leader, 186
Climate, 12-13, 32-33, 35, 38, 43, 52-53, 62, 66, 73, 80, 83, 89, 113, 139,
    145-146, 187, 191-192, 194, 197, 257, 260
Club Buffet, 121
Coad, Jim, 207-208
Coe, B. E., 86
Coffee Pot Bayou, 137, 143, 177-178, 198, 200, 204, 209, 223
Coffee Pot Golf Course, 204, 223
Coleman, W. W., 103
Coliseum dance hall, 204, 238
Columbian Exchange, 17-18
Columbus, Christopher, 17
Compromise of 1877, 41

Investment Bankers Association of America, 252
Iowa, 60, 133, 252
Irish-Americans, 135, 252
Italian-Americans, 56
Ittner, William B., 242

J
Jackson, Andrew, 29
Jackson, Kenneth, 309
Jacksonville, Fl., 44, 142
Jacobs family, 207
Jagger, Douglas, 65
Jamaica, 19
James, Harry, 204
Jannus, Tony, 142-143, 164-165, 201
Japanese, 298-299, 307, 319
Jenness, L. Y., 58, 83
Jesuits, 24
Jessup, Ga., 87
Jews, 17, 38, 135, 207-208, 303
Jiminez, Jose, 26
John's Pass, 35, 129, 326
John's Pass Bridge, 326
Johnson, Arthur L., 153
Johnson, Hayworth, 263
Jones, Sam, 328
Jonsberg, F., 201, 232
Jordan Park, 270, 272, 292, 306-307
Joseph Conrad, U.S.S., 298, 315
Judge, R. C. M., 71
Jungle area, 18, 202, 232-233, 299, 310
Jungle Country Club Hotel, 202, 232, 307
Jungle Golf Course, 202, 233, 299
Jungle Prado, 202

K
Kennedy, Dr. George, 71
Kenneth City, Fl., 309
Kentucky, 133, 137-138, 199
Kerensky, Alexander, 60
Key West, Fl., 31, 40, 44, 49, 207
Kids and Kubs, 261, 282, 320
Kiehnel, Richard, 203, 273
Kimball, Timothy, 42
King, George, 47-48, 61, 63-64, 75, 86
Kissimmee, Fl., 47
Knight, Peter O., 140
Knights of Pythias, 127
Knoxville, Tenn., 263
Ku Klux Klan, 41, 187, 207-208, 268, 303

L
La Bahia de Caballos, 20
La Bahia de Espíritu Santo, 21, 24
La Bahia de la Cruz, 19
La Bahia de San Fernando, 25
La Bahia de Tampa, 25
La Plaza Theatre, 126, 142, 159, 161, 179, 196, 201, 218, 239, 247, 261, 295, 321, 335
Labor unions, 187, 251, 260-262, 288, 311-312
Lake, James B., 127
Lake Apopka, 52
Lake George, 29
Lake Maggiore, 26, 41, 137, 189, 213, 220, 266, 309
Lake Vista subdivision, 220-221
Lakeland, Fl., 268
Lakeview House, 75
Lakewood Country Club, 204
Lakewood Estates, 137, 199

Landon, Alf, 264
Lang, Al, 136-137, 143-144, 147, 177, 188, 261, 291, 309, 311, 323
Lang Field, Al, 309, 322-323, 329
Lassing Park, 198
Latham, Bird, 175
Laughner, Aymer Vinoy, 202, 235
Lawrence, Bradford, 142
Lazzeri, Tony, 204
Le Moyne, Jacques, 16
League of Nations, 187
League of Women Voters, 188, 270
Legislature, Florida, 53, 64, 139-142, 312
Lee, Ivy, 79
Lee, Young G., 65
Leggett, Dr. Gilbert, 305
Leland, Glenn V., 269
Lend-Lease Act, 298
Leonardi, Vincent, 40, 42
Lesseroux, Maurice, 207
Levick, John (Juan Levique), 30-31, 35, 38
Lewis, J. M., 87
Lewis, Leora, 189
Lewis, Sinclair, 188
Libraries, 122, 142, 168, 307
Little Bayou, 40
Little Coe Channel, 86-87
Little Manatee River, 21
Little St. Mary's, 304
Livingston, B. F., 106
Livingston, Lillian, 106
Lodwick, John, 186-187, 193-194, 203-205, 214, 252, 254, 261
Loehr, Nellie, 188
Lohr, Specs, 284
Long, Huey P., 264
Long Bayou, 257
Long Island (N.Y.), 12
Long Key, 187
Lonstreth, H. M., 65
Longwood, Fl., 52
Los Angeles, Calif., 60
Louisiana, 20, 35, 42, 46-47, 52-53
Louisville, Ky., 137-138
Louisville Courier-Journal, 138
Loyal Temperance Legion, 121
Lund, Soren, 201
Lynching, 129-130, 132, 142, 172
Lyon, France, 31

M
Maas Brothers department store, 308, 325
MacDill Field, 301
Madeira Beach, 266, 326
Madison, Ark., 138
Madrid, Spain, 25
Magdalena, 22-23
Main Street, 188
Maine, 42, 133
Manasota culture, 14-15
Manatee, 127
Manatee River, 19, 29, 31, 42
Manhattan Hotel, 54, 70
Manila, Phillipines, 298
Manual Training School, 84, 107, 109-110
Marconi, Guglielmo, 84, 98, 107, 201
Martinez de Cos, Garcia, 24
Mary Disston, 47
Maryland, 31, 38, 52, 133
Mason Hotel, 201, 232
Masonic order, 38, 64, 142

Massachusetts, 26, 133, 201-202, 232
Mattie, 57-58
Mayan Indians, 15
Maximo Point, 30, 53, 131
Mayes, Dick, 283
McAdoo, W. D., 187
McCray, Arline, 294-295
McCray, Grant H., Sr., 294-295
McCray Foundational School, 294-295
McCutcheon, R. J., 291
McDonald, Rex, 204
McEachern, A. C., 267
McKay, Captain James, 38
McKinley, William, 79, 84, 96
McMullen family, 39
McPherson, Aimee Semple, 204
McPherson, William J., 47, 49
McRae, Annie, 122
Meador, J. T., 65
Meares, Mabel, 109
Medical Bulletin, 83
Meloche landfill, 198
Mencken, H. L., 202
Menéndez de Avilés, Pedro, 23-24
Merchants' Association, 270
Mercy Hospital, 127, 206, 269, 307, 310
Merrell, Herman, 121
Merrell, Mary, 121
Merrick, George, 137, 203
Methodist Episcopal Church, 155, 211, 244
Methodist Town, 269
Mexican War, 32, 38
Mexico, 15, 19-22, 32, 38
Miami, Fl., 203, 273
Miami Beach, Fl., 186, 195
Miami Herald, 191
Miccosukee Indians, 27
Michigan, 44-45, 54, 60, 84, 96, 132-133, 146
Michigan State Society, 146
Miller, G. A., 50
Miller Tent City, 189
Million Dollar Pier, 190, 199, 247-249, 256, 259, 261, 264, 269, 275, 280, 284-285, 295-297, 304, 309, 313, 322, 334
Ministerial Association, of St. Petersburg, 269
Minorcans, 27, 39
Minshall, Stanley, 312
Miranda, Abel, 39-40, 42, 44, 46
Miranda, Eliza, 39-40
Miranda, Thomas, 45
Miranda, William B., 46-47
Mirror Lake, 58, 64, 82, 137, 204, 239, 244
Miruelo, Diego, 18
Mississippi, 133
Mississippi River, 21, 41
Mississippi Valley, 15
Mississippian culture, 15, 17
Mitchell, Henry, 81
Mitchell, James J., 129
Mitchell, Noel, 94, 136-137, 140-143, 145, 174, 188-190, 192-194, 205-206, 214, 217, 225
Mitchell's Courthouse Subdivision, 141
Mix, Tom, 204
Mizner, Addison, 137
Modernistics, 294
Moffett, David, 64, 73
Moffett, Janie, 73
Mocoso, 21
Moore, Elijah, 289
Moore, James, 25

Morgan, Richard J., 65
Morison, Samuel Eliot, 19, 21
Moscoso, Luis, 21
Moses, J. C. "Honeybaby," 268
Moses, J. P., 305
Mound Park Hospital, 26-27, 310
Mount Olive Primitive Baptist Church, 127
Mule Branch, 47
Mullet Key, 53-54, 83, 301
Municipal Negro Swimming Pool, 330
Municipal Pier (1973), 337
Municipal Recreation Pier (1913), 142, 190-192, 199, 211
Muñoz, Juan, 23

N
Napoleon I, 31
Narváez, Panfilo de, 15, 18-21
Narváez Park, 198
Nashville, Tenn., 263
National Airlines, 280
National Association for the Advancement of Colored People, 266, 268-269
National Biscuit Company, 137
National Campfire Girls, 123
National Guard, 260
National Park Association, 123
National Register of Historic Places, 198
National Urban League, 270, 307
Neal, William, 144
Neeld, R. E., 45
Neeld, William P., 45
Negro News Page (*St. Petersburg Times*), 293, 303, 305
Neolithic Revolution, 14
Nevada, 42
New Cadiz, Fl., 47-48, 61, 63
New Deal, 258-260, 264, 266, 269-272, 290, 299, 303
New England Society, 146
New Hampshire, 133, 201
New Jersey, 129, 132-133, 136, 142, 146, 199, 201
New Orleans, La., 35, 42, 46-47, 52-53
New York, 52-53, 60, 128, 133, 142, 144, 146, 193-194, 196, 200-202, 205
New York-New Jersey Society, 146
New York Yankees, 143, 202-204, 241, 261, 283, 309
New River, Fl., 31
New Smyrna, Fl., 27
Newspapers, 47, 49, 64-65, 78, 84-85, 132, 138-140, 186, 190-191, 208, 268, 292-293, 303, 305, 307, 311
Nichols, E. H., 130
Nikko Inn, 299
Nineteenth Amendment, 188
Noel, Raymond, 267-268, 281
Nolan, David, 196
Nolen, John, 124, 266-267
North America, 12, 22
North Carolina, 60-61, 133
North Dakota, 84
North St. Petersburg subdivision, 197
North Shore subdivision, 113, 137, 217, 255
Norwood, Arthur, 47, 72, 81-82, 94, 124, 183

O
Oakland, Fl., 52-53, 56-57
Ocala Star, 132
Odd Fellows, 64
Ohio, 133, 137, 144, 146, 186, 226
Ohio State Society, 146, 226
Oklahoma, 30
Old Northeast, 200

Raymond Arsenault is professor of history and director of the Honors Program at the University of South Florida, St. Petersburg. He has taught at the University of Minnesota and at the Université d'Angers, in France, where he was a Fulbright Lecturer in American Studies in 1984-85. From 1980 to 1987, he served as associate director of the Fulbright Commission's Summer Institute on "Regionalism in America," at the University of Minnesota. A specialist in the social and political history of the American South, he is the author of *The Wild Ass of the Ozarks: Jeff Davis and the Social Bases of Southern Politics* (1984) and "The End of the Long Hot Summer: The Air Conditioner and Southern Culture," *Journal of Southern History* (1984), which was awarded the Green-Ramsdell Prize by the Southern Historical Association; and the editor of *Crucible of Liberty: 200 Years of the Bill of Rights* (1991). He is coeditor of the Florida History and Culture Series published by the University Press of Florida. He lives in St. Petersburg with his wife and two daughters.